Sustainable Leadership

"Avery and Bergsteiner have done a masterful job at fleshing out the honeybee metaphor that drives sustainable organizations. They have identified 23 leadership practices that enable organizations to survive and thrive in both good and bad economies. They offer specific examples and leadership tools to bring these practices to life. They show that companies who adopt and adapt these ideas have higher employee, customer, investor, and community returns. This is a book worth reading, and using!"

—**Professor Dave Ulrich**, Ross School of Business, University of Michigan, and Partner, The RBL Group

The business case for operating along sustainable principles is becoming very clear. Sustainable organizations outperform their peers on many criteria, including corporate social responsibility, employee satisfaction and—surprisingly for some—even financially.

Sustainable Leadership: Honeybee and Locust Approaches presents an evidence-based view of how 23 leadership practices facilitate outcomes that go beyond what is commonly referred to as the triple bottom line—environmental sustainability, corporate social responsibility, and financial success. The book centers on a powerful metaphor of honeybee and locust behaviors, which illustrate two leadership philosophies with very different outcomes for a business and its viability. Gathering evidence from scholars combined with observations from successful firms around the world, the book presents a bundle of principles, behaviors, and beliefs that forms a sustainable leadership system.

This engaging, insightful book offers a set of principles that can be adapted in many ways to underpin sustainable leadership in different situations. It provides evidence and a rationale for building a business case to change towards more sustainable practices.

Gayle C. Avery is Professor of Management at Macquarie Graduate School of Management, Australia, and co-founder of the Institute for Sustainable Leadership. She has authored a number of books on leadership and sustainability.

Harald Bergsteiner was Adjunct Professor at Macquarie Graduate School of Management, Australia, and is a co-founder of the Institute for Sustainable Leadership.

Sustainable Leadership

Honeybee and Locust Approaches

Gayle C. Avery and Harald Bergsteiner

Routledge
Taylor & Francis Group

NEW YORK AND LONDON

First published 2011
by Routledge
711 Third Avenue, New York, NY 10017

Simultaneously published in the UK
by Routledge
2 Park Square, Milton Park, Abingdon, Oxon OX14 4RN

Routledge is an imprint of the Taylor & Francis Group, an informa business

To purchase this book in Australia and New Zealand, please contact Allen &
Unwin, PO Box 8500 (83 Alexander Street), St Leonards NSW 1590, Australia.

© 2011 Gayle C. Avery and Harald Bergsteiner

The right of Gayle C. Avery and Harald Bergsteiner to be identified as authors
of this work has been asserted by them in accordance with sections 77 and 78
of the Copyright, Designs and Patents Act 1988.

Typeset in Bembo by Midland Typesetters, Australia

Library of Congress Cataloging-in-Publication Data
Avery, Gayle, 1947–
Sustainable leadership : honeybee and locust approaches / Gayle C. Avery,
Harald Bergsteiner.
p. cm.
1. Leadership. 2. Corporate culture. 3. Social responsibility of business. I.
Bergsteiner, Harald. II. Title.
HD57.7.A939 2011
658.4′092--dc22
2010042510

ISBN 13: 978-0-415-89138-7 (hbk)
ISBN 13: 978-0-415-89139-4 (pbk)

Contents

Practice Boxes, Figures and Tables

Preface

Sustainable Leadership contrasts two very different approaches to running organisations. Research and practice show that one approach, 'Honeybee' leadership, is likely to be more sustainable than the other, and to add more value overall. Our title reflects a metaphor, in which honeybees and locusts have represented creation and destruction since at least biblical times. Honeybees build community and ecosystems. Locusts swarm together and eat green fields bare.

'Diana of the Ephesians', also known as Artemis (Acts 19, 23–41), was pictured with beehives and other fertility symbols. Her priests and priestesses were called 'bees' and her community was the 'hive'. Bee colonies consist of a queen and many specialists, such as drones and foraging workers. Other specialists engage in various hive duties such as brood-rearing, comb construction, house-cleaning, defence and temperature regulation. Under ideal conditions a colony of honeybees can produce more than 90 kilograms of surplus honey in a year. However, the honeybee's most significant contribution is pollinating plants that affect about one-third of the human diet, and much of what animals and insects eat. Without bees, our lives would be impoverished by a general lack of fruits, vegetables, flowers and other plant products. Thus, honeybees are essential for maintaining a large part of the ecosystem. The honeybee is not only productive; it is a symbol of cooperation, thrift, diligence, forethought and healing.[1] It stings only for defence purposes.

National Geographic describes locusts as sometimes solitary insects with lifestyles much like grasshoppers.[2] Alone they are relatively benign. However, throughout history humans have feared the devastation that locusts can bring when they form swarms. According to the Bible, a plague of locusts was one of the ten punishments inflicted on the Egyptians for not releasing the Israelites from their bondage. Under favourable environmental conditions that produce many green plants and promote breeding, millions of locusts can congregate into thick, ravenous swarms. Swarms are highly mobile and can cover vast distances, such as flying from Africa to the UK. Ravenous swarms can devastate healthy crops and cause major agricultural damage. This results in misery through famine and starvation because each locust can eat its own weight in plants – every day. Estimates are that desert locust plagues threaten the economic livelihood of a tenth of the world's humans. Swarms of locusts eventually die as suddenly as they erupt. Although locusts have survived as a species the cost to other life forms is high, and the impact on the environment can be catastrophic.

In a similar way, honeybee and locust behaviours illustrate two leadership philosophies with very different outcomes for a business and its viability. Many researchers and management gurus point out that honeybee behaviour is likely to be more sustainable and lead to better organisational performance than its locust counterpart. In *Sustainable Leadership*, we gather the evidence from scholars and combine it with observations from successful firms around the world. The result is a bundle of principles, behaviours and beliefs that forms a sustainable leadership system.

The ideas behind *Sustainable Leadership* came from observing successful businesses that operate on 'sustainable' leadership principles.[3] We wanted to help readers understand the what, the why and the how underlying sustainable enterprises. In this book we present an evidence-based view of how 23 leadership practices facilitate outcomes that go beyond what is commonly referred to as the triple bottom line – environmental sustainability, corporate social responsibility and financial success. We add to this: brand and reputation, customer satisfaction and a broader conception of long-term stakeholder value. Sustainable leadership blends these practices into an integrated system in which the practices reinforce one another.

The business case for operating along sustainable principles is becoming very clear: sustainable organisations outperform their peers on many criteria. Sustainable enterprises are widely admired – as a result of their being responsible corporate citizens. Sustainable enterprises often enjoy 'Best Employer' status (meaning that they tend to win the talent war). Surprising for some – sustainable organisations can and do outperform their peers financially. This occurs through a bundle of practices that combine to provide competitive advantage. We focus on these sustainable practices in this book, providing insight into what other enterprises do and why. This will hopefully trigger reflection on practices inside your own enterprise. We do not claim to have the perfect solution for every business. We offer a set of principles that can be adapted in many ways to underpin sustainable leadership in different situations.

Looking beyond the firm itself, there are many other reasons for operating on sustainable leadership principles. One reason is that the very survival of the earth is imperiled by the rate at which humans are exploiting natural resources and polluting the planet. A major rethink is required to address the resulting human and environmental consequences. And business has its part to play in this process. Another reason why it is important to operate on sustainable principles is that society suffers when business does not take account of its impact on local communities.

What can business leaders do to create enterprises that are more sustainable both internally and externally? Here we can draw on the honeybee and locust metaphors. For example, the high degree of specialisation of bee populations enables the hive to generate surpluses sufficient to benefit others without in any way endangering the sustainability of the hive itself. External beneficiaries of the surplus, such as beekeepers, tend the hives for their own as well as for the hive's benefit. Locusts, on the other hand, with their single-minded and self-destructive greed, do not attract locust-keeper friends to look after their well-being in times of need.

In the business world, some organisations operate similarly to honeybees. They collaborate and generate value for themselves, their communities and their environment. Others serve their own self-interests. They consume whatever lies in their paths like locusts. This book shows how employing honeybee-like practices creates sustainable enterprises. Locust-like practices tend to deliver less value for the enterprises themselves, and in the long run impoverish the communities and environments in which they operate.

Sustainable leadership practices are generally associated with long-term success, but simply engaging in such practices does not guarantee long-term success. One reason is that organisational performance is relative. This means that even though company A's good performance has not changed, if competitors substantially improve their performance then company A's relative position has deteriorated. Thus, sustainable practices can be expected to continually evolve and develop.

A second reason is that businesses need to get two basic things right: what they do, and how they do it. This book focuses on the how, illustrating it with living examples. Finally, even having sustainable practices in place does not prevent managers from making poor strategic decisions that affect the sustainability of their organisation. Fortunately, Honeybee leadership makes this less likely.

This book is intended to help readers distinguish between honeybee and locust leadership principles. It provides evidence and a rationale for building a business case to change towards more sustainable practices. Those who want to assess the extent of these practices in their organisation might consider applying the Sustainable Leadership Questionnaire. Further information about the authors' assessment instrument is available in Appendix A.

notes

1   Carl Hayden Bee Research Center, a cooperative venture between the United States Department of Agriculture and the University of Arizona

2   http://www3.nationalgeographic.com/animals/bugs/locust.html; accessed 27 April 2007

3   Our terms 'honeybee' and 'locust' were derived independently of Elkington's (2001) *The Chrysalis Economy*.

Acknowledgements

Heartfelt thanks are due to many people for their support during the writing of *Sustainable Leadership*. Not least are the representatives of the organisations we visited in collecting data for this book, who so openly shared information about their enterprises. We are grateful to some of our academic colleagues who contributed case material and examples. In particular, our thanks are due to the many research students who stimulated and challenged our thinking, over and over again! The people who influenced us are too numerous to mention individually without running into the danger of inadvertently overlooking someone.

However, Andrew Schuller deserves a special acknowledgement for his commitment to seeing this book published. We are also grateful to Elizabeth Weiss and her team at Allen & Unwin, who have enthusiastically supported this book. We would also like to thank the librarians at Macquarie University who tirelessly acquired materials for us and addressed our on-line library challenges.

Finally, we appreciated being able to spend time writing in the inspiring alpine environment at Geiern, in the heart of the Bavarian Alps. On-line technologies and the support of our colleagues made this possible. Finally, we extend our gratitude and love to our friends and family, who put up with our absences during many writing retreats – and are still on speaking terms with us!

Gayle C. Avery
Harald Bergsteiner

1

Sustainable Enterprises

Sustainable Leadership is about why some businesses stay at the forefront of their industry, no matter what is going on around them. Why these firms outperform their peers over the long term – while surviving wars, depressions, recessions, oil crises and intense global competition. Why they can adapt to changes in markets, regulations, consumer behaviour and technologies and many other challenging events and continue to flourish. Do these sustainable enterprises have a secret to share with us?

In trying to answer these questions, we expose the special ways in which many highly successful and sustainable businesses operate. We reveal much of the scholarly evidence supporting these 'honeybee' principles and their associated practices. We examine the business case behind each principle, showing why and how practices based on that principle pay off for organisations.

In writing this book, we have drawn on practices in 47 enterprises and the personal experiences of senior executives from more than 35 of them. The result highlights how 23 mostly intangible factors embedded in the leadership of 'sustainable' businesses differ from conventional business practices and mainstream academic thinking. Intriguingly, academic research shows that while each individual principle or practice contributes to organisational performance, exceptional performance is likely to be achieved when the practices are combined in appropriate ways.

Along the way, we have come to challenge many entrenched ideas about leadership. For a start, we join the growing army of critics of the popular business model that permeates much of the business and political thinking around the world. This model is based on the assumption that a corporation's primary purpose is to maximise short-term returns for investors.

Some would agree that maximising short-term shareholder value is the sole purpose of a business. This approach traditionally underpins what managers are taught in business schools (see Box 1–1). In *Sustainable Leadership*, we show that outstanding organisations typically do the very opposite of these teachings. Using findings from research and practising managers, we explain how and why companies that challenge conventional wisdom perform better financially, environmentally and socially over the long term.

A long-term perspective is fundamental to the notion of sustainable leadership. But it is not sufficient, because mere survival is not enough. Sustainability is a necessary foundation for corporate success, but it is not the main game. The main game is to create enduring value for all stakeholders, including investors, the environment, other species and society. To achieve this, sustainable practices provide an essential foundation.

Box 1–1: What business schools traditionally teach

Given that graduates can expect a career of between one to four decades, the effects of a business education on management practice are important. However, many professors (and others) criticise business schools for not helping the practice of management, contrary to their mission. According to Canadian Professor Henry Mintzberg,[1] business schools are teaching the wrong skills by turning out managers who are mainly informed, analytical and efficient decision-makers. Many other essential skills are not part of the curriculum, including developing wisdom and learning to generate, integrate, disseminate and use ideas and knowledge. Even more importantly, managers need to build organisational culture, master politics and empower others to make the most of their talents.

Professor Denise Rousseau, President of the American Academy of Management in 2005, argues that professors contribute to the 'dumbing down' of managers. Few professors prepare managers to challenge conventional wisdom, solve problems or evaluate evidence underlying effective managerial behaviour. One consequence is that myths and unsupported ideas that teachers learned in their own university training are passed on to new generations of students. To counter the habit of simply perpetuating the same old myths, a Swiss management institute boldly advertised that 'mainstream thinking is mostly wrong'.[2]

According to the late Professor Sumantra Ghoshal, many of the worst excesses of recent management practices stem from what is taught in business schools. Focused solely on shareholders, managers are trained to exploit suppliers, customers and employees. There is little mention of trust or a partnership with these stakeholder groups, or of taking their concerns seriously. Ghoshal criticised these and other destructive ideas for having no basis in research – they have just become part of many managers' mindsets. Ghoshal contrasted 'the ruthlessly hard-driving, strictly top-down, command-and-control focused, shareholder-value-obsessed, win-at-any-cost business leader' with an alternative leadership philosophy.[3] Here, the interests of a range of stakeholders are considered over the long term.

The idea that corporations need to justify their existence by contributing to society as a whole is very different from what most business schools have traditionally taught. Yet this is the basis of sustainable leadership.

Not only do business schools traditionally teach poor ideology; some of the leading management consulting firms have also championed a win-at-any-cost, short-term approach to running organisations. Box 1–2 relates what two well-known management consulting firms have said about doing business. Fortunately, this is changing as more people examine the evidence.

Box 1–2: What some management consultants recommend

Two vice presidents of the Boston Consulting Group promoted the 'hardballing' approach in the April 2004 issue of the *Harvard Business Review*.[4] They described the approach thus:

plagiarize with pride . . . steal any good idea . . . As long as it isn't nailed down by a robust patent . . . squishy issues – leadership, corporate culture, customer care, knowledge management, talent management, employee empowerment – [have] encouraged the

> making of softball players . . . The nicest part of playing hardball
> is watching your competitors squirm.

Such calls for unethical and antisocial behaviour are puzzling
given evidence that firms with a reputation for ethical and fair
behaviour perform better financially.[5] Perhaps the explanation
lies in the myth that business leaders need to be tough and
ruthless.

In the September 2005 issue of the *McKinsey Quarterly*,
two senior McKinsey consultants argued that the European
approach of considering stakeholders and social issues in
their business activities essentially makes a firm uncompetitive
– and advised managers to be 'as unEuropean as possible'.
Without substantiating evidence, articles like these reflect poor
understanding of national values and corporate competitiveness
in global comparisons, to say the least.

These are extreme views, and not representative of all
consultants. Furthermore, consultants' ideas seem to be changing.
In 2007, two McKinsey consultants interviewed prominent US
sustainability gurus including Al Gore, financial expert David
Blood and opinion poll researcher Daniel Yankelovich. This rather
late interest in the social and environmental aspects of sustainable
leadership follows a 2006 McKinsey study indicating that most
executives now believe that business has more obligations to
society than it used to have.[6]

Another key influence on people's thinking typically comes
from the media. Like their readers, journalists often reflect the
traditional views found in business schools rather than principles
of sustainable leadership. That there is confusion is not surprising,
given estimates of more than 300 definitions of sustainability. The
business-as-usual nature of much of what is written in the popular
media is worrisome, given its influence in our society. But this is
also changing. The question is: what do you change to?

Sustainable Leadership presents an alternative view of corporate
leadership from the traditional approaches found in conventional
academe, consulting, the media and much managerial practice
around the world. Some people will read this book and think: my
organisation already does a lot of this. For example, an Australian
bank, Westpac, shifted towards sustainable leadership over a decade
ago. As both the then chairman and CEO of Westpac jointly
concluded in their 2007 sustainability report:

We have come to understand that sustainability is not a program, nor even a set of priorities. It is an overarching management approach. In our terms: managing long, that is for the long term not the short term; managing broad, in the sense of meeting the legitimate needs of all stakeholders; and managing around a set of values. We do not run the company for today's market or for the short term – as ultimately, the only returns that matter are long term.[7]

The challenge lies in maintaining those principles with future CEOs and in turbulent times.

While these and other aspects of sustainable leadership will not be entirely new for readers associated with sustainable firms, four things will be new in this book. First, we identify and describe 23 key factors that underlie sustainable leadership. This provides a framework for understanding the practices contributing to sustainability. Second, using published research we show how and why these factors contribute to improved organisational performance. This provides a basis for making the business case for sustainable leadership. Third, we present evidence and a conceptual framework showing how sustainable leadership practices provide competitive advantage when they are combined. This reminds us that sustainable leadership emerges from the interplay of many factors. Fourth, our Sustainable Leadership Pyramid provides a framework to assist managers in examining the extent of sustainable practices throughout their organisation. The pyramid also provides guidance on where to start with changes that need to be made.

Even in workplaces that already embrace some of the principles and practices described here, other practices will be new. Or existing practices can be improved upon, or given greater importance. Or the framework that we have developed may simply aid strategic decision-makers in ensuring that all bases have been covered. Equipped with this information, practitioners of sustainable leadership may find themselves better able to recognise, promote and deal with threats to their approach.

The cases dotting this book show how different kinds of businesses actually implement and practise sustainable leadership. We see that there is no one 'right' way within the overall sustainable leadership paradigm. But these living cases can inspire new ways of strengthening already sustainable workplaces.

> *The main game is to create enduring value for all stakeholders.*

Other readers will be amazed that businesses thrive by doing the opposite to what their organisation always understood to be good practice. For these readers, *Sustainable Leadership* will be provocative and challenging. However, if they truly care about shareholder value, they will need to accept that both research and practice show that enterprises embracing sustainable leadership principles typically outperform their competitors over the long term.

This book's questioning of current orthodoxies may disturb some readers so much that they will refuse to engage with these different ideas at all. Here it helps to recall the words of management professor Gary Hamel. Hamel calls upon managers to 'deconstruct your management orthodoxies . . . loosen the grip that precedent has on your imagination. While some of what you believe might be scientific certainty, much of it isn't.'[8] Hamel goes on to point out that great companies are managed in unorthodox ways, rather than following the same old management principles. Other management writers are also urging managers to question every belief they hold. In 2008, following the global financial crisis, once successful enterprises – from banks to automakers and others – went out of business or came under government control. Why was the leadership in these firms unsustainable? Was it just bad luck?

This book will quite possibly challenge some readers' fundamental beliefs about leadership and how to run an enterprise. We offer this challenge in the knowledge that it is based on current research evidence, as well as on discussions with executives from some of the world's most successful and admired organisations. Not engaging with what these organisations can teach means denying yourself and your shareholders the opportunity to join their ranks.

Knowing how successful organisations practise sustainable leadership helps identify and challenge unsustainable practices. Addressing unsustainable practices becomes a bit like turning around a large ship that has run off course. First you need information about just how far the ship is off course and what caused it to go off course. Then you need charts and maps that help you steer the ship back in the desired direction. In *Sustainable Leadership* we chart the route to sustainable leadership using current examples and research.

What is sustainable leadership?

Sustainable leadership helps an organisation endure over time and weather the inevitable storms that beset an enterprise. Both terms 'sustainable' and 'leadership' have to do with moving towards some future state.

In *Sustainable Leadership* we define leadership in a systemic way – going beyond the popular idea of leadership residing in a powerful individual or an elite group. For us, leadership is reflected in the system of principles, processes, practices and values that a firm adopts in pursuing its future. Of course, leadership involves individuals – both leaders and followers. But effective leadership is about how those individuals interact with one another; their stakeholders; the organisation's systems, processes and culture; and the external environment. This in turn influences how firms allocate their financial, human and other resources. Clearly, this can be done in many different ways, but in this book we focus on two widely differing philosophies underpinning organisational leadership. We will see evidence that one approach is more sustainable than the other. Unfortunately, the less sustainable model represents business-as-usual for many corporations.

Being a leader these days is fraught with challenges that were not even conceived of a decade ago. Today, political, corporate and government leaders have to confront 'new' issues like climate change, corporate social responsibility, talent shortages, uncertain financial markets, fuel costs and crises over lack of food and water in many parts of the world. This is all in addition to the more expected challenges in a dynamic, global, networked and high-tech world that everyone was starting to get used to. The context for leadership has suddenly changed. Sustainability is on many leaders' lips.

What does sustainability historically refer to? Essentially, it means living within our means, living within the earth's resources. Many organisations, such as the World Business Council for Sustainable Development, the United Nations and the UK government, define sustainable development as *development that meets the needs of the present without compromising the ability of future generations to meet their own needs*. In the developed parts of the world humans are clearly living beyond their means, leaving too little for coming generations. According to the 2006 *Living Planet Report* issued by the global conservation organisation WWF, on current projections humanity will be using two planets' worth of natural resources by 2050. This presupposes that those resources have not run out by then!

The effects of not reducing our global consumption of scarce resources will far exceed the costs of moving towards more sustainable living now, according to Sir Nicholas Stern's report on the costs of climate change. The 2007 *Stern Report* calls for collective action around the world to stem the anticipated severe consequences of climate change on human health and quality of life. Living within the earth's resources is important, but so is sharing the wealth and well-being more equitably with other humans. Thus, a sustainable future may well require moderating economic growth to allow for social well-being and ecological balance to be restored. This in turn requires a major rethink of business-as-usual that goes beyond simply being 'green'.

The world is not inactive. For example, the World Business Council for Sustainable Development (WBCSD), a CEO-led coalition of some 200 international companies, is striving to create sustainable development through economic growth, ecological balance and social progress. Nearly half the members are from the *Fortune* 500, but the WBCSD reaches more than 1500 business leaders worldwide. Two-thirds of these leaders are in the developing world and emerging economies.

A few words of caution. Sustainable leadership is not about altruism or charity work, or just being 'green'. A strong business case can be made for operating on sustainable principles. CEOs who are members of the WBCSD pursue sustainable development for business reasons. According to the WBCSD, sustainable leadership makes firms more competitive, more resilient, faster to respond and more appealing to customers. It also helps attract talented employees, as well as make businesses more attractive to investors and insurers. Being sustainable is important. After all, enterprises that fail to perform financially cannot survive, let alone thrive.

However, enterprises that thrive can afford to be altruistic. Not all are. But, as we will see, operating on sustainable principles can add financial and other value to a firm.

Sustainable leadership practices are not a magic formula for making life easy for their adopters. On the contrary, making the right short-term decision to serve the long-term interests of an organisation can be quite hard. For example, taking an ethical stance against corruption can be a difficult decision when competitors are paying bribes. However, doing so can pay off because people working in organisations that employ sustainable leadership practices tend to be more committed to that enterprise. Outcomes like these can raise the firm's resilience to weather the inevitable storms that beset every business at some stage.

Finally, being sustainable is not an all-or-nothing position. There are degrees of commitment to sustainable leadership, as we see next.

Degrees of commitment to sustainable business practices

Sustainable businesses try to meet the needs of the present without affecting the ability of future generations to meet their own needs. They aim for longevity. Enterprises reject, adopt or embrace business practices that contribute to sustainability for a variety of reasons and with different degrees of commitment. Australian Professor Dexter Dunphy and his associates propose a scale with six levels of commitment to sustainability. These levels range from Phase 1 or anti-sustainability, through degrees of acceptance to Phase 6 or complete internalisation.[9] Dunphy initially proposed these phases to reflect where companies or individuals are in terms of their attitudes and behaviour towards the environment and corporate social responsibility. However, they can be extended to cover other aspects of sustainable leadership such as people practices. The six phases of commitment to sustainability are:

Phase 1 – Rejection: Businesses in the rejection phase refuse to adhere to regulations. Their executives, often believing that a business's only responsibility is to maximise its own profits, try to obtain exemptions or otherwise get around laws and other initiatives. Corporations in this category might employ political lobbyists to seek exemptions from sustainability criteria. They may seek exemption from minimum wages, ethical standards or pollution regulations, for example.

Phase 2 – Non-responsiveness: Here, managers do not actively campaign against sustainability initiatives like those in Phase 1 do. For them, ideas about sustainability are simply irrelevant to their business. Many companies, driven by short-term thinking, fall into this category. As UK management expert Charles Handy pointed out, according to these managers 'the business of business is business'.[10] Managers in this phase try to ignore various standards and regulations or may simply be unaware of them.

Phase 3 – Compliance: Businesses comply with regulations affecting employees, the environment and corporate social responsibility because they have to. These organisations are not interested in sustainability – often because they believe it costs too much money – but they do want to be law-abiding citizens.

Phase 4 – Efficiency: Here, managers recognise the advantages of sustainable practices. They pursue the cost savings that can be made by using water and energy more efficiently, retaining their staff and other sustainability opportunities. Rational management supports sustainability initiatives that bring immediate and easily identifiable cost savings. Getting to this stage requires the investment of time, money and commitment that some businesses may not be willing to give.

Phase 5 – Strategic proaction: For firms at this stage, sustainability is part of their business strategy. It brings them competitive advantage. For example, fostering excellent employee relationships may attract talented people – important when there is a worldwide shortage of talent. Good employees can make a firm become renowned for service, creating a competitive advantage like US fashion retailer Nordstrom has enjoyed for decades. Customers may be more willing to buy from socially responsible businesses than from their competitors, advantaging the responsible firms.

Phase 6 – The sustaining enterprise: This stage reflects the ideal of sustainable leadership. Enterprises in this phase pursue sustainable initiatives because creating a sustainable world is the right thing to do. Many organisations described throughout this book provide examples here. Organisations at this stage of sustainability implement their sustainable leadership principles wherever they operate, even when local regulations tolerate lower standards. This is because these firms believe it is the responsible thing to do. Phase 6 enterprises will not usually publicise or boast about their activities to gain an advantage; they act according to their principles. Of course, at Phase 6 firms enjoy the economic and competitive advantages won at previous sustainability phases.

> *Sustainable leadership is not about altruism or charity work.*

You may wish to reflect on which phase your own organisation operates in and which phase it ought to be in. Using the metaphor of honeybees and locusts, we can say that Phases 1-3 represent degrees of locust-like attitudes to sustainability, with Phase 1 signifying extreme locust behaviour. Honeybee leadership falls into Phases 4–6, with Phase 6 reflecting the 'highest' form of honeybee commitment to sustainability. Clearly many firms will fall between the extremes of Phases 1 and 6.

Leadership and its cultural context

Examples of sustainable business leadership can be found all over the world. The case studies used in this book reflect the global nature of sustainable leadership principles. Not surprisingly, the highest concentration of sustainable enterprises occurs in regions where sustainable thinking has widespread support among the community. Research shows, for example, that American and British CEOs tend to favour the short-term shareholder model, whereas CEOs in continental Europe have traditionally preferred leadership that engages with a range of stakeholders.[11]

The principles of sustainable leadership also operate at national levels. Gayle Avery discusses this in detail in her book *Leadership for Sustainable Futures: Achieving Success in a Competitive World*. She notes that at least two forms of capitalism have coexisted for decades: Anglo/US and Rhineland capitalism. Anglo/US capitalism has various alternative names, including neo-liberalism or liberal market economics, common law, market-oriented or the shareholder-centred model. Similarly, Rhineland capitalism is variously known as coordinated or social market economics, stakeholder-centred capitalism or simply as the Continental model.

One basic difference between the Rhineland and Anglo/US economic models is the extent to which business and society regard themselves as partners. Rhineland capitalism is characterised by a high level of partnership between business and society, whereas Anglo/US capitalism does not require business to partner with society.[12] Instead, Anglo/US capitalism sees that the 'economic, legal, and social mission of corporations is to maximise their owners' wealth'.[13]

While various other forms of capitalism can be identified, Anglo/US and Rhineland are considered the most prevalent forms in advanced industrialised societies. However, the Anglo/US approach is far more dominant. This is supported by the strong influence of US business, popular culture, education, military and economic might and politics, as described in Box 1–3.

Box 1–3: Why is Anglo/US capitalism so widespread?

Why has Anglo/US capitalism been more widespread than its polar opposite, the Rhineland approach? Is it just because its major proponent, the USA, also happens to be a global superpower? There are many reasons for the dominance of US thinking in the world, including its military power, which allows it to dictate to other countries. Furthermore, US financial power currently dominates world stock markets. The world learned this the hard way with the collapse of its financial systems in 2008. The long-standing popularity of the US dollar for international trade is yet another factor supporting the spread of Anglo/US capitalism. However, the US dollar's dominance is being challenged by the euro.

Furthermore, US financial beliefs have spread beyond the business world to politics and everyday life. US government policies promote the Anglo/US system by influencing major institutions such as the International Monetary Fund and the World Trade Organization.[14] These organisations were created to promote economic stability and help countries in crisis. Now they promote or even dictate to needy countries what is perceived as good for the Anglo/US financial community. As US economist and Nobel laureate Joseph Stiglitz concluded, what might be good for the US can be inappropriate for other countries. An understanding, known as the 'Washington Consensus', was formed between the International Monetary Fund, the World Bank and the US Treasury about the 'right' growth policies for developing countries. Stiglitz argued that the Washington Consensus has been harmful to those countries' environment, democracy, human rights and social justice.

The spread of US values worldwide is another factor favouring Anglo/US capitalism. This has occurred in many ways, helped by English becoming an almost universal language for mass communications and the Internet. The US exports its culture via films, television and music. Its elite universities gain from attracting bright people from abroad. In turn, US culture and business practices are exported home with the returning graduates. Another influence is that most English-language academic journals are published in the US but are read by managers and professors around the world. Unfortunately for a global world this flow of information is still one way, with most US managers and academics not reading what foreigners have to say.

Through these and other mechanisms, US business philosophy continues to dominate daily life in much of the world. The emergence of China, India, South America and the European Union as economic powers raises the question of how long the US economy will continue its dominance – and with it the Anglo/US approach to running businesses.

Obviously, the form of capitalism practised in a particular region influences how easy or difficult it is to adopt sustainable principles. However, this does not mean that firms wishing to pursue sustainable practices are condemned to stay out of countries that favour Anglo/US capitalism, or vice versa. Geography does not determine an enterprise's leadership philosophy. Many family businesses around the world adopt sustainable leadership principles, as we discuss below. Ideas based on Anglo/US capitalism can take hold in Rhineland countries. This happens when corporations list on international stock exchanges or when private equity groups, hedge funds and other investors buy up Rhineland companies.

In short, the influence of both forms of capitalist thinking can be found all over developed regions of the world. Examples of firms following Rhineland principles also occur in developing economies. Examples include Huawei Technologies (telecommunications industry) in China and the Siam Cement Group and Kasikorn Bank in Thailand.

Hence, it is important to emphasise that the terms 'Anglo/US' and 'Rhineland' capitalism are *not* to be understood in a geographic sense. The terms simply refer to where the concepts were first introduced. This is not uncommon with other ideas. For example, the Kyoto Protocol gets its name from the Japanese city where a global environment agreement was signed. The Shengen Accord was named after the town in which an agreement to open Europe's borders was signed. In a similar way, Rhineland capitalism derives its name from a 1959 conference held in Germany on the banks of the Rhine River. Unfortunately, some people interpret the terms 'Rhineland' and 'Anglo/US' capitalism in a geographic sense. While this is understandable it does suggest a geographic divide that we do not intend, and hence we have derived our own terms, explained next.

> *. . . the terms 'Anglo/US' and 'Rhineland' capitalism are* **not** *to be understood in a geographic sense.*

Locust vs Honeybee leadership

The two forms of capitalism described above have strikingly different implications for the way organisations are led. Anglo/US capitalism has created an extreme form of corporate leadership based largely on business practices originally promoted by the Chicago School. We call this the Locust approach, which reflects a tough, ruthless, asocial and profit-at-any-cost business philosophy.

Similarly, Rhineland capitalism has sired a form of corporate leadership that we call the Honeybee approach, which is sophisticated, revolves around a focus on stakeholders including society, and is sharing. Enterprises operating under the Honeybee philosophy are found in their highest concentration in areas influenced by

Rhineland capitalism. However, Honeybee leadership occurs in businesses located in many different countries. This includes in the heartland of Anglo/US capitalism, the USA, at such companies as Colgate, SAS software and Marriott. Locust leadership also operates in countries that traditionally embrace Rhineland capitalism. Major German corporations such as Daimler AG and Deutsche Bank provide good examples of firms that have moved away from the Rhineland approach towards more locust-oriented behaviour.

What is the difference between Locust and Honeybee leadership? The prevailing belief underpinning the Locust approach is that business has one purpose only – to generate a continuous stream of profit and growth for its shareholders. On the face of it, this sounds reasonable. However, the drive to deliver regular profits, growth and shareholder dividends, quarter by quarter, has engendered a particular approach to leadership. The 'hardballing' within Locust leadership requires managers to be tough and ruthless, and to do whatever is necessary to perform well in the short term. The immediate rewards that flow from Locust management can be very enticing for those receiving them – mostly managers and short-term traders. These rewards reinforce the Locust philosophy, encouraging a focus on the short-term.

We use the labels 'honeybees' and 'locusts' to represent the extremes of particular leadership philosophies. As discussed above, firms will differ in the degree to which they display practices belonging to either kind of leadership. In the next sections, we introduce Locust and Honeybee leadership in more detail.

Locust leadership

Under the most extreme form of Locust philosophy (tough, ruthless, asocial and profit-at-any-cost leadership), managers achieve their objectives by polluting the air and water wherever they can get away with it. Locust executives will send competitors out of business, pay pittance wages in emerging economies, or devise elaborate tax evasion or tax avoidance schemes. Giving or taking bribes, 'creative accounting' (fiddling the books) or otherwise being unethical are all part of the game. In other words, the Locust philosophy is based on the idea that one's own advantage can be achieved only by making others suffer. This is a zero-sum game.

Promoters of the Locust model have cloaked themselves in a mantle of respectability by calling it the shareholder value model. In this way, these people have hijacked the moral high ground by claiming that they are the true champions of shareholder value. That Locust leadership delivers better shareholder value is not just a misconception but also a deception. In this book, we explain why Honeybee leadership rather than Locust leadership actually drives long–term shareholder value.

At times, the Locust approach works well for some. One reason for this is that even in a 'dog-eat-dog' environment there have to be winners and losers. But what if a new player comes along who plays by different and more sustainable rules? This happened in the US car industry, where for decades General Motors (GM), Ford and Chrysler dominated. Each tried to be tougher, more ruthless and more asocial in order to be the top dog. The situation changed dramatically for all three enterprises when Japanese car-makers entered the US market. These new competitors invested large amounts of money in training their employees, treated their employees and suppliers relatively well, operated long term and most importantly provided customers with quality at an affordable price. By 2007, Toyota had become the world's largest car company and GM, Ford and Chrysler were all in dire straits. Was it sustainable leadership practices that helped Toyota? Was it Locust leadership that hindered the US competition? Or was it the combined effects of these two leadership philosophies that created such a dramatic gulf between them?

Locust philosophy has been fostered by financial analysts, academics, journalists, management consultants and many investors. Many people do not know or believe that there is any other way of doing business. However, mounting evidence that the Locust approach is not the most profitable and sustainable is resulting in more and more people questioning this philosophy.

The immediate rewards that flow from
Locust management can be very enticing for
those receiving them . . .

Honeybee leadership

The Honeybee, or sophisticated, stakeholder-oriented, social and sharing approach to leadership, provides a contrast to the many variations on the popular Locust philosophy. Honeybee leadership focuses on the long-term and delivers its outcomes more responsibly for more stakeholders. Honeybee leadership assumes that a company can be sustainable only if its operating context is sustainable, and if the basic needs of all involved parties are taken into account. A sustainable enterprise considers all its members as well as the interests of future generations. A business led under Honeybee philosophy cares for and develops its people, tries to protect the planet, cares for the local communities in which it operates and protects its image and brand through ethical behaviour.

Picking up on the holistic nature of the Honeybee approach, the term 'stakeholder value approach' has gained currency. This term captures only a part of the Honeybee philosophy. There is a danger in referring to Honeybee leadership as simply a stakeholder approach. The problem is that it reinforces a widespread misconception that Honeybee leadership is not concerned about creating shareholder value. Nothing could be further from the truth. The difference lies in the Locust approach's almost exclusive focus on shareholders to the exclusion of other stakeholders.

For a long time, the Honeybee model was believed to be less successful financially. Then detailed analyses by eminent economists such as Britain's Will Hutton and top executives such as France's M. Albert, President of Assurances Générales de France, started to indicate otherwise. A vast amount of research now establishes that the long-term Honeybee approach is generally more sustainable than Locust short-termism.[15] In later parts of this book, we cover some of this research. Finally, the collapse of Enron, Worldcom and other large firms in 2002, as well as more recent major shakeouts in the financial industry, have led many opinion leaders to question business models based on short-termism and poor ethics.

Honeybee or Locust?

Writers sometimes refer to a war between the two approaches, and some assert that the Locust model could be winning.[16] However, we will see that individual Honeybee practices tend to outperform practices common in Locust firms. This does not mean that Honeybee enterprises are invulnerable. Sometimes external events affect the business badly, or poor decisions are made that dampen business performance. For example, VW's takeover of Porsche in 2009 can be traced back to Honeybee-Porsche's decision to try to take over VW just before credit dried up during the global financial crisis. A poor strategy in hindsight.

Furthermore, competitors improve or deteriorate at different times, making it hard for a firm to stay ahead. As a result, 'a company can get better and fall further behind its rivals at the same time'.[17] Many external factors clearly affect company performance and, as always, managers run the risk of setting strategies that do not work. It is foolish to assume that all Honeybee companies always perform better than all Locust firms, or that less successful firms are necessarily badly managed. There is no guarantee of high performance in a dynamic world where organisations have to compete and take risks.

However, we will demonstrate that each individual element in the Honeybee model has the potential to add value to a firm and so enhance its long-term performance. This can happen for many reasons. For a start, choice of Honeybee or Locust leadership philosophy heavily determines the way resources are allocated within a business. For example, Honeybee leadership values systemic innovation so highly that, even in difficult years, funding for research and development (R&D) is not cut. Honeybee employees continue to be rewarded and encouraged to innovate in management, processes, services and products. By contrast, R&D is often one of the first budgets to be reduced in a Locust organisation experiencing difficulty meeting its quarterly figures. Another example is training. Honeybee leadership continually invests considerable resources in staff training, whereas a Locust CEO would be prepared to cut the training budget drastically to meet short-term financial targets. We will show that these quick fixes are dysfunctional from a long-term point of view. A business lacking skilled workers and new products will almost certainly struggle to thrive.

Not knowing about alternatives prevents managers from making informed choices. The Locust approach has many influential advocates and is widely practised. But even those who see opportunities and a need for improvement seem to be unaware that a business case can be made for the radically different Honeybee leadership principles.

Questioning business-as-usual

Many executives are preoccupied with day-to-day business and have little time to question and reflect on what they are doing. This is unfortunate if it occurs throughout a firm because the capacity for reflection may be fundamental to leading a sustainable enterprise.[18] Reflection enables an enterprise to learn and change. Various events can trigger reflection – errors or failures, exposure to new ideas, external shocks, or other major crises and events affecting an enterprise. Our hope is that this book will encourage readers to reflect on their current business practices and the effects of these practices on the long-term sustainability of the organisation.

Some leading management thinkers from the US and the UK have already reflected on the drawbacks of the Locust approach. They are calling for a move away from these leadership practices, arguing for changes towards what we now identify as Honeybee principles and practices. Box 1–4 summarises some of the individual changes that leading thinkers are advocating. *Sustainable Leadership* contributes to the debate by explaining how these and other initiatives interact to drive organisational success through Honeybee leadership.

Box 1–4: What the critics say

Management experts who have studied all kinds of organisations to identify factors that provide competitive advantage are urging Locust firms to change their ways to become more sustainable. For example, Warren Bennis[19] calls for a top leadership team rather than the lonely CEO at the top. Bennis wants a long-term perspective in decision-making and a healthy open transparent climate to deter corruption and maintain ethics.

Stephen Covey[20] observes a lack of genuine empowerment of employees. He points to the need to remove our individualistic focus. Firms should operate in emotionally binding teams in which people act in the interests of the group, rather than out of self-interest. Covey also calls on leadership to provide people with a sense of purpose. This requires ensuring that employees are committed to a common vision and set of principles for achieving the vision.

For Margaret Wheatley,[21] leaders are destined to fail if they distance themselves from their staff. Further, she argues that managing knowledge is really about managing quality relationships between people.

Tom Peters[22] reminds us that talent is the be-all and end-all of every organisation. This means retaining and developing staff. For Gary Hamel,[23] a business's only weapon in going forward is having systemic innovation everywhere in the enterprise.

Change is inevitable for every organisation to survive and thrive, according to the late Peter Drucker.[24] By this, he did not mean changing CEOs every three years and adopting hire-and-fire policies! Drucker called on management to treat stakeholders, including organised labour, with respect. He warned that leaders need to balance the long- and short-term interests of different stakeholder groups.

Charles Handy[25] challenges leaders to face the fact that environmentally and socially responsible actions are not reserved for rich corporations. This is a duty for all enterprises and individuals – what is more, it pays off. Lawrence Mitchell calls for introducing trust into organisations.[26] Doing so would allow managers to reveal the decent human beings hidden inside their corporate personas.

These and other elements of sustainable leadership are supported by leading management thinkers. They are practised by Honeybee leadership.

Growing up with business practices that are rarely challenged, it is easy to take them for granted. We simply assume that that is the way things have always been done. We often do not question these ideas. Fortunately, management science can explain why some common Locust leadership practices are on the wrong track. For example, many unethical practices are at least partly attributable to pressures on managers to produce consistent shareholder returns as well as growth. The resulting damage to society and to organisations of fraudulent behaviour can be huge. According to one estimate, over $15 trillion of investor capital was destroyed through financial scandals in 2002 alone.[27] Substantially more value was wiped off the books in 2008 due to extreme volatility in the financial markets resulting from essentially unethical practices. Clearly this has not benefited shareholders.

*. . . environmentally and socially responsible
actions are not reserved for rich corporations.*

There is a destructive flaw in the short-term Locust model, even when fraud is not involved.[28] This flaw stems from the sole focus on the short-term interests of investors, rating agencies, fund managers, the stock markets and their analysts. Most of these groups are not interested in a particular business's future. They are concerned about making quick money from relatively short-term deals. Over-emphasising short-term profits discourages long-term investing and planning – key contributors to an organisation's future. Paradoxically, then, the pursuit of profit can threaten Anglo/US capitalism itself and its offspring, the Locust approach.

However, no matter how business entities are defined or perceive themselves, they are social entities. As such, they need to justify their existence and contribution to society as a whole.[29] Citizens in many countries are beginning to demand this. In 2004, more than half the population in Canada and the UK and 41 per cent in the USA favoured legislating for more corporate social responsibility – even if this meant increasing unemployment and/or raising prices.[30] How much more support would this approach garner if people were told that bottom lines can be expected to improve! A 2006 McKinsey survey concluded that about 84 per cent of executives believed that business has a broader contract with society than has traditionally been the case.[31] How much more support would this approach attract if people realised that it is more sustainable?

Many writers are calling for businesses to reinstate the moral and social dimensions of what they do.[32] So are legislators in many countries. The King of Thailand has instigated a 'sufficiency economy' for the entire nation (see Box 1–5). The Chinese government refers to creating 'harmony'. Increasingly, in many developed economies businesses are being forced by law, regulation and social pressure to take more account of the environment and society in their activities. This challenges the Locust model, with its focus on short-term financial performance and the interests of selected stakeholders.

> ### Box 1–5: The Thai sufficiency economy philosophy
>
> His Majesty King Bhumibol Adulyadej's Sufficiency Economy Philosophy for Thailand aims at ensuring balance and sustainability in many domains, including in business organisations. The philosophy comprises the three components of 'moderation', 'reasonableness' and a 'requirement for a resilience system', plus two underlying conditions of 'knowledge' and 'ethics/virtues'. Dr Sooksan Kantabutra[33] examined the business practices of 299 small and medium-sized Thai enterprises from six industries and three other large enterprises. All were regarded as sustainable because they had survived the 1997 Asian economic crisis. The researchers found some business practices common to these enterprises that are consistent with the King's philosophy. These enterprises adopted a long-term perspective in running their organisations, not just focusing on short-term profitability. They genuinely valued their employees and did not lay off staff during the economic crisis. The businesses were accountable to a wide range of stakeholders, including society and the environment. Innovation in products and business processes was nurtured, particularly by using local knowledge and wisdom.

Finally, managers themselves are recognising the need for sustainable management. Increasing numbers of corporations are claiming to make sustainability core to their business strategy. For example, one of the ten group goals that Munich-based global chemical company WACKER Chemie explicitly aims at is: 'Sustainable management: focusing on coming generations – we cannot afford to mismanage our future'.[34]

Why don't more companies use Honeybee philosophy?

The evidence that we present later in this book shows that the Honeybee model is more sustainable and profitable in the long run. If this is so, why do business schools, management consultants and managers persist with the Locust model? Among the many reasons, let us look at four key ones: the Locust model represents rarely questioned conventional wisdom, people tend not to use evidence in making decisions, some of what is put forward as evidence in support of the Locust approach is ideological propaganda, and fundamental change is difficult to make.

1. The lure of conventional wisdom   *Status Quo*

To act on conventional wisdom, by definition, means to go with the majority; that is, to play safe. Psychologists tell us that when managers and other people know that they will be held accountable for their decisions, they tend to go with the most acceptable alternative among the choices they think they have.[35] If things do not work out, managers can at least claim that they only did what everybody else was doing. Therefore, other factors beyond their control must account for the failure.

This tendency to go with the herd is so powerful that people not only ignore evidence that conventional wisdom is flawed but also they will even doubt their own judgement. A classic experiment demonstrated that people modify their correct judgement even about the relative length of a line when subjected to group pressure from those around them.[36] In a sense, going with the herd is a way of solving problems that has often worked in the past. The assumption is that it may well work again.

In practice, life without these rules of thumb, known as heuristics, would be unthinkable. People cannot go back to basic principles on all the decisions that need to be made.[37] Of course, to maintain cooperation (as one would hope for within organisations) some consistency in people's behaviour, and hence predictability, is essential. Consistency helps to produce and maintain a climate of trust, fairness and commitment. However, when the herd is heading into an abyss, following conventional wisdom is no longer viable. Conventional wisdom is very powerful – but limiting.

2. People discount evidence when making decisions

Contrary to strong popular belief, people tend not to make decisions using evidence. If decisions are not evidence-based, what are they based on? In answering this question let us look at the decision-making processes of a group of people whose job essentially is to make decisions – magistrates.

Magistrates expend a great deal of effort assembling and evaluating evidence in order to avoid pre-judging matters before a court. Or so one would like to think. In fact, Canadian research shows that magistrates' attitudes are greatly affected by many other factors.[38] Some influences relate to how the magistrates feel about the people involved. Others relate to the magistrates' essentially stable, well-to-do, conservative, Anglo-Saxon, largely Protestant backgrounds. The research shows that in 50 per cent of instances one can predict magistrates' decisions, knowing *nothing about the case* but knowing only three specific things about the magistrate. This shows that how people make decisions is not so much about what the facts are but about who the deciders are.

Many countries have adopted a jury system, hoping that a group will produce more balanced judgements than a single judge. Unfortunately, juries do little better. Asking mock-jurors in the US to evaluate new evidence revealed that 75–85 per cent of the potential jurors allowed personal biases to override the facts in their evaluations.[39]

Journalists are supposed to be trained in objective reporting, but are they any better at using evidence? The popular media like to titillate their readers with all kinds of opinions based on assumptions rather than facts. Let us look at an example. One set of statistics claims that multinational corporations are growing larger than many countries in size and power. Thus, multinationals are projected to pose a general global threat. This interpretation is based on misleading data comparisons. Looking closely shows that the political and economic power of multinational corporations is overstated and is not increasing: 'The 37 largest corporations that appear in the list of the 100 largest economies create value added that represents less than 4 per cent of the value added created by the top 37 countries in that list.'[40]

What about managers? Given the substantial biases in judges who are trained to make non-prejudicial decisions, it is not surprising that lay people such as managers are even more prone to making decisions without evaluating the evidence. Managers either act out of habit or base their decisions on their own experiences, prejudices and illusions rather than on evidence.[41] People also claim to feel more in control of making decisions than research suggests they actually are.[42]

In short, we humans are fallible decision-makers. Our decisions are subject to a large number of errors and biases. This may be behind the assertion that one should never let a fact get in the way of a strongly held opinion! Thus, it is not surprising that Locust managers continue to make decisions based on their existing beliefs, even if they know about the evidence that Honeybee leadership is potentially more sustainable and profitable.

3. Ideology as behaviour engine

Given that people do not tend to make decisions based on facts, it is no wonder that ideology can influence outcomes. One example relates to CEOs. In an attempt to make CEOs more accountable, remuneration packages, including stock options, are often linked to share price movements. The belief is that rewarding CEOs for short-term gains with shares in their enterprises will align their interests with those of shareholders. Management scientists have shown this to be a myth because there is little evidence that it actually works.[43] Indeed, such practices can be counter-productive when they dissuade managers from making essential long-term decisions that might adversely affect short-term share prices, and hence their own wealth. Nonetheless, stock options remain a popular addition to CEO packages. This situation is not helped by the fact that CEO tenures are steadily decreasing in length. The long-term performance of companies is of less and less interest to short-term CEOs.

Most of us lovingly hold on to our prejudices. Scholars have identified many long-standing beliefs in management and elsewhere that conflict with or ignore the available evidence.[44] Three of these beliefs are that forced rankings in performance reviews work, downsizing is effective, and managers make decisions objectively on the basis of facts.

As decision-makers become subject to greater accountability, the beliefs underpinning their actions will come under increased scrutiny. This should raise the quality of decisions, given evidence that people are inclined to make better decisions when they expect to have to account for their actions.[45] Otherwise, decisions continue to be based on beliefs, prejudices and ideology!

4. Resistance to major change

If firms managed on Honeybee leadership principles outperform Locust enterprises, why do people resist changing to the Honeybee way? There are practical reasons for managers and employees to resist change. For a start, change disrupts an organisation's systems. When systems appear to be functioning reasonably well, changes can adversely affect performance in the short term. This can have repercussions for managers held accountable for short-term results. It also puts many other employees out of their comfort zones as systems and processes change. Not changing is the comfortable way to go.

A second reason for resistance is that change entails direct and indirect costs of many kinds. For example, learning new ways of doing things can be expensive if people with different skills and training, or new technologies, are needed. Costs like these can be fairly readily identified. However, hidden factors such as how employees relate to each other can also prevent change. Altering existing relationships changes the way people do their work and share information.[46] All these and other factors make major change costly in various ways, particularly for employees who are accountable for short-term outcomes. Even where an organisation accepts the need to do things differently, hidden costs, obstacles and other agendas can thwart change.

Third, managers may be cautious about introducing changes unless they believe that those changes will definitely benefit their business. They are often waiting for 100 per cent certainty. Hopefully the evidence in this book will contribute here. Some people believe, for example, that Honeybee principles are not suited to high-tech or service industries. The experience of enterprises such as Kärcher, Munich Re, Nordstrom, Novartis, SAS software and many others suggests otherwise. To satisfy the sceptics, research is needed to determine which elements of Honeybee leadership are most effective in which situations. However, some sceptics will insist on waiting until all the evidence is in before changing. Others will at least consider the costs of not acting immediately – could waiting damage the business?

Radical change, of course, entails the risk of failure. To manage this risk, prudent managers introduce change in a staged way. This takes time. Thus, a fourth explanation for why companies are not rushing to change to Honeybee leadership could have to do with the speed with which new ideas can be implemented. Adopting innovative practices tends to happen gradually, often by trying a few elements. Three phases seem to occur in the spread of new ideas, such as adopting Honeybee leadership.[47]

1. At the first stage, managers try one or two individual Honeybee practices to achieve efficiencies. An example would be creating teams to help innovate and raise the level of quality in a business. When this single practice becomes successfully embedded, the company starts to see this decision as an astute one.

2. At the second stage, spurred on by the initial success, the business introduces some more Honeybee practices. Although it appears to make good sense to take a gradual approach, this can cause problems. Experimenting with some of the Honeybee practices without adopting the full package may result in reduced growth, particularly compared with the results after introducing the first new practices. This can happen because the system is adjusting to all the changes while still being hampered by its remaining Locust practices. For example, introducing autonomous teams to a manufacturing business requires many adjustments. Managers need to delegate decision-making to the teams. This requires team members to have the skills, motivation and values to be able to be trusted to act autonomously in a competent, motivated and responsible way. This can be a new experience for both managers and team members. In organisations used to high staff turnover, management may be reluctant to commit large amounts of money to training teams. But without training, autonomous teams are likely to fail. Former team supervisors need to adjust to having their roles change from that of boss to team member, with speakers often elected from the team. It also means making changes to the performance management and reward systems to foster teamwork. Furthermore, learners make mistakes that can be costly. Problems arising as learners, systems and processes adapt can interfere with productivity and business performance. If change is not competently managed, managers disappointed with the lack of progress will probably be tempted to abandon the changes. Thus, during the second stage organisational performance can drop. This is of particular concern to Locust leadership, where managers are evaluated on short-term objectives.

3. At the third stage, the full bundle of sustainable Honeybee principles needs to be implemented as a system. Here productivity gains associated with the entire bundle should show up in improved performance over time. But do they always result in improvements? Why do Japanese practices seem to work better in Japanese firms than in the USA? In exploring this question, researchers concluded that adopting only individual elements rather than multiple elements was the likely problem. Few US firms adopting Japanese practices implemented the full range of innovative human resources practices associated with Japanese management. Many managers who adopted isolated practices were disappointed in the results. However, companies that introduced all the Japanese practices showed gains in overall business performance. This suggests that the practices form an integrated bundle rather than a set of isolated practices.[48] All relevant facets of the bundle need to be implemented at this stage.

In short, introducing fundamental changes in leadership philosophy can be hampered by at least four key issues. First, there is the attraction and security of sticking with conventional wisdom. Second, change initially creates both financial and intangible costs. Third, managers, like the rest of us, do not base most of their decisions on evidence but on ideological beliefs. Finally, major change is fraught with risks. The chance of a dip in short-term performance during the change process is high. Therefore, why should managers change from Locust to Honeybee leadership philosophy, particularly if their rewards are based on short-term outcomes?

What might help in changing towards Honeybee leadership? Professor David Ulrich and his colleagues propose a four-step model for managing major change.[49] Although their model was developed for human resources transformations, the systemic approach they have taken is helpful for other kinds of change processes. Ulrich and his team propose four questions to help implement change:

1. Why make this change? This requires change agents to build the business case, providing everyone in the organisation with a

clear rationale for why they should support the proposed change. The rationale should take account of the business context and provide a business case for why this change matters. *Sustainable Leadership* provides a foundation for the business case.

2. What outcomes are expected from making the change? Change 'costs' people in many different ways as we have already seen. Therefore, people need to understand the benefits the organisation will derive from the change. This book highlights some of the expected outcomes from changing to Honeybee leadership.

3. How do we make these changes? Major transformation requires changes in strategy, practices and individuals' attitudes and behaviours that need to be addressed systemically. One change affects another, and these in turn influence other practices and outcomes. *Sustainable Leadership* emphasises the systemic nature of sustainable leadership.

4. Who should be involved in the change? This means engaging others to help with the change – team leaders, line managers and individual employees whose daily work routines and practices will be affected. Many organisational members need to be involved in defining and implementing such widespread leadership changes.

Clearly these steps are not linear, they need to happen concurrently. For example, helping colleagues understand why the change is necessary (Step 1) and the benefits to the business (Step 2) will engage more people in the change process (Step 4). Ulrich points out that these steps should not be regarded as a fixed recipe for managing change, but need to be tailored to individual enterprises in ways that make sense for each business.

Notwithstanding impediments to changing from a Locust culture to a Honeybee one, pressures for change are increasing. Among other things, those holding Locust enterprises to account for their often lacklustre performance relative to industry leaders will want explanations about why Honeybee practices are not being adopted. In addition to expecting sustainable financial performance, critics and shareholders of Locust firms will expect them to meet major external challenges. These challenges include climate change, changing social expectations and a global shortage of talent. Locust executives and their stakeholders will need to rethink the way their organisations are led. Interestingly, as we will see later, Wal-Mart – one of the largest US corporations – has recognised the need for sustainable leadership.

Those in a position to demand explanations need to be equipped with facts and arguments to be able to press their claim. The rest of this book deals with those arguments. Our aim is to provide information for managers to base their decisions on, and we explain to the interested reader how we obtained that information in Appendix B.

The intention is not to provide a 'one-size-fits-all' approach to leadership. Rather, we use examples from many different kinds of organisations to show how differently the sustainable leadership elements can be implemented in practice. Nor are we trying to claim that the organisations illustrating Honeybee leadership will never change. Sometimes Honeybee managers are unaware of the intertwined, systemic nature of their practices and come under pressure to change them. Or Locust leadership decides to adopt sustainable practices, as happened at Westpac Bank in Australia, for example.

Summary

Sustainable leadership refers to achieving futures in which humans live within their ecological and social means, without exploiting other parties. Business has a significant role to play in developing a sustainable future, and an increasingly strong interest in doing so. But will business-as-usual get us there?

Sustainable Leadership is about two diametrically opposed philosophies used for running businesses, going beyond the triple-bottom-line elements of financial, social and environmental considerations. Some organisations are already operating under sustainable leadership principles. We refer to these as Honeybee organisations, and contrast them with Locust enterprises.

Honeybee firms operate on a philosophy of leadership regarded as sophisticated, stakeholder, social and sharing. Locusts adopt leadership approaches that are tough, ruthless, asocial and profit-oriented-at-any-cost. These approaches are not distinguished by their raw materials, facilities, equipment or even the management formulae that they apply. The fundamental difference lies in how they use 23 intangible elements of leadership, known as 'sustainable leadership practices'.

Customers, employees and suppliers are key players in a Honeybee enterprise. There, managers also see themselves as the guardians or stewards of the business for future generations. As such, they plan for the long term and protect the firm's reputation through ethical practices. They care for the environment as well as their local communities.

In its extreme form, Locust leadership takes a short-term, shareholder-based approach to managing a business. Overall, Locust leadership represents what some regard as business-as-usual for many corporations. It is reinforced by powerful institutions such as business schools, management consultancies, media and governments. Nonetheless, management thinkers and many managers around the world are increasingly questioning the Locust philosophy as they call for corporations to become more sustainable. There are sound business reasons underpinning Honeybee practices, as we show in the following chapters.

Although they developed from Rhineland and Anglo/US economic theories that dominate in different regions of the world, Honeybee and Locust leadership principles refer to philosophies and practices that are found across the globe. Some social contexts may support one philosophy more than the other. But sustainable leadership can operate successfully in enterprises everywhere.

How committed an enterprise is to sustainability is highlighted using Dunphy's six phases of sustainability. Locust leadership generally falls into Phases 1–3, at best in Phase 4. Honeybee leadership begins at Phase 4, but is most likely to operate in Phases 5 and 6 where sustainable practices provide competitive advantage as well as being morally right.

Sustainable leadership has to do with generating (common)wealth over the long term. It is a contradiction in terms to claim to be both sustainable and focused mainly on the short term. One excludes the other. Although Locust leadership claims to generate shareholder value, the evidence shows that Honeybee leadership does it better. The difference is that the Locust approach emphasises short-term shareholder value, whereas Honeybee leadership produces better long-term value for its investors and other stakeholders.

Notwithstanding the benefits stemming from Honeybee leadership principles, there are various reasons why Locust managers are not rushing to adopt them. These include the lure of sticking with conventional wisdom, the habit of making decisions based on existing beliefs and ideology rather than on evidence, and the risks entailed in making major changes. As long as shareholders, market analysts and opinion leaders remain relatively ignorant of alternatives, Locust managers are encouraged in their practices.

But this is changing – pressures are mounting for change towards more sustainable leadership. Managers now have to decide whether they want to risk being singled out as defenders of an essentially indefensible way of doing business or face the risks associated with changing over to a more sustainable business model.

Our primary interest lies in the less well known of the two philosophies, namely in Honeybee leadership. Both research and modern management thinking indicate that Honeybee principles are financially, environmentally and socially more sustainable than their widespread counterparts under the Locust approach. A firm adopting Honeybee practices derives significant competitive advantage, as we explain later. This includes the potential for better financial performance.

Students, managers and business academics are overwhelmingly exposed to Locust leadership. There is a huge bias in the academic, popular and manager-targeted literature favouring the Locust approach to business. We therefore want to expose our readers to an alternative approach to doing business and to show how it actually works in practice. In the following chapters, we introduce and describe 23 leadership practices that distinguish the Honeybee and Locust approaches. We show how successful businesses implement the Honeybee elements wholly or in part, explain how such practices form a self-reinforcing system, and demonstrate how that system drives business performance and hence sustainability. And we use the published research evidence to make the business case for each Honeybee practice. Furthermore, we will show that Honeybee leadership can be practised irrespective of its form of ownership, including in publicly listed corporations.

notes

1   Mintzberg, 2004
2   Advertisement, *Der Spiegel*, 2005, Issue 20, p. 36
3   Ghoshal, 2005, p. 85
4   Stalk and Lachenauer, 2004, pp. 67–8
5   Eberl and Schwaiger, 2004
6   McKinsey, 2006
7   http://www.westpac.com.au/manage/pdf.nsf/6917F4B5AF7459EDCA2573AE007DFE7B/$
    File/SIR07_ChairmanCEO.pdf?OpenElement, p. 3; accessed 27 January 2008
8   Hamel, 2006, p. 81
9   Dunphy, Griffiths and Benn, 2003
10 Handy, 2002, p. 53
11 Stadler *et al.,* 2006
12 Mitchell, 2001
13 For example, Copeland and Dolgoff, 2006
14 Stiglitz, 2002
15 For example, Albert, 1992, 1993; Champlin and Knoedler, 2003; Gelb and Strawer, 2001;
    Ghoshal, 2005; Hutton, 2002; Kennedy, 2000; Malik, 2002; Mintzberg, Simons and Basu, 2002;
    Mitchell, 2001; Stiglitz, 2002
16 For example, Hoffmann, 2004
17 Rosenzweig, 2007, p. 16
18 Shuttleworth, Aynsley and Avery, 2008
19 Bennis, 2003
20 Covey, 2003
21 Wheatley, 2003
22 Peters, 2003
23 Hamel, 2003
24 Drucker, 2003
25 Handy, 2002
26 Mitchell, 2001
27 Malik, 2002
28 Malik, 2002
29 Mintzberg, Simons and Basu, 2002
30 Globescan, 2004
31 McKinsey, 2006
32 For example, Hutton, 2002; Kennedy, 2000; Mitchell, 2001; Stiglitz, 2002
33 Kantabutra, 2009
34 See WACKER Chemie AG annual report 2006, p. 30
35 Simonson, 1989
36 Asch, 1963
37 Klein, 2001; Martignon, 2001; Todd, 2001
38 Hogarth, 1971
39 Carlson and Russo, 2001
40 De Grauwe and Camerman, 2002, p. 320
41 Kane, 1996; Rousseau, 2006; Tetlock, 1985
42 Martz, Neil and Biscaccianti, 2003
43 Pfeffer and Sutton, 2006
44 For example, Pfeffer and Sutton, 2006; Rousseau, 2006
45 Schlenker, 1997
46 Gant, Ichniowski and Shaw, 2002
47 Hogan and Mühlau, 2003
48 Ichniowski, Shaw and Prennushi, 1997
49 Ulrich *et al.,* 2009

2

Elements of Sustainable Leadership

How can Honeybee leadership be recognised? In her book *Leadership for Sustainable Futures*, Gayle Avery identified 19 specific elements that characterise Honeybee leadership philosophy. She showed that how Honeybee firms handle these elements is diametrically opposed to the tough, ruthless, asocial and profit-at-any-cost Locust philosophy. *Sustainable Leadership* builds on Avery's work, exposing four more practices that drive long-term organisational performance: staff engagement, self-managing employees, trust and valuing employees. We show how all 23 elements contribute to the competitive advantage of a Honeybee firm, and make the business case for implementing these practices. The aim is to provide guidance for those enterprises seeking to become more sustainable.

This chapter introduces the sustainable leadership elements and the varied organisational forms in which Honeybee leadership occurs – from private to public enterprises.

Distinguishing Honeybee and Locust leadership

Table 2–1 shows the 23 sustainable leadership elements derived from observations of companies and supported by published research. The elements are arranged in three groups: 14 foundation practices, six higher-level practices and three key performance drivers. For the sake of brevity, we refer to the twenty practices and three key performance drivers collectively as practices, although strictly speaking the three key performance drivers (innovation, staff engagement and quality) are not practices. In this chapter we explain what the three levels refer to, and then show that the practices reinforce each other in creating a leadership system.

Foundation practices can be embarked upon immediately if senior management decides to do so. They do not require other practices to be in place first. Foundation practices include programs for training and developing staff, managing labour relations, retaining staff, succession planning, valuing employees, deciding whether the CEO's role is to be that of 'hero' or top team member, initiatives for ensuring ethical behaviour, whether a long- or short-term perspective predominates, how organisational change is managed, orientation towards or away from the financial markets, promoting environmental and social responsibility, the firm's attitude towards stakeholder interests, and the role of vision in driving the business.

Although these are all called 'practices', some more precisely reflect broad principles and attitudes. However, what distinguishes the foundation elements from other practices in Table 2–1 is that they could be introduced tomorrow if the management will is there.

> *Foundation practices can be embarked upon immediately . . .*

Not so for the next level of practices. Relevant foundation practices must be in place before these *higher-level practices* can emerge. Higher-level practices comprise devolved decision-making, employee self-management, team orientation, an enabling organisational culture, managing knowledge and trust.

The foundation and higher-level practices collectively feed into a third level of practices, called 'key performance drivers'. The three *key performance drivers* are innovation, staff engagement and quality. They drive performance essentially by providing what customers are looking for.

It is important to note that the order in which the elements are shown in Table 2–1 does not reflect any order of priority in importance. It represents the order in which the elements are discussed in this book.

Table 2–1: Sustainable leadership elements comparing Honeybee and Locust approaches

LEADERSHIP ELEMENTS	HONEYBEE PHILOSOPHY sophisticated, stakeholder, social, sharing*	LOCUST PHILOSOPHY tough, ruthless, asocial, profit-at-any-cost*
FOUNDATION PRACTICES		
1. Developing people	develops everyone continuously	develops people selectively
2. Labour relations	seeks cooperation	acts antagonistically
3. Retaining staff	values long tenure at all levels	accepts high staff turnover
4. Succession planning	promotes from within wherever possible	appoints from outside wherever possible
5. Valuing staff	is concerned about employees' welfare	treats people as interchangeable and a cost
6. CEO and top team	CEO works as top team member or speaker	CEO is decision-maker, hero
7. Ethical behaviour	'doing the right thing' as an explicit core value	ambivalent, negotiable, an assessable risk
8. Long- or short-term perspective	prefers the long term over the short term	short-term profits and growth prevail
9. Organisational change	change is an evolving and considered process	change is fast adjustment, volatile, can be ad hoc
10. Financial markets orientation	seeks maximum independence from others	follows its masters' will, often slavishly
11. Responsibility for environment	protects the environment	is prepared to exploit the environment
12. Social responsibility (CSR)	values people and the community	exploits people and the community
13. Stakeholder consideration	everyone matters	only shareholders matter
14. Vision's role in the business	shared view of future is essential strategic tool	the future does not necessarily drive the business

HIGHER-LEVEL PRACTICES

15. Decision-making	is consensual and devolved	is primarily manager-centred
16. Self-management	staff are mostly self-managing	managers manage
17. Team orientation	teams are extensive and empowered	teams are limited and manager-centred
18. Culture	fosters an enabling, widely shared culture	culture is weak except for a focus on short-term results that may or may not be shared
19. Knowledge-sharing and retention	spreads throughout the organisation	limits knowledge to a few 'gatekeepers'
20. Trust	high trust through relationships and goodwill	control and monitoring compensate for low trust

KEY PERFORMANCE DRIVERS

21. Innovation	strong, systemic, strategic innovation evident at all levels	innovation is limited and selective; buys in expertise
22. Staff engagement	values emotionally committed staff and the resulting commitment	financial rewards suffice as motivators, no emotional commitment expected
23. Quality	is embedded in the culture	is a matter of control

* Readers interested in anagrams may have noticed that *sophisticated, stakeholder, social, sharing* can be written as *FourS* (pronounced 'force') and *tough, ruthless, asocial, profit-at-any-cost* can be written as *TRAP*. This is no accident.

What do these 23 elements represent? Looking at Table 2–1 again, the words or phrases in the middle and right-hand columns represent the two extreme ends of a Honeybee–Locust spectrum. At the left end of the spectrum (middle column), the elements interact to create 'pure' Honeybee leadership philosophy. On the far right of the Honeybee–Locust spectrum (right-hand column), the elements reflect 'pure' Locust leadership. The individual leadership elements in the table and their contribution to organisational success are discussed in Chapters 3 and 4.

The elements in Table 2–1 can be used as a quick checklist to assess a firm's prevailing leadership philosophy. Given the dynamic and 'chaotic' nature of real firms, it is rare to find 'pure' types in which an organisation is 100 per cent consistent with Honeybee or Locust leadership on all elements. Most likely a mixture will result – whether intentional or not. Sometimes this mixture can be historic, perhaps reflecting the personal preferences of a founder.

Changes to the prevailing leadership philosophy can occur because of dramatic events such as mergers and acquisitions, or taking on additional major shareholders. Global pressures from the financial markets or political changes can produce changes in the systems. Disruption to the prevailing leadership philosophy can also arise as a result of a deliberate or unintended shift from one leadership approach to the other.

Elements form a system

The sustainable leadership elements in Table 2–1 do not operate in isolation. Two largely self-perpetuating leadership systems result. The particular combination of elements can reflect either the Honeybee or Locust philosophy, or some mixture. At the two extremes, the 23 elements work together to reinforce each other – positively or negatively. For example, taking a long-term or short-term perspective affects many other practices. A short-term perspective is likely to require cutting training and innovation, shelving plans for reducing emissions and possibly laying off workers to please investors in the next quarter. This may even require taking ethical shortcuts and ignoring the interests of other stakeholders, such as employees and suppliers. Inevitably, it will be associated with unpremeditated organisational change and disruptions to an enabling culture, and disturbed labour–management relations.

Under a long-term perspective, investors would most likely be in for the long haul and tolerant of short-term fluctuations in results. Internal cuts for short-term reasons are unlikely to happen under a long-term strategy. Thus, the firm's innovation continues, its knowledge is retained and expanded via training and development, stakeholders (including the environment and community) are considered and abrupt unconsidered change averted.

The relationships between the practices are illustrated in Figure 2–1, which depicts the so-called Sustainable Leadership Pyramid. The pyramid shows how the 23 elements listed in Table 2–1 interact at three levels to influence five performance outcomes. Not only do interactions between the elements arranged in the pyramid occur bottom-up and top-down, practices on the same level also influence each other. Thus, the system is dynamic.

Figure 2–1: The Sustainable Leadership Pyramid

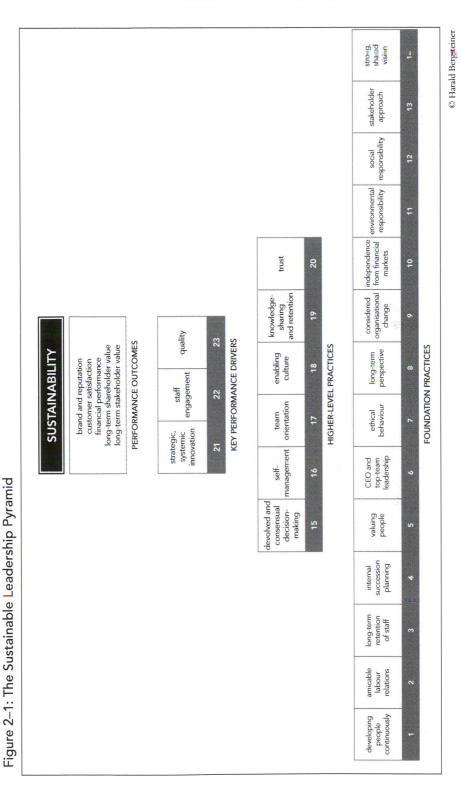

SUSTAINABILITY

brand and reputation
customer satisfaction
financial performance
long-term shareholder value
long-term stakeholder value

PERFORMANCE OUTCOMES

strategic, systemic innovation	staff engagement	quality
21	22	23

KEY PERFORMANCE DRIVERS

devolved and consensual decision-making	self-management	team orientation	enabling culture	knowledge-sharing and retention	trust
15	16	17	18	19	20

HIGHER-LEVEL PRACTICES

developing people continuously	amicable labour relations	long-term retention of staff	internal succession planning	valuing people	CEO and top-team leadership	ethical behaviour	long-term perspective	considered organisational change	independence from financial markets	environmental responsibility	social responsibility	stakeholder approach	strong, shared vision
1	2	3	4	5	6	7	8	9	10	11	12	13	14

FOUNDATION PRACTICES

The essential difference between the foundation and the higher-level practices is that each of the foundation practices can be initiated at any time. Their introduction does not depend on the presence of other practices, although each practice may reinforce one or more other practices.

By contrast, each higher-level practice depends on the presence of particular foundation practices. For example, having decided to create a Honeybee organisation, management can introduce training programs for its people at any time. However, trust cannot be bought and taught the way skills can. Rather, trust depends on the organisation implementing and embracing many of the foundation practices. Developing and maintaining trust requires people to be trained and developed, amicable labour relations, a commitment to long-term staff retention, internal succession plans, valuing people, ethical behaviour, considered organisational change, environmental responsibility, social responsibility, taking a stakeholder approach and sharing a strong vision. Hence, trust is classified as a higher-level practice.

Similarly, the key performance drivers depend on the presence of some or all of the lower-level practices. For example, research shows that achieving high quality requires a team orientation, empowered employees who can make decisions, knowledge management and trust. Thus, the third-level practices emerge from the lower-level practices.

Finally, all 23 elements drive five performance outcomes that contribute to organisational sustainability. We examine the performance outcomes next.

Performance outcomes

Measuring the performance of a business can be very challenging, particularly finding appropriate criteria.[1] Just relying on accounting and financial measures such as 'cash flows still to come in' does not reflect the many other important outcomes of an organisation's performance; nor does measuring fluctuations in the share price.

While the weighting and importance of common performance indices will vary from firm to firm, five outcomes appear to contribute to enterprise sustainability. These performance outcomes are:

1. excellent brand and reputation
2. enhanced customer satisfaction
3. solid financial and operational performance
4. long-term shareholder value and
5. long-term stakeholder value.

Let us briefly discuss what these performance measures refer to, although this is not an easy task given that definitions vary widely across different academics and practitioners.

Brand and reputation

Brand and reputation encompass outsiders' beliefs about what distinguishes an organisation from its competitors. For our purposes, brand and reputation reflect attributions that people make to a firm based on the firm's past actions or those of its products and services.[2] Both brand and reputation may be used to predict future actions. Perceptions of brand and reputation are associated with different aspects of a firm, as well as with different stakeholder groups. For example, in a world experiencing a shortage of talent, an attractive 'employer brand' provides competitive advantage in the labour market. A company with a good 'products and services brand' will be attractive to customers. Thus, the quality of a firm's brand and reputation can have important effects on the behaviour of customers, employees and other stakeholders. As one writer put it, 'reputation management can be about managing what happens inside an organisation to influence external perception'.[3] The quality of a firm's reputation has been related to heightened financial performance and customer satisfaction.[4] Researchers frequently advise firms to dedicate as much effort as possible to establishing a favourable reputation, to gain competitive advantage.

Customer satisfaction

Customer satisfaction refers to the extent to which a company's products or services fulfil customer needs compared with competitors' offerings. Customer satisfaction relates to other measures of business performance, including financial performance.[5] Satisfying customers may be an effective way of enhancing shareholder value because of the strong relationship between those two performance measures. Customer satisfaction reflects other critical measures as well, such as customer loyalty, profits, market share and growth.[6] Increasing customer satisfaction improves future cash flows, thus creating benefits for a firm. This is because satisfied customers are likely to stay with the business, adding real value to the firm. New customers are costly to acquire, and income derived in the year after acquiring a customer essentially just covers the cost of acquiring that customer. Thereafter the takings from a typical customer tend to increase for at least another six years.[7] The increase in revenue over this period is roughly sixfold, largely because satisfied customers are willing to pay a premium for quality, purchase more and refer others. This in turn reduces operating costs. Hence, customer satisfaction is an important measure of organisational performance, and is essential to a firm's long-term viability.

Financial criteria

Clearly, firms need to be financially successful to be sustainable and remain in business. Financial and operational performance may sound very straightforward, but in fact measuring these concepts is complex and controversial. Many different measures are used including profits, sales and revenues, growth in capital, net worth, stock market measures, costs, market share and changes to it and shareholder returns. Other popular measures include return on equity (ROE) or economic value added (EVA).[8] Appropriate accounting measures are critical to all organisations but especially to managers in firms that base many decisions on short-term reported earnings.

The 'optimal' financial measure is controversial. Some scholars have suggested combining individual measures to create a financial scorecard in order to minimise the flaws in each metric, although in practice this does not always work either.[9] The elements in the financial score card are often contradictory and may not be tied to wealth creation. Combining the measures also runs the risk of compounding the flaws in each individual component, making the measurement error larger. A rather surprising criterion for financial performance relates the marketplace's expectations about a firm's performance to changes in its stock price. In this case, managing the expectations of the financial markets becomes an important leadership activity.

Thus, far from financial measures being objective and consensual, there is huge disagreement among experts as to the most appropriate way to measure financial performance. Yet financial performance is vital to a firm's survival.

Long-term shareholder value

Clearly, investors expect a return that makes it worthwhile putting their money into a business. Considerable controversy surrounds what actually drives shareholder value and how to measure it. One definition is that shareholder value is created when the equity returns of a firm exceed the cost of that equity. Financial managers and analysts typically regard such measures as earnings per share, return on assets and dividends as an indication of a firm's value. This is problematic because research has found little correlation between a firm's performance in the share market and its historical accounting returns.[10] Thus, actually demonstrating shareholder value is very difficult because accounting measures do not reflect a company's value or its change in value during a reporting period.[11] Fluctuations in share price and other short-term financial indicators are not enough to reflect or create long-term shareholder value. Thus, individual financial metrics do not relate well to shareholder returns.

Various suggestions have been made for generating long-term value for shareholders by adopting rather different financial initiatives. These include rewarding employees at all levels for delivering superior long-term results, and requiring senior managers to share the risks of ownership just as shareholders do.[12] However, shareholder value over the long-term appears to be driven by factors other than conventional short-term financial measures. The evidence indicates that just as important as financial measures in creating long-term shareholder value are the interactive effects of many of the 23 sustainable practices identified in this book.

Long-term stakeholder value

Research shows that accounting for stakeholder interests, in addition to shareholder interests, is integral to creating sustainable value.[13] However, actually measuring stakeholder value in financial or other quantitative terms is very challenging. Charreaux and Desbrieres[14] attempted to do this using procedures comparable to those used for assessing returns to shareholders. In the process, these writers proposed that resources beyond just financial returns should form part of value creation for sharing with stakeholders in the long term. They concluded that, given stakeholders' many interests, it is better to measure stakeholder value using more qualitative than quantitative criteria. However, few scholars appear to have measured stakeholder value in any consistent way.

One approach to creating stakeholder value is based on seeking Pareto optimality in making decisions. This is based on the principle that the implications of decisions can benefit some individuals or groups at the expense of others. A Pareto improvement arises when some stakeholders benefit from a firm's activities but no other stakeholders are actually made any worse off. Pareto optimality arises when no further Pareto improvements can be made. This requires the interests of a wide range of stakeholders to be considered in a firm's activities.

Sustainability

Sustainability is the ultimate outcome for a business. Longevity is an indicator of sustainability, as is the capacity to weather storms that inevitably beset a business. However, many factors contribute to creating a sustainable enterprise, including the five outcomes identified above. First, financial survival is crucial in both the short and long terms. Creating sustainable businesses requires meeting customer needs and establishing a strong, positive brand and reputation in various arenas. Sustainable enterprises develop a solid social core that emerges from the support of various stakeholders, including employees, suppliers and local communities. Finally, sustainable enterprises create value not only for their shareholders but also for a range of stakeholders over the long term.

The importance of the outcome factors listed above is evident from research showing that in practice they relate to one another in complex ways. For example, a study of industrial enterprises in Israel examined the relationships between CEOs' beliefs about the organisation's reputation, customer satisfaction and other more traditional performance measures.[15] The results showed, for example, that reputation is influenced by customer satisfaction, while customer satisfaction links quality of products and services to the firm's reputation. In turn, reputation is associated with growth of the enterprise and increased customer orders. Interestingly, reputation is not linked to 'hard' measures such as market share, profitability and financial strength.

In studying the effects of the 23 sustainable leadership elements on organisational performance, researchers have used many different measures. This makes direct comparison of studies difficult. Therefore, in collecting evidence from the literature we have had to accept the definitions and measures that individual research teams have reported in their results. However, wherever possible, we have referred to a broad range of studies to try to compensate for the variability in definitions and measures that researchers have used.

Missing elements?

Some readers may be surprised that certain elements or practices do not appear explicitly in Table 2–1 or Figure 2–1. A pragmatic reason for this is that in creating the Sustainable Leadership Pyramid it was not feasible to include every possible practice. Only those elements that discriminate between Locust and Honeybee leadership have been included.

Some practices have been subsumed under other headings. For example, research suggests that a strong customer orientation contributes to organisational sustainability. While not an explicit element in the pyramid, customer orientation is covered in two places: under stakeholders, and as part of the organisational performance measure of customer satisfaction.

Corporate governance is another key factor that influences organisational performance and affects all businesses, but does not appear explicitly in Table 2–1. Corporate governance refers to how companies are run, and to what extent, and how, stakeholders' interests and rights are taken into account. Good corporate governance aims at creating sustainable enterprises, and preventing fraud and damaging scandals. It requires companies to be administered in transparent, ethical ways to maintain the confidence of investors and other stakeholders.[16] The omission of this important concept from the Sustainable Leadership Pyramid may surprise some readers, but there is a good reason for it.

Corporate governance codes and laws are being widely introduced to ensure that companies in most developed parts of the world are well managed and transparent in their dealings. In this respect, corporate governance requirements are growing increasingly similar around the world. Even though the way they achieve these ends may differ in detail,[17] corporate governance affects Locust and Honeybee organisations alike. Good corporate governance becomes part of the global operating context, rather than being a choice made by individual leaders or boards.

Therefore, because implementing transparent corporate governance is required of all kinds of leadership, the broad concept of corporate governance has not been included among the 23 elements in our model. This practice *per se* is not a distinguishing element of sustainable leadership; it applies to all enterprises. However, specific components of this topic have been incorporated into our model. In particular, the corporate governance elements of labour–management relations, ethics and consideration for stakeholders are found among the 14 foundation practices.

A third example covers variables that do not contribute to organisational outcomes. For instance, 'internal auditing', which is a continuous process of examining and comparing the organisation's performance against standards and expectations, has not been included. This is because research has shown that internal auditing *per se* does not contribute to organisational performance.[18] Furthermore, it is a practice that could characterise both Locust and Honeybee firms.

A fourth example of a topic that is not addressed directly in the Sustainable Leadership Pyramid is strategy. One reason for this is that adopting Honeybee or Locust leadership is itself a decision with strategic intent. Many resourcing actions and responses to environmental changes and opportunities flow from the fundamental strategic decision to adopt sustainable leadership principles.

Finally, our focus in this book is on the intangible factors that underpin sustainable leadership. Discussion of tangible resources such as available capital, facilities, equipment and raw materials therefore falls outside the scope of this book. Many other writers focus on the tangible factors. We accept the view that intangible factors, such as the capacity for innovation and managing knowledge, are more likely to create competitive advantage than simply physical resources.[19]

> *Good corporate governance becomes part of*
> *the global operating context, rather than being*
> *a choice made by individual leaders or boards.*

Forms of sustainable enterprise

The examples used in this book show that Honeybee enterprises can be found all over the world and in many different organisational forms. In this section, we point out that Honeybee leadership occurs in both privately held and publicly listed enterprises.

Family businesses are often Honeybee

Based on the available research evidence, enterprises that are still related to their founder or are family-owned or family-run are more likely to operate under Honeybee than under Locust leadership philosophy.[20] That is, they are more likely to operate under sophisticated 'stakeholder, social and sharing leadership' than under 'tough, ruthless, asocial and profit-at-any-cost leadership'. There are clearly exceptions!

It is difficult to define a family business. The term can include publicly listed enterprises still associated with their founders, as well as firms that are not listed on a stock exchange. Family businesses can range from publicly listed firms such as Marriott International Hotels under Bill Marriott as chairman and CEO, to privately held firms. Family businesses often face succession problems and complications arising from family relationships that do not affect most non-family businesses. However, researchers have uncovered widespread Honeybee leadership in family businesses, as we discuss next.

An essential part of being a sustainable enterprise under any leadership philosophy is being financially viable. Interestingly, considerable evidence shows that overall firms that are still related to their founders financially outperform their independently owned and managed peers. This was shown when the performance of family firms was compared with the Standard and Poor's (S&P) index.[21] It was also evident from a study of the largest family businesses in

America.[22] Despite scepticism that family firms face from banks, investors and venture capitalists, overall they tend to perform well financially.[23]

One widespread characteristic of family businesses is that they strive for independence from the financial markets. Privately held family businesses are notably reluctant to sell shares to outsiders.[24] Similarly, to safeguard their independence, family businesses try to grow from their own resources rather than accept external funding. When growth has to be financed externally, they prefer to do it with debt rather than equity. This is often because the debt that family businesses typically take on is more patient money, especially when it comes from owners or friendly banks. Nonetheless, this is changing because banks are increasingly willing to sell customer debt, sometimes with dire consequences for the corporate borrower.

Research shows that SMEs (small and medium-sized enterprises) and privately held businesses typically remain staunchly independent of external capital, even if this limits growth.[25] However, independence from the capital markets does not mean limiting financial success, as a study of privately held German companies showed.[26] This is matched by examples from practice. For example, Rohde & Schwarz, radio and IT communications and measurement experts, refuse to borrow from banks. The story within this firm is that when a banker calls, the company turns the tables on the banker. It asks if the banker is seeking a loan from Rohde & Schwarz! This company goes from strength to strength financially under its current leadership philosophy. It often exceeds its 15 per cent annual growth targets – without using outside capital.

Family firms generally take a long-term perspective,[27] another Honeybee characteristic. Without external pressures from the capital markets, family firms often find themselves in a better position to make necessary long-term investments, thereby achieving better long-term results. Innovation is also important to family businesses. Research shows that they are more likely to initiate and implement new ideas than other firms.[28] In addition, even among the *Fortune* 500 companies, those classified as family businesses lay off staff less often than their non-family peers, thus retaining employees and their knowledge.[29]

Another Honeybee principle often found in family businesses is an emphasis on ethical and socially responsible practices.[30] Of course, there are always exceptions, but family businesses value their reputation and family name. Reputation may also prompt family businesses to protect the environment more than publicly listed firms, and to place a strong emphasis on retaining and investing in their staff. Furthermore, family businesses tend to focus on offering high-quality products and services.[31] This may again be because negative publicity affects the family name and thus the people involved directly.

In later chapters we will see examples of family businesses that operate on virtually all of the Honeybee principles. The result is that many family-owned and family-run companies outperform their Locust peers over the long term.[32] Of course, not all family businesses perform well. However, researchers predict that family businesses that thrive will exhibit Honeybee principles like independence from the financial markets, non-heroic CEOs, strong vision and values, long-term investment horizons, a focus on developing the firm's capabilities through training and development, treating employees as a priority and ensuring low staff turnover.[33]

> *. . . family businesses . . . strive for*
> *independence from the financial markets.*

Public companies can operate sustainably too

Publicly listed companies such as BMW (automobiles), Holcim (building materials supplier), Marriott (hotels) and Nordstrom (fashion stores) – all of whom still have family members on the board or actively managing them – operate on Honeybee principles. Being publicly listed therefore does not preclude adopting sustainable leadership principles.

What about public corporations that are not associated with or controlled by their founders in any way? Our research has uncovered public corporations around the world that adhere to Honeybee principles. Managers of these enterprises are not necessarily even aware of the concept of Honeybee leadership, yet successful publicly listed global companies with professional management can and do display strong Honeybee leadership. Examples cited throughout this book come from many different industries and countries. These include China's Huawei (technology), German-based Allianz and Munich Reinsurance (financial and insurance industry), Roche (pharmaceuticals) from Switzerland and US-based Colgate (soap and other consumer products), Continental Airlines and IBM (services).

Public corporations under professional management face particular challenges in adopting a long-term perspective and serving the interests of multiple stakeholders. Financial markets and investors exert pressure for short-term growth and profits. Managers are usually enticed into focusing on the short-term share price through share options that form part of their compensation packages. Even where companies seek to address this problem by tying manager compensation to the longer-term performance of the business, Locust executives can still be under pressure to maintain consistent company performance for the shareholder. To achieve quarterly results acceptable to the market, R&D, training or staff will be cut if deemed necessary. Honeybee organisations see such short-termism as undermining their competitiveness (through loss of knowledge, expertise, morale and employee engagement) and brand (by breaking commitments to stakeholders). This poses a direct threat to long-term survival, and hence is not sustainable.

> *. . . successful publicly listed global companies*
> *with professional management can and do*
> *display strong Honeybee leadership.*

Summary

Chapter 2 provides the framework for discussing the 23 sustainable leadership elements. The elements are divided into three broad groups, starting with 14 foundation practices. These are regarded as basic for two reasons. First, any one of them can be embarked upon at any time. Second, without them, achieving the higher-level practices and the performance drivers would be very difficult. The foundation practices in turn drive six higher-level practices and three key performance drivers. The manner in which these 23 elements are practised therefore indicates the Locust or Honeybee leanings of a firm.

The 23 elements contribute to five performance outcomes that create corporate sustainability. In particular, sustainability is driven by financial performance, customer satisfaction, brand and reputation, and long-term shareholder value. Taken together, these four outcomes contribute to the fifth, long-term stakeholder value, which ultimately underpins sustainability.

Not every variable relevant to sustainable leadership has been included in the 23 elements. There are various reasons for this, including whether an element distinguishes between Locust and Honeybee leadership. For example, corporate governance, while affecting how all businesses are run, is a requirement for both Locust and Honeybee enterprises. However, components of corporate governance, such as ethics and a stakeholder approach, are already elements of sustainable leadership. Other factors such as the tangible resources available to a firm have been excluded largely because they do not distinguish between the Locust and Honeybee approaches and their outcomes, or they apply equally to both models.

Finally, we have seen that Honeybee leadership can be practised irrespective of the form of ownership – whether the entity is a family business, a public company still associated with its founders or a public company in which ownership and management are separated.

In the following chapters we describe the 23 elements in the Sustainable Leadership Pyramid. We show how each contributes to enhancing organisational performance, beginning with the 14 foundation practices in Chapter 3. We discuss management thinking, practical examples and formal research relating to each element. Chapter 4 covers the higher-level practices and key performance drivers. Finally, in Chapter 5 we examine how all 23 elements reinforce one another to underpin organisational performance and sustainability.

notes

1   Meyer, 2005
2   Thomas, 2007
3   Chun, 2006, p. 105
4   Carmeli and Tishler, 2004a; Roberts and Dowling, 2002

5   Anderson, Fornell and Mazvancheryl, 2004; Bird, 1995; Gates, 2000; Matzler *et al.*, 2005; Sitzia and Wood, 1997
6   Anderson, Fornell and Lehman, 1994; Bolton and Drew, 1991; Hurley and Estelami, 1998; Rust and Zahorik, 1993
7   Reichheld and Sasser, 1990
8   De Wet and du Toit, 2007
9   Copeland and Dolgoff, 2006; De Wet and du Toit, 2007
10   De Wet and du Toit, 2007
11   Rappaport, 2006
12   Rappaport, 2006
13   Pitelis, 2004
14   Charreaux and Desbrieres, 2001
15   Carmeli and Tishler, 2005
16   For example Hilb, 2006
17   O'Sullivan, 2003
18   Carmeli and Tishler, 2004a
19   Hitt *et al.*, 2001
20   Avery, 2005
21   Anderson and Reeb, 2003
22   Lee, 2004
23   McConaughy, Matthews and Fialko, 2001
24   Westhead, Cowling and Howorth, 2001
25   Heffes and Sinnett, 2006; Poutziouris, 2001
26   Venohr and Meyer, 2007
27   Adams, True and Winsor, 2002; McConaughy, Matthews and Fialko, 2001
28   Gudmundson, Tower and Hartman, 2003
29   Stavrou, Kassinis and Filotheou, 2007
30   Adams, True and Winsor, 2002; Gallo, 2004; Wittmeyer, 2003
31   Adams, True and Winsor, 2002; Poza, Alfred and Maheshwari, 1997
32   For example Adams, True and Winsor, 2002; Heffes and Sinnett, 2006; Kleiman, Petty and Martin, 1995
33   Miller and Le Breton-Miller, 2003

3

Foundation Practices

A commitment to sustainable leadership requires owners, boards and managers to choose between two very different approaches to running organisations: the Locust approach (tough, ruthless, asocial and profit-at-any-cost) and the Honeybee approach (sophisticated, stakeholder, social and sharing leadership). Ideally, the choice falls on the approach that demonstrably and logically delivers the better outcomes.

However, the problem is not so simple. Strategic decisions need to be made on 14 foundation and six higher-level practices that influence three key performance drivers. What are these factors that need to be considered? Why are they important? How do they contribute to business success?

The foundation practices are described in this chapter, along with research showing how the elements contribute to organisational performance. The higher-level practices and key performance drivers are described in Chapter 4.

The foundation practices, which are discussed in turn, are:

1. investment in developing and training people
2. fostering cooperative or tolerating antagonistic labour relations
3. retaining staff or treating employees as a replaceable resource
4. focusing succession planning on internal or external prospects
5. signalling to employees how much they are valued

6. whether a 'heroic' CEO or a top team manages the business
7. attitude towards ethical behaviour
8. favouring short-term or long-term perspectives
9. approach to organisational change
10. dependence on or independence from the financial markets (or from political masters in the case of government organisations)
11. environmental responsibility
12. social responsibility (CSR)
13. range of stakeholders to be considered and
14. whether vision drives the business.

The above list does not represent any particular order of importance. The relative importance of the foundation practices is likely to vary with each firm's situation.

Developing people

Honeybee leadership values a skilled workforce and invests heavily in training and developing staff. Not only technical skills are developed but also people's interpersonal and management skills. Programs are planned and updated to ensure that employees develop the social and technical competencies needed to pursue changing business goals. This seems to be what employees want, too. A survey of nearly 13,000 employees found two main characteristics distinguishing Best Employers from other employers: the opportunity for career development through learning, and the quality of work life.[1]

Training is not just for elites, but is spread throughout Honeybee organisations. Special programs are available to apprentices and young graduates to help them gain company experience. University graduates are often offered systematic, company-wide development programs. Many Honeybee companies 'grow their own managers'. They develop people from junior levels, through to middle and senior management.

In the Locust world, training and development tends to be selective. The bulk of employer-provided training focuses on managers and key technical personnel. Development programs are much rarer for front-line workers. This lack of training for customer-facing and production workers reflects a key downside of short-termism. Because people are not expected to stay with the company for long, it is considered uneconomic to invest in them.[2] After all, no one wants to train people to work for a competitor.

If employers do not provide training and development, the onus for training shifts to the employee. However, since employees in Locust firms have an expectation to work for many different employers, there is little incentive to acquire skills specific to their current employers' needs. The fact that developing specialised skills tends to be expensive provides a further disincentive to acquire such skills to Locust employers and their employees alike.

Clearly, people employed by Locusts – who are more vulnerable to being laid off than Honeybee staff – are well advised to acquire more general skills. They can then take their general skills to the next employer, rather than acquire skills specific to a particular employer. This contrasts with the Honeybee practice of investing heavily in training and developing employees, who then become highly skilled at what the employer requires. Of course, if workers are too finely focused on current needs this can reduce their flexibility in adapting to change, so continuous development is important.

> *. . . no one wants to train people to work*
> *for a competitor.*

Training is a heavy investment in most Honeybee manufacturing companies. For example, at BMW teams enjoy a weekend of group training every three years – in addition to specific skills training for individual team members. The team decides who needs which training. Each year, the company spends more than €100 million on training and developing its 90,000 or more associates. This is roughly the equivalent of a medium-sized university's budget. Typically, about half the BMW employees take advantage of the training courses on offer. Similarly, US-based consumer goods firm Colgate offers staff over 150 training programs each year. This is in addition to continuous coaching and on-the-job feedback. At different times, specific training needs are addressed. For example, in 2003 following major corporate scandals elsewhere in the US, about 2500 Colgate managers were schooled in business integrity as part of the company's commitment to strong ethical practices. At German automaker Porsche the entire workforce is highly skilled to meet the company's strategic needs. Training starts with apprentices, who are schooled in a separate area for three years before working on the main production line. The apprentice training area is equipped with the latest technology, which is continually updated. Every employee at Porsche has the chance to engage in lifelong learning, including developing technical, social, personal and methodological skills. These opportunities are discussed in performance management dialogues between managers and their staff. Comprehensive, strategic management training has been developed in association with a well-known business school. In Box 3–1, read more about developing employees at China's Huawei Technologies.

Box 3–1: Huawei Technologies – developing stakeholders globally[3]

China's largest manufacturer of telecommunications equipment, Huawei Technologies, was founded in 1988. It has become a leader in the global telecom market, with innovation at its core. Huawei's landscaped campus gardens in Shenzhen reflect company strategy to stimulate creativity and innovation among its roughly 61,000 employees. The company claims that nearly half the workforce (43 per cent) is engaged in research and development, with only 6 per cent in administration.

Huawei emphasises learning and development for various stakeholders. In seeking to become a learning organisation Huawei invests heavily in employee learning, including formal study and skills development. The company's university is responsible for in-house training for staff and customers as well as an orientation program for new employees. New employees attend a series of training courses covering 1–6 months on such topics as corporate culture, product knowledge and marketing and sales skills. Further training for employees covers management and technical skills. Huawei University's 200 full-time trainers service staff and customers globally in 28 training centres. Customers receive training on products, technical matters and management.

Development plans are created for all employees, tailored to their needs. This ensures that a career plan is available for everyone. A dual career program enables employees to choose between following a career in management or taking a professional/technical path. A competencies and vocational qualification system allows staff to continually improve their skills. Since Huawei's culture values and rewards results, the performance management system emphasises self-motivation and self-improvement. Managers are expected to use goal-setting, coaching, appraisals and communication to help employees raise their performance and competence.

New recruits are expected to share the company dream of enriching life through communication. Stories of successful Huawei employees from around the world prepare prospective employees for some of the experiences, challenges and rewards that the company offers. Developing managers who share the vision and corporate culture is considered a high priority for maintaining a sustainable business.

It is not only manufacturers who invest heavily in developing their people. Service companies such as Allianz (global finance house) and Marriott (hotels) also spend significant amounts on training. The Allianz Management Institute provides leadership-oriented qualifications for the entire insurance and finance group. It collaborates with international universities and research centres. Similarly, other financial institutions such as HSBC (UK), Munich Reinsurance (Germany) and Westpac (Australia) invest heavily in developing their people's skills. HSBC averaged US$750 on each of its nearly 223,000 employees for training in 2003. In 2007, Australia's Westpac Banking Corporation spent A$678 per head for training its 28,018-member workforce.

> *BMW . . . spends more than €100 million on training and developing . . . roughly the equivalent of a medium-sized university's budget.*

Evidence that developing people pays off

Developing employees' skills pays off in many ways, including through increased productivity and profits and shareholder value.[4] For example, US public companies that invest extraordinary amounts in training and developing their people reportedly outperform the Standard & Poor's stock index by between 17 and 35 per cent.[5] Therefore, developing staff pays off financially.

Sometimes employers fear that training their people will drive up wages. The expectation is that employees could demand more money for their new skills, thereby making the firm less competitive. This fear is unwarranted for several reasons. First, OECD research indicates that wages do not rise where employees develop specialised skills that are not easily transferable to other employers.[6] This specialisation actually restricts the job market for those candidates, keeping wages in check. Second, even if wages were to rise, training can be justified on two performance grounds. Employees with specialised knowledge in using technology, dealing with customer needs and understanding the business become more productive. Furthermore, research confirms that people's value to a business rises when they become specialised in that company's knowledge and activities.[7] A third reason is that employing skilled workers reduces the need for expensive supervisors.[8] The high levels of skill and commitment of Honeybee employees supports self-managing employees. This lessens the need for supervisory staff, whose only contribution to the value chain is to ensure that those who are paid to add value actually do so. Therefore, considerable research shows that training and development pay off for shareholders in cost savings, share price increases and enhanced productivity.[9]

The picture looks bleaker for enterprises with high staff turnover. Research shows that shareholder value can decrease by 5.6 per cent if employees are in effect developed for their next job rather than their current one.[10] The investigators attribute this decrease in value to trained staff leaving if a promotion is not imminent, and taking their new skills to a competitor. Therefore, those researchers advise Locust enterprises against training staff during economic downturns.

The direct and hidden benefits of training are often overlooked in evaluating labour costs and productivity. A skilled workforce supports the three key performance drivers shown in the Sustainable Leadership Pyramid (see Figure 2–1), namely staff engagement, innovation and quality. Among the higher-level practices within the Sustainable Leadership Pyramid, training and development can enhance self-management and teamwork as well as strengthen the organisation's culture and promote trust. This makes the strategic decision to invest in widespread training and development fundamental to sustainable leadership.

Labour relations

Honeybee employers rely heavily on their highly skilled workforce. This requires cooperative relations between employer, employees and/or employee representatives where they exist. Hence, collaboration with unions is an important part of Honeybee leadership philosophy. This is easier where trade unions are recognised as part of the business landscape, as in much of continental Europe. In Germany, for instance, unionisation is not mandatory for smaller enterprises, but beyond a certain size companies are legally required to involve unions even if only one worker asks for it.[11] Unions in parts of Europe enjoy protected status under the law and are closely involved in running larger enterprises. In some cases, the company pays the salary of one or more employees to focus solely on union matters. In return, European unions are obliged to support industrial conditions that stimulate organisational success as part of a partnership with the business.[12]

Locust leadership characteristically takes an antagonistic approach to unions. Employer antagonism is embraced by many Australian, UK and US unions. These unions often prefer to distance themselves from employers so that they can criticise them and fight for worker rights. This reinforces the generally adversarial nature of the relationship between management and unions in these countries. In the UK aerospace industry, for example, union–management partnerships have not been very successful. This is partly because attempts at collaboration did not filter through to individual workers. Additionally, management did not change its short-term, shareholder-value-at-any-price and cost-cutting perspectives to adopt the long-term stakeholder approaches needed in a partnership culture.[13] The researchers were not surprised that the old management–union antagonism continued under this Locust management philosophy.

Labour–management collaboration is easier where there is a small number of unions and relatively centralised and coordinated collective bargaining.[14] Employees are able to participate at different levels in decisions affecting their future and that of their employer. Employee influence can be quite strong. In some parts of Europe, the supervisory boards of firms with more than 2000 employees are required by law to have staff representatives make up 50 per cent of the membership. As a result, unions represented at board level in large European enterprises are involved in making key business decisions. Relationships are necessarily more collaborative than is usual under Locust leadership.

Employee representatives can also be useful in managing change. Once convinced of the need for change, employee representatives can help their colleagues accept and implement new decisions. In this respect, employee representation can assist both management and staff in dealing with the human side of change.

However, it is not only in Europe that Honeybee companies value cooperative relationships with employee representatives. At Colgate's US headquarters, a special vice-president for labour relations was employed to foster excellent labour–management relations. Collaboration with unions assists this consumer goods manufacturer in achieving its business objectives. Read about another example of a collaborative attitude to labour relations at Continental Airlines in Box 3–2.

Some global companies like Stockholm-based Atlas Copco (construction equipment) and Marriott International Hotels relate differently to unions in different parts of the world. Relations are cooperative or adversarial depending on local customs. In some countries a very different concept of unions prevails, as in China where unions tend to be like government authorities. Swiss-based retailer Migros protects the rights of supplier employees to union membership, even when those employees work in other countries.

Employee representatives can also be useful in managing change.

Box 3–2: Labour relations at Continental Airlines

US-based Continental Airlines seeks mutual agreement with the unions that represent about 42 per cent of its employees. In the 2007 letter to shareholders, CEO Larry Kellerman described Continental's relationship with unions in the following words: 'The respectful and consensual process we followed demonstrated the profound strength of our culture of Working Together, when

contrasted to the hostility and brute force used by most of our
large network competitors.'

How the unions felt about the process is not recorded, but
they agreed to cuts in wages and benefits during loss-making
years. In 2004 the company signed a 'partnership accord' on
a new approach to labour–management relations, which the
company claims was based on open, honest communication and
trust.[15] Then, in the same year, Continental Airlines announced
that it needed to reduce its payroll costs by changing wages,
work rules and benefits for most US-based management and
clerical employees. All employee groups eventually accepted
the new arrangements, with the prospect of doubling the rate of
employee profit-sharing once positive figures were restored.

Top executives also took a pay cut at the same time. The
board of directors cut its compensation and all its 2005 stock
option grants. Management reduced its own benefits and
suffered cuts along with staff. In 2007, the company began to
return to consistent profitability and directed substantial funds
to employee pension funds and profit-sharing. This recovery in
a troubled industry is at least partly due to the cooperation of
various stakeholders, including unions.

Evidence that healthy labour relations pay off

Fears that unionism inevitably leads to higher costs and lower profits
appear unfounded. Research indicates that unionism is linked to
higher productivity, and the increased productivity offsets any rises
in wages that may occur with union representation.[16] Contrary to
popular belief, in OECD countries union participation does not
adversely affect national unemployment figures – but can actually
help reduce unemployment.[17]

Early studies suggested that trade unions had a negative effect on
business performance, at least in the US and UK where antagonistic
labour–management relations are traditional.[18] However, other studies
challenge this. French researchers found that trade union presence
has no adverse effect on an organisation's financial performance.[19]
Other international data showed that positive union–management
relationships can enhance the adoption or sustainability of a
firm's innovations. A study of the airline industry concluded that
labour relations indirectly affect overall reputation and company
performance, largely through their effects on customers.[20] In the
once antagonistic labour climate of the UK, a study of 200 firms

showed that unionism was positively related to how innovative a business was.[21] Recently, UK firms seem to be shifting towards more cooperative union–management relations, with workers and management treating each other as partners. This has occurred partly because participative management is seen as a good thing to have, and because employee participation is presumed to lead to improved job satisfaction and productivity[22] and enhanced financial performance.

Similarly, traditional labour–management antagonism may be lessening in the US. Investigations of labour relations in the airline industry revealed that business performance may improve in the presence of trade unions.[23] No doubt the increased conflict and deterioration in workplace culture historically associated with antagonistic unions did not help firm performance. Rather, business performance appears to improve when unions are present and relationships among employees, supervisors and managers are cordial. Researchers suggest that in the case of the US airline industry, increased productivity stems from greater cooperation and effort in turning aircraft around more quickly, allowing the machines to be used more efficiently. Thus, the quality of labour–management relationships matters.

A similar finding was made among Japanese firms, where companies that openly shared information with employees and their representatives enjoyed higher profits and productivity and lower wage costs.[24] Israeli researchers concluded that several factors contribute to the performance of public sector organis-ations, including labour relations.[25] Thus, in many different contexts cooperation between management and unions appears to pay off financially for an enterprise, certainly in the medium to longer term.

By itself, unionism can have positive or negative effects on a firm's performance, depending on the nature of the relationship with management. When accompanied by other factors, such as flexibility, teamwork and cooperative relationships, union representation can be positive for productivity and financial performance.[26] Deciding to develop amicable relationships with the representatives of the workforce can be introduced at any time, and appropriate actions instigated. For a start, communication can be opened and meetings set up, representatives of management can be appointed for the purpose, and positive messages sent to employees and unions.

In short, a major difference between Honeybee and Locust leadership philosophy rests on how much management strives to cooperate with unions. The Locust attitude is one of conflict, whereas Honeybee leadership seeks cooperative relationships. Of course, it requires a reciprocal attitude on the part of the unions for collaborative relationships to develop, but striving for partnership with unions is a decision that management can take immediately. This makes it a foundation practice in the Sustainable Leadership Pyramid. Leading commentators are already calling for a rethink of the relationship between business, labour and government to create 21st century organisations that are not only globally competitive but also offer high quality of life and well-being for workers.[27]

Staff retention

Layoffs have long been common under Locust leadership. For example, GM's 2006 annual report on progress made that year euphemistically states in the letter to shareholders: 'More than 34,000 US workers participated in the GM attrition program.' Regularly laying off staff provides a firm with the flexibility to adjust quickly to changes in the market.[28] It also allows firms to attack competition through lower prices. This can be an advantage in producing cheap commodity items and in restructuring an enterprise quickly.

However, in sectors where innovation and quality are important, a hire-and-fire approach brings disadvantages. Among other things, continual changes in staffing make it difficult to impart and retain essential skills and knowledge. This in turn hampers efforts at achieving high quality and innovation. Furthermore, the so-called survivors of layoffs often operate in fear that they may be the next to go. They may suffer stress from having to take on extra work previously done by newly departed colleagues. Survivors are less likely to take the risks needed to get an organisation out of trouble – risks associated with creating new products and markets or targeting new customer groups. Thus, taking a short-term approach to people, such as issuing short-term contracts, works against being innovative.[29]

Employers can increase the chances of staff staying with them in various ways. Retention starts with recruiting people whose values align with those of the firm. This was shown in a US study that tracked the early careers of 171 auditors in eight large public accounting firms.[30] Those auditors whose values most closely matched the firm's values reported feeling most satisfied and actually remained with the firm longer than their less well-fitting peers. Analysing the results of 172 studies revealed that those people who do not fit their organisations tend to look for work elsewhere.[31] The main benefit of ensuring a fit between employees and the organisation appears to be its positive association with organisational commitment and job satisfaction – as well as employees' intention to stay.

Employers can also enhance retention by managing employees' career aspirations. When a multinational manufacturer aligned the organisational culture and employees' career motives, employees perceived their organisation more positively and expressed a greater desire to stay.[32]

Under Honeybee philosophy, employees are the heart and soul of the enterprise – workers play a key role in creating value for the firm. Honeybee enterprises try to retain their people even in difficult times. Continually laying off staff breaks the silent agreement between Honeybee management and labour, namely that job security is offered in return for employee loyalty. The Honeybee approach includes offering a choice of career paths in an effort to retain employees who want different kinds of careers. Once, the traditional career path led from technical positions to senior administration. Now, parallel technical or professional careers aid in keeping workers who want to remain technicians, specialists or project managers.

. . . employees are the heart and soul of the enterprise . . .

Few employees leave Honeybee enterprises other than to retire, although staff fluctuation numbers vary with industry. Staff turnover is of the order of 2–3 per cent at Honeybee companies such as Swiss building materials supplier Holcim and German chemical firm WACKER. Turnover is close to zero at Aesculap, and no one has ever been sacked at this leading German surgical instrument maker. Even Germany's Fraunhofer Society, part of whose research and development mission is to release research scientists into industry once they have received some commercial training, has an annual staff fluctuation of only about 12 per cent. Staff departures at US software producer SAS are around 4 per cent yearly, very low compared with the 20 per cent elsewhere in the IT industry. Staff fluctuation at Marriott International Hotels is low by hotel industry standards. For example, in Hong Kong the hotel industry experienced 29 per cent staff turnover overall in 2003. In that same year, staff turnover at the JW Marriott in Hong Kong was under 9 per cent. The savings of not having to recruit, induct and train new staff reflect positively on a firm's bottom line.

Sometimes it is unavoidable that employees need to be laid off, and a firm benefits from doing so in an employee-friendly way.[33] Employees cope better if the organisation displays a concern for staff when work is redistributed or jobs are threatened. Employers can provide counselling for both those going and for the survivors, for example. Downsizing seems to be more effective when it is planned in advance, rather than used as a quick fix for a financial loss.

In difficult times, Honeybee enterprises try to retrain and redistribute employees within the organisation. For example, Marriott did this during the SARS epidemic in Hong Kong. The percentage of hotel room bookings was reduced to single-digit numbers during the epidemic. However, the JW Marriott Hotel in Hong Kong had developed a quality reputation for its restaurants. During the SARS epidemic, Marriott's restaurant business boomed. The company quickly retrained its under-employed housekeeping staff to wait on tables, rather than sacking the housekeepers and hiring new waiters. In this way, Marriot staff did not lose their jobs during the SARS epidemic. The company benefited by retaining its skilled housekeepers and was fully prepared for the return to normal business that followed.

Companies often use the need to restructure as an opportunity to rid themselves of staff – a practice known euphemistically as 'downsizing'. However, when global reinsurer Munich Re restructured its Munich head office in 2001–02, it kept its promise that no employees would lose their jobs during the process. The whole change management process was handled in a highly structured way and was implemented in record time. This was possible because it had support at all levels of the organisation. On the other hand, IBM (see Box 3–3) is concerned with injecting regular new blood into its workforce each year, and this involves shedding existing staff. This Locust practice is inconsistent with other practices at IBM that are more Honeybee in orientation.

Box 3–3: A constant flow of new blood at IBM

Although IBM wins awards for its leadership, people focus, training and innovation, it 'rebalances' its workforce regularly. Managers argue that constant rebalancing of the skills base is necessary because of the fast-paced changes in their global industry. In short, IBM parts company with about 20,000 employees each year. In 2002, 6 per cent of IBM's workforce was shed within a relatively short period. This created a culture of fear according to insiders, even though displaced workers are well supported by outplacement and other programs to help them find other work. To balance its approach of shedding employees, IBM is developing a new relationship with its staff that involves providing opportunities for workers to retrain for completely new roles and to continue learning. According to the company's 2007 annual report, IBM retrains retiring IBMers to transition to second careers in teaching, government service and non-governmental organisations.

Evidence that retaining staff pays off

Contrary to conventional wisdom, companies benefit financially by retaining staff whenever possible. Managers often forget that staff turnover is expensive. Replacing a US call-centre customer service representative costs roughly a year's wages, while replacing higher-level staff costs between one and two years' salary and benefits.[34] A six-year study of 904 university graduates hired by six public accounting firms estimated the difference in related human resource costs at the various firms at about US$6 million.[35] Whether employees stayed or not depended on the organisation's values. These estimates are likely to be conservative because many costs are indirect and hence difficult to quantify. Hidden costs include lost productivity while the new employee is learning the job, training costs and time spent conducting exit interviews and briefing search consultants or advertising agencies.

Retaining well-trained and loyal
staff . . . enhances organisational performance.

Apart from saving on recruitment costs, retaining employees can also create hidden, non-financial advantages for a firm. For example, retaining staff preserves and capitalises on linkages that form between long-term employees and enable ideas and skills to be shared in unique ways. This creates competitive advantage that other businesses cannot copy.[36] On the other hand, when employees leave, knowledge and expertise is lost to a firm and may end up serving a competitor. Laid-off staff can take customers with them. This can be costly given the high costs of acquiring a new customer compared with retaining an existing one.[37]

Various studies show that employment security is part of a bundle of practices associated with higher productivity.[38] Interestingly, firms that retain staff are not plagued by the high rates of absenteeism, sick leave and internal migration that are a frequent cost of layoffs.[39]

Overall, despite certain short-term improvements to financial metrics, firms shedding staff tend to experience more long-term financial difficulties than their counterparts.[40] Certainly shareholders miss out on the financial benefits of retaining staff. Keeping voluntary turnover low contributes about 3.2 per cent to a company's value, while a strong commitment to job security adds an additional 1.4 per cent according to global research.[41]

Another consequence of staff layoffs can be damage to the firm's reputation, as shown in a study of *Fortune*'s most admired companies in America that laid off staff between 1984 and 1994.[42] While executives rated the laying-off firms negatively, stock analysts tended to be even *more negative* in their appraisals of downsizing firms. This was surprising, given how analysts often lobby firms to downsize. One of the reasons for this damage to reputation is likely to be that the trustworthiness, credibility and commitments underpinning corporate reputations were broken.

Thus, while laying off staff may result in some immediate cost savings, it rarely leads to increased organisational performance. Rather, it tends to produce medium- to long-term losses once hidden people costs are taken into account. Nonetheless, for new Locust CEOs, chasing such short-term cost savings can be highly tempting when the next quarterly result is tied to their own short-term rewards. Since the resultant bonus payments to the CEO occur at the same time as the staff layoffs, the trust between top management and staff is severely tested, if not destroyed. Some of these hidden costs stem from the so-called survivor syndrome whereby people remaining with the business feel insecure or angry, or experience other emotions that diminish their performance. The evidence shows that workers feeling insecure about their jobs perceive their organisations poorly — as ineffective in responding to change, managing morale and delivering on customer performance and effectiveness.[43] Such workers are prone to suffer from poor health, which can be expensive for an employer. The good news is that employers who continue to invest in and care for their people can minimise negative effects such as productivity losses and absenteeism, even after layoffs.[44]

Similar findings emerge from research into small businesses. Enterprises reporting strong financial growth tend to have employees with high levels of involvement in the firm and intentions to remain with it.[45] The same research shows that these firms also outperform their competitors. Thus, retaining well-trained and loyal staff wherever possible enhances organisational performance, including for small business.

The bottom line is that businesses that lay off staff only as a last resort are financially ahead of companies that regularly downsize. Retaining staff supports various higher-order outcomes in the Sustainable Leadership Pyramid: it allows knowledge to be retained, fosters trust and supports quality, staff engagement and innovation. Overall, retaining staff enhances financial performance, as well as brand and customer satisfaction, outcomes important to sustainable leadership. Staff retention is regarded as a foundation element in the Sustainable Leadership Pyramid because conditions aimed at keeping staff can be initiated at any time.

Succession planning

Planning for the future, while retaining staff, requires systems for identifying successors for roles in an organisation. Honeybee leadership prefers to promote people from within the firm rather than hire new workers. In periods of rapid growth, filling every role from within is not feasible; in these circumstances, even Honeybee firms recruit externally. However, newcomers are carefully selected and inducted into the existing organisational culture.

Some Honeybee firms will not appoint outside managers directly to top positions. Instead, new recruits are slotted into the company's succession plan and mentored for a year or two to ensure that they fit the role and culture. If all goes well, the newcomers are promoted to the top posts. Since not all staff members reach senior management levels, other measures to foster development need to be coupled with internal promotion.

A US study found that high-performing visionary companies are six times more likely to promote an insider to CEO as other US companies.[46] The researchers concluded that it is not the quality of leadership that most separates excellent companies from others but the *continuity* of quality leadership. This continuity preserves core organisational values, maintains a strong and consistent culture and helps ensure that long-term plans and strategies remain on target. Hiring senior executives from outside the organisation puts core values and cultural identity at risk, as do frequent changes at the top. This makes it hard to become and remain successful.

> *Hiring senior executives from outside the organisation puts core values and cultural identity at risk . . .*

Locust leadership prefers to hire new talent from outside the firm. Locust managers are often perplexed at the Honeybee practice of growing and developing senior management from inside the organisation. 'Where do new ideas come from?' they ask. From a Honeybee point of view this is the wrong question. The role of senior management in a Honeybee enterprise is not to be the source of innovation. Honeybee CEOs have the task of ensuring that the organisational culture, practices and systems foster widespread and continuous innovation. Organisations could not survive if innovation were simply filtered down from CEOs and other top executives, whether employed for the short or long term. Just how seriously some Honeybee businesses take staff succession and development can be seen in the following examples.

The board of US consumer goods manufacturer Colgate is extensively involved in succession planning, particularly at senior levels. Board members discuss and evaluate potential successors to key executives, rather than leaving this important matter to lower levels of management. Swiss building materials supplier Holcim has an explicit goal of appointing internally to vacant positions. This is organised around a complex succession plan and a pool of well-developed managers. The company's objective is to ensure that the managers of today have the professional, social and personal competencies needed to make the company successful in the future. To this end, Holcim uses targeted management development programs designed to stretch and challenge its future leaders. You can read about the extent of promotion from within at US-based global delivery firm UPS in Box 3–4.

A special challenge for many organisations is to increase the proportion of women in management positions. Although women make up about half the intake from universities at global reinsurer Munich Re, for example, retaining females long enough for them to move into senior management positions is difficult. To this end, the company sponsors a kindergarten and has set targets and strategies for increasing the number of executive women significantly.

Box 3–4: Promoting from within at UPS

American UPS describes itself as 'the world's largest package delivery company, in terms of revenue and volume, and a global leader in supply chain solutions.'[47] UPS is regularly America's 'most admired' company in the transport industry. Founded in 1907, this messenger company had grown into a US$51.5 billion corporation with about 426,000 full-time and part-time employees operating in more than 200 countries by 2008. Its goal is 'to run a financially sound business, in a socially responsible and financially sustainable manner, to ensure our on-going ability to positively impact the stakeholders with whom we interact every day'.[48] A key element in achieving this goal is people.

UPS has long had a strong preference for promoting existing staff into more senior positions and encouraging people to have long-term careers in the firm. This means that part-time employees become full-time, and some then move into management. Under this policy, 2008's full-time UPS manager averages 15 years of service. This creates a management team with expertise that the rest of the industry can only envy, and supports an enabling culture.

Some statistics from the company's sustainability report include:

- 4551 part-time employees advanced to full-time in 2008
- more than 50 per cent of UPS's current full-time drivers were once part-time employees
- 75 per cent of full-time management employees were promoted from non-management positions
- most vice-president-level employees started in non-management positions
- 8237 employees were promoted into management for the first time in 2008
- 99 per cent of global managers work in their home countries.

To achieve the required degree of internal promotion, the company formalises career development. Under UPS's succession planning, employees are identified early to fill the next level of executive leadership and then are prepared for advancement.

The company claims that this promotion-from-within policy has underpinned its ethical culture for nearly one hundred years. The values of ethics and integrity can be passed on to younger generations because of the level of experience and length of service of employees developed from within the company. However, in recent years UPS has noticed that its culture of strong processes, procedures and hierarchy was not particularly attractive to younger recruits. Young drivers were reluctant to learn the ropes and stay with the company in adopting its approach to the new generation. UPS now makes employees responsible for their performance and career path within the company's promote-from-within policy.

Evidence that succession planning pays off

Although promoting people from within requires extensive attention to developing people for new roles, researchers have found that this pays off for an enterprise in various ways. Internal succession planning not only provides a perspective for employees to advance their careers but has also been associated with successful enterprises.[49] Organisations with high-quality leadership development and succession management programs are associated with higher performance on six financial indices: return on equity, return on assets, profit margin, market–to–book ratio, net sales and total assets.[50]

Sourcing senior management from within the business adds value. At top levels internal succession is associated with positive financial performance for the firm, and high-performance companies from around the world prefer to appoint CEOs from within, making succession as seamless as possible.[51] By contrast, externally appointed CEOs underperform the market by about 5.5 per cent compared with companies led by insiders.[52] One reason for this is that internal promotions retain knowledge in the business, whereas outside hires rarely bring, or have little interest in investing in, firm-specific knowledge. Notably, when organisations are performing poorly, the chances increase that an outsider will be appointed as CEO compared with when performance is good.[53]

Internal promotion can help retain staff at all levels, another Honeybee principle. In a global survey of 900 companies, human resources professionals reported that 65 per cent of people promoted internally into leadership positions remained with the company and were regarded as successful.[54] The remainder did not perform well, and this was attributed largely to their poor people skills.

Succession planning is particularly vital in the many developed economies facing an ageing population and declining growth in the workforce over the coming decades. This makes replacing staff increasingly challenging. Regions heavily affected include parts of Europe, Japan, New Zealand, Australia and increasingly the USA. Therefore retaining staff and planning for their career development is becoming increasingly important to a firm's very survival in those economies, let alone planning for growth.

Like other foundation elements in the Sustainable Leadership Pyramid, succession planning can be introduced at any time. Associated with promoting from within are several other essential Honeybee practices designed to foster quality and innovation. These include extensive training and development for new roles and responsibilities, and retaining knowledge for the firm. Research shows that promotion opportunities provide employees with intrinsic motivation,[55] and are more likely to occur where trust is high.[56] Thus, appropriate succession planning influences, and is in turn influenced by, other sustainable leadership elements.

Valuing employees

The strong value that Honeybee leadership places on caring for employees emerges from much more sophisticated and complex ways of approaching efficiency, adaptability and productivity than Locust companies adopt.[57] Considerable attention is given to trying to raise organisational performance just by managing operations and technology better, and via cost savings and other financial measures. However, a firm's performance can also be raised by focusing on the value that employees bring to the business.

Supporting this view are findings that specific people practices promote strategic advantage for firms. Many of these practices characterise Honeybee enterprises. Examples include providing security of employment, recruiting for cultural fit, sharing information, employee participation and empowerment, self-managing teamwork and multiskilling and training staff across different activities.[58] Other important people practices include fostering a relatively non-hierarchical culture, ensuring that wage differences are not too extreme and promoting from within wherever possible.

Certainly, offering incentives such as bonuses or employee ownership emphasises that an employee's contribution is valued in a material way. However, the actual benefits to the business of employee profit sharing and ownership are far from clear.[59] Another practice thought to characterise high-performing businesses is to pay very high wages,[60] but again this is not always the case in Honeybee organisations. Interestingly, of the various human resources practices found to benefit organisational performance, employee ownership of company stock is the only one not universal in Honeybee enterprises. In practice, ownership and high wages are not necessary to retain employees bound by loyalty, firm-specific skills and a feeling of being valued.

> *. . . much more sophisticated and complex*
> *ways of approaching efficiency, adaptability*
> *and productivity . . .*

For various reasons, Locust leadership seems to find it more difficult to employ the above people principles than Honeybee companies do. This may be because under Locust philosophy, employees are regarded as a cost rather than as an asset. Workers in Locust organisations are liable to being laid off or having their work outsourced. This signals to people that they are not valued, thereby reducing people's commitment to their employer. Finally, if employees are viewed as a cost, managers may overestimate the importance of money as a motivator.[61] Intangible factors such as interesting work and opportunities for personal development and recognition can be even more attractive to employees than just money.

Let us look at some practical ways in which some Honeybee enterprises demonstrate that they value their employees. At US-based Marriott International Hotels, high wages and incentives are not used to retain high-flying staff because this goes against the firm's collaborative culture. This hotel group recognises that employee life-work balance is essential, so it supports its associates in coping with their complex lives. The employer helps with visa and housing problems, elder- and childcare, and domestic abuse. Both associates and their families are covered by subsidised medical care, and the company assists its employees in saving for their retirement through the company's profit-sharing system. Recognising the efforts of employees is an everyday event as well as an annual ritual at Marriott. Associates' small achievements are recognised in daily team meetings, and at parties and other festivities that celebrate the staff's contribution to the company during the annual Associate Appreciation Week.

US-based Colgate also recognises employees as the key driver of its success. Living the values of caring, global teamwork and continuous improvement at this global consumer goods company involves managing people with respect and caring for people's contributions. The company shows that it values its associates' contribution not only through rewards and recognition but also by providing many benefits.

At America's Continental Airlines, creating shareholder value is important. As at Marriott and Colgate, this is achieved by treating employees well. Continental Airlines regards happy, loyal employees as key to its success. There, employees are paid well and participate in the company's financial success, receiving about 30 per cent of the company's pre-tax earnings. Employees also earn a monthly bonus if flights are on time. Its tradition of valuing employees enabled Continental Airlines to ask its 37,680 staff members not to leave the business in 2002, but to stay and help the troubled company.[62] The workforce responded and rebuilt the company.

Typically, companies led by Honeybee principles provide outstanding employee benefits and recognition that exceed those offered by most of their competitors (see Box 3–5 for what software company SAS does). This generates strong loyalty that assists the enterprise in difficult times. Feeling valued provides employees with reasons why they should stay with the company and not shift to a competitor. This helps retain people, with all the benefits that entails.

Box 3–5: Valuing employees at SAS

Like many Honeybee organisations, US-based SAS software wants its employees to enjoy coming to work. It goes to great lengths to ensure that this happens. Headquartered in Cary in North Carolina, SAS does not offer stock options to its employees. Instead it offers many other benefits, including one of the highest motivators for creative people: challenging work.[63] SAS makes extensive efforts to let its people know that they are highly valued. The company is set in splendidly landscaped grounds, boasting 34,000 flowers, 40 hectares of lawn and a fitness centre. Of course, the company takes care of the big issues such as childcare with family friendly practices and on-site medical facilities, and provides profit-sharing and bonus schemes. However, often small things signal how much the company values its people. For example, at the company-run gym, SAS employees find their sports clothes laundered and waiting for them the next day.

Everyone is expected to balance work with his or her personal life. SAS employees often lunch with their children on campus, and most leave for the day at around 5 pm. This is part of a strategy to take distractions and menial tasks away from employees so that they can concentrate on doing what they like doing and on what is important. These savings in precious worker time can be directly costed and justified when assessing benefit programs.[64] No wonder SAS is regularly awarded for being an outstanding employer. No wonder its annual staff turnover is extraordinarily low for the IT industry at 4 per cent. Is it any wonder that SAS's financial results continually climb as well?

Evidence that valuing employees pays off

Behind valuing employees is the belief that a satisfied and happy workforce enhances customer satisfaction and in turn raises financial performance. That this happens is well supported by research evidence dating back over 50 years.[65]

Positive work environments demonstrably pay off in financial performance compared with negative environments. For example, employees at the 100 Best Companies to Work For in America receive extraordinary benefits, experience high job satisfaction, have fun at work and find opportunities to balance their personal and work lives. Public companies among the 100 Best Companies have realised substantial advantages in financial performance compared with publicly listed companies in general, starting with better financial performance than peers in their industries.[66] Between 1998 and 2004 'Best' companies outperformed the Standard & Poor's index by almost four times, and their cumulative returns have outstripped those of the rest of the market. Similar findings have been made with organisations rated as Best Employers by Hewitt Associates and by others as Great Places to Work.

Studies consistently show that investing in people is good for the bottom line even in more mainstream firms not on 'best' lists.[67] For example, shareholder value increases with a skilled, motivated, adaptable workforce and by creating an employee-oriented workplace.[68] The way entrepreneurs in small businesses develop and treat their people affects employment growth in the business.[69] Additionally, global research shows that flexible work arrangements that take individuals' needs and wants into account, such as flexitime, working from home and job-sharing, can increase shareholder returns by around 3.5 per cent.[70]

Similarly, so-called innovative human resources practices have been used to great effect. In one situation, they were used to offset many of the unfortunate features of working in call centres with highly controlled and measured work environments.[71] Instead, employees were encouraged to take responsibility for their work both as individuals and in the newly introduced teams and to make suggestions for improvements. Careful selection and recruitment, extensive training and development and a new career structure were part of the new call centre workplace. In addition, a deliberate attempt was made to create a fun environment so that people would enjoy coming to work – unlike in traditional call centres where stress is the dominant experience. These measures were associated with increases in productivity and reduced absenteeism in both call centres studied.[72] Call-centre workers' earnings also rose in most cases, along with their morale and commitment to the job.

Although researchers have not clearly established just how valuing staff improves the bottom line,[73] the overall evidence is compelling. Caring for people is associated with better business performance as evidenced by higher cumulative stock returns, stronger operating performance and greater return on average assets. Valuing employees also helps in being able to recruit, develop and retain the best people. According to US research, MBA graduates at 11 top business schools ranked a future employer's reputation for caring for its staff about 95 per cent as important as the financial package itself.[74]

It is not clear whether happy employees produce higher performance, high-performing companies make employees happy, or both interact to form a virtuous spiral. Regardless of why, the evidence indicates that the additional cost of looking after employees does not come at the expense of financial results. On the contrary, taking care of employees is associated with better financial returns.

The decision to introduce ways of valuing employees can be taken at any time, and hence makes this a foundation element in the Sustainable Leadership Pyramid. This element links to retaining staff, succession planning, training and development, as well as to supporting an enabling culture.

CEO and top team

Under the Locust view, the CEO is the hero who leads from the front and sets the direction for the firm from the top. New Yorker

Donald Trump personified this in the television series *The Apprentice*, in which he became infamous for gleefully telling employees they were fired. On a more positive note, UK-based Sir Richard Branson of Virgin Enterprises presents himself as an inspiring version of the CEO, a visionary hero. Both of these men are owners of their companies, thus further accentuating their 'heroic' status. However, hero status was also accorded – at least for a time – to professional leaders such as legendary Jack Welch of GE fame and infamous 'Chainsaw Al' Dunlap, as well as to lesser lights.

Underpinning the heroic leader view is an assumption that the CEO alone, or primarily, is responsible for organisational performance. Often this extends to the idea that this performance can be measured through the share price. Therefore, the CEO should be rewarded with stock options for essentially doing the shareholders' bidding. This belief can make others in the organisation feel undervalued by overemphasising the contribution of a single individual. It is also based on the illusion that leaders control events. Heroic leader myths reinforce a focus on charismatic individuals rather than on distributed leadership, playing down ideas that leadership is part of a broader system. This potentially devalues the contribution made by the rest of the organisation.

All leaders ought to be held to account for the success or failure of their business. This rarely happens to top Locust leaders. These CEOs are treated as media stars when things go well but are seldom held accountable in a meaningful way for poor results. Measured by the number of firings and forced resignations, the failure rate of many CEOs is in fact high.[75] However, catastrophic failures occasioned by CEOs and high officials in government generally are dealt with less severely than more minor mistakes made by lowly workers. Poor performance, immorality or even criminal actions are rarely reflected in the golden packages of departing CEOs. Thus, Locust CEOs are given preferential treatment when things are going well – and a different kind of preferential treatment when things go wrong.

A team-based approach is more characteristic of Honeybee executive leadership. Here, strategic decisions are typically taken by a top management team. The role of the so-called CEO can be either that of speaker of a group of equals or as the final authority.

In 2006 Helmut Panke, then CEO of BMW, was rated the most popular CEO in Germany. At that time he is reported as saying: 'I don't let that affect me. When things are going well for an enterprise, it influences the way managers are evaluated. I am part of a successful team.'[76] Although most Honeybee CEOs keep a low personal profile, there are always exceptions. See Box 3–6 about the CEO of Novartis, a Swiss-based pharmaceutical giant, who adapted his behaviour to cultural context.

. . . the illusion that leaders control events.

The CEO-as-speaker role rotates among top team members in some Honeybee organisations. This makes it unwise for individuals to profile themselves unduly during their tenure as CEO. If overdone, playing the hero role may upset others in the top team. The team speaker role is institutionalised in law in some countries, but strongly performing organisations appear to voluntarily embrace top team leadership.[77]

Well-known management experts, such as Warren Bennis, support a more team-based approach at the top of corporations.[78] They urge firms to reduce their dependence on the charismatic all-powerful CEO. Team leadership allows a firm to pursue a consistent course, with people and resources heading in the same direction. A team focus at the top promotes sustainability by ensuring that strategy, decision-making, corporate culture and management styles continue seamlessly in the event that something happens to the CEO.

As business becomes more complex, sharing accountability, resources and problem-solving at the top is unavoidable. Sharing responsibilities makes good sense because the quality of decisions tends to increase when several people contribute.[79] The idea of collaborative leadership at the top can challenge some managers, especially because of top team members' conflicting priorities and accountabilities. Given that there are numerous examples to the contrary, such scepticism appears unfounded.

Top team leadership is strong in Honeybee enterprises such as US-based Colgate and SAS software. Colgate is considered remarkable for the skill and depth of its top team, as well as for its consistently high financial returns. Current chairman and CEO between 1984 and 2007, Reuben Mark maintained a very low personal profile while promoting strong teamwork at the top.[80] Similarly, early on James Goodnight, founder, chairman, major shareholder and president of SAS software, empowered his top management team to enable him to indulge in his personal passion for computer programming.[81]

Box 3–6: Novartis' CEO caught between two worlds

Dr Daniel Vasella is the former CEO and current chairman of Novartis, a pharmaceutical company headquartered in Basel, Switzerland. Novartis was formed in 1996 from three very old European pharma companies: Geigy, Ciba and Sandoz. A new enterprise with roots nonetheless dating back to the 18th century, Novartis operates in about 140 countries through 360 independent affiliates. The largest market is in the USA, followed by Europe. To promote awareness of the merged new company in the USA, Vasella presented himself to the American media as a heroic CEO. Such behaviour back in Switzerland elicited heavy criticism from his fellow citizens. For heads of large corporations to profile themselves in this typically Locust manner is not acceptable. More modest Honeybee behaviour is expected.

Evidence that top-team leadership pays off

Research into top teams is complicated by the differing definitions of top team that apply in different enterprises.[82] For a start, smaller firms tend to have fewer members in their top teams than larger corporations, so their composition will be different. Research suggests that because larger teams provide more information, better decisions tend to result from larger top groups.[83] However, psychological research concludes that there is an upper limit to the ideal size of any group, depending on its purpose.

Various studies suggest that top-team leadership is more sustainable than relying on heroic CEOs, starting with evidence that organisational outcomes are better predicted by considering the characteristics of top management groups than of individual CEOs.[84] Among organisations recognised as having achieved greatness, the CEOs at the time of greatness were humble and team-oriented.[85] Outstanding firms practise top-team leadership, and the competency of the top team is important to business performance.[86] Furthermore, team leadership occurs at the top of the 11 most successful, or 'winning', organisations in Australia.[87]

Stakeholders can be confused or unsettled under new leadership if everything is likely to change. Spreading the top roles over a team helps manage the risk of a single member making mistakes.

The complementary nature of managerial and other essential skills at the top is a crucial intangible business success factor, according to evidence from 93 Israeli firms.[88] Since all the essential skills are unlikely to be found in a single person, firms led by a top team possessing these skills collectively are more likely to exhibit above-normal performance than firms without these skills or led by single CEOs. Overall the evidence suggests that there are considerable advantages to organisations being led by top teams rather than by heroic solo CEOs.

'Heroic' decision-making disbenefits strategic decisions in particular, and a study of the world's 2500 largest public corporations indicates why this might be so.[89] The researchers concluded that in the early 21st century CEOs are viewed rather like top athletes. Heroic CEOs enjoy well-paid careers, as long as they continue to perform at exceptional levels. If growth and high share prices stumble, the corporate athlete is voluntarily or involuntarily retired. Under a succession of heroic leaders organisations are more likely to chop and change direction, strategy and style as each newcomer wants to leave his or her mark. This makes it difficult for an enterprise to achieve greatness, particularly if core values are affected.

Danger lurks for top teams led by powerful CEOs where members do not share the same objectives and interests.[90] With a particularly powerful CEO or other member presiding over a top team, as is likely to occur in Locust enterprises under heroic CEOs, members are less willing to speak openly and share information. This can even contribute to an organisation's decline by undermining the top team's opportunity to openly and accurately assess potentially threatening information. Furthermore, senior leaders are likely to centralise their power when their organisation is threatened.

Extending leadership beyond one all-powerful individual to a top-management team is part of the Honeybee approach.

Team-based leadership can be introduced at any time after an organisation decides to shift towards Honeybee leadership, making it a foundation practice in the Sustainable Leadership Pyramid.

Ethics

Corporate and individual behaviour is coming under increasing scrutiny from both inside and outside business. Public perceptions in various countries are that business ethics are generally low. More than two-thirds of Americans polled in the early 21st century reported that only some, very few or no companies acted fairly and honestly. This should worry boards and leaders alike as it comes at a time when the business world has been plagued with corporate scandals and fraud cases. Research shows that misrepresenting corporate financial statements is more likely to occur when top management's compensation is tied to financial performance. Manipulating the firm's earnings may occur, particularly when organisational performance falls below managers' aspirations.[91]

Management expert Warren Bennis[92] argues that openness and transparency will help deter corruption. Others favour laws against wrong-doing and fraud. However, Honeybee organisations seek to deter wrong-doing by embedding ethical behaviour in the organisation's culture. They require their people to do the right thing, binding people to a set of principles, codes of conduct and values that support ethical behaviour. Sound ethics not only protect brand and reputation but also ensure that a firm's resources and technical skills are put to appropriate use. In these ways, ethics become an integral part of good leadership.

What do managers themselves think? Even back in 1999, about 80 per cent of managers agreed that being ethical is good for the bottom line. More than 87 per cent disagreed that one's ethics have to be compromised in order to be competitive.[93]

Ethical practices can take many forms, as the following examples show. Research-based organisations such as Fraunhofer and Novartis require their staff to adhere to the principles of good scientific practice and ethics in research. Swiss pharmaceutical giant Novartis' achievement in ethical practices was recognised when it received the 2006 Award for Business Ethics from the European

Business Ethics Network. A further instance of ethical behaviour involving considerable amounts of money comes from German car-maker Porsche. In developing its new factory in Leipzig, Porsche refused state government subsidies to which it was entitled. While any company could benefit from extra money, Porsche argued that mature industries such as its own should not be given taxpayer funds. Accepting public money went against Porsche's ethics. Management believed that taking government subsidies would damage the company's credibility.

However, ethics should involve more than just avoiding fraud and scandals. Honeybee organisations seek to become virtuous; that is, people aspire to act in the best way they can. Ethical firms encourage positive organisational behaviour, not just avoid bad behaviour.[94] Read about what Swiss retail conglomerate Migros means by the 'moral market' in Box 3–7.

Box 3–7: The moral market at Migros

Visitors to Swiss retailer Migros in Zürich are surrounded by symbols of the organisation's values. Entering the headquarters building, the visitor sees a giant arrow indicating how much electricity the solar panels on the roof are generating. The visitor soon encounters the bust of Migros' founder and a replica of one of the trucks with which he started the business. Not so evident at the front entrance to its headquarters are the moral and ethical values that Migros practises. To experience these values in action, the visitor enters the supermarket. There huge 'engagement' signs direct attention to the many ethical value-added labels on the supermarket shelves, and to the choice of three price categories for many basic items – each of which offers quality and value for money.

Without going behind the scenes, the visitor will not realise that suppliers to one of Switzerland's largest supermarket operators must meet agreed standards for workers around the world. One rest day per week and a maximum working week of 48 hours have to be guaranteed – even by suppliers in emerging economies. These suppliers must also avoid harming the environment, whether it is by overfishing certain sea creatures or destroying rainforest to plant trees for palm oil.

The casual observer is also unlikely to be aware that Migros is owned by about 2,000,000 customers, as the founder's last testament provided for. Only the most observant will have noted that despite the huge profits many supermarket operators derive from tobacco and alcohol, none of these products are found in Migros supermarkets. However, this commitment is being somewhat eroded by Migros subsidiaries. Migros focuses on what its founder called the moral market – and still achieves around CHF20 billion annual turnover from 81,000 staff in about 528 stores. Migros is listed among *Fortune*'s 500 largest enterprises.

Evidence that commitment to ethical behaviour pays off

Acting ethically pays off for an enterprise, not only by protecting its reputation but also financially. Ethical companies are likely to generate higher market value than their less ethical competitors, as an analysis of the performance of ethical S&P 500 companies between 2000 and 2004 showed. Financial outcomes for ethical firms were consistently and substantially higher than the remaining S&P companies.[95] In 2004, the average additional value created by the ethical companies was $9.4 billion. This confirms similar findings among major UK companies that being virtuous – that is, encouraging positive behaviour in employees – pays off on various financial measures.[96]

Not only do ethical companies outperform unethical businesses but also unethical or unlawful behaviour can be expensive. Cheating on reporting requirements, falsifying expense accounts, paying or accepting kickbacks, fixing prices, stealing from employers and taking bogus sick days cost industry billions of dollars.[97] Damage to reputation can be irreparable. Illegal behaviour is rarer in organisations perceived as being employee- or community-focused, compared with their competitors.[98] This suggests that firms that care for employees and the community are likely to see less illegal behaviour than firms that disregard the needs of these stakeholders.

Research indicates that a firm's reputation relates positively to its future financial performance.[99] Part of this benefit comes from attracting motivated employees. Stanford University researchers found that MBA graduates would sacrifice salary to take challenging work at corporately responsible firms.[100] Employees are likely to better understand and commit to a strategy when they think their leaders have high ethical standards,[101] which is valuable given the importance of employee commitment in achieving visions, particularly in turbulent times.

Thus, the evidence favours being ethical over unethical. It is puzzling why more organisations do not voluntarily adopt ethical practices. Enterprises stand to benefit substantially from a more ethical, self-accountable workforce and by protecting their brand and financial viability. Encouraging an ethical stance can begin immediately, which is why ethical behaviour is a foundation element in the Sustainable Leadership Pyramid. A code of conduct can be introduced, and training in ethics commenced along with other initiatives.

> *. . . encouraging positive behaviour . . . pays*
> *off on various financial measures.*

Long-term vs short-term perspective

The time perspective is one of the major differences between the Locust and Honeybee approaches. Locust leadership is focused primarily on the short term, whereas the Honeybee model values the long term. Clearly a balance between these two time horizons is essential for all businesses, but is difficult to achieve when short-term pressures jeopardise long-term goals. This was evident from the 2008 *McKinsey Quarterly* survey of 586 company directors. The survey concluded that board directors would like to spend more time developing a long-term strategy and increasing long-term shareholder value. Most directors' time currently appears to be spent on meeting short-term financial and regulatory requirements, and not on developing strategy.

Achieving a solid performance over the long term is a major management challenge. Honeybee firms accept that results in some reporting periods will be outstanding, in others only modest. Locust managers are under pressure to grow profits in each reporting period. According to the Locust view, taking a long-term perspective, while sensible and necessary, is an option that tends to be compromised by short-term pressures. Honeybee enterprises resist these pressures in the knowledge that overall performance is better when it is averaged over longer timeframes.[102] The length of these timeframes varies with industry. In fast-paced sectors annual averaging will suffice, whereas in others five years or even longer intervals may make sense. Examples here include the aircraft construction industry and reinsurance.

US-based Professor Alan Kennedy[103] points out that companies locked into short-term thinking have often mortgaged their future long-term profitability to make their balance sheets look better now. To achieve quarterly returns acceptable to analysts and shareholders they may have cut R&D, lost knowledge and wisdom by sacking employees or postponed training or new projects — all vital for a firm's long-term sustainability.

Being sustainable and prosperous in the long term is virtually impossible when all decisions are driven by short-term pressures. The long term affects various aspects of the business. For example, sustainable enterprises value long-term relationships with stake-holders and alliance partners, and collaboration with other firms. These 'assets' are not usually reflected in the balance sheet, making it difficult to quantify their effects. However, they form part of an organisation's intangible assets and require time to develop. Realising a long-term vision may require forgoing short-term financial gains until organisational strategies, systems and resources have been aligned to fit the vision.

Executives face a conflict of interest if they are rewarded financially for pursuing short-term goals. A Locust CEO can improve the next quarterly result by immediately cutting staff numbers. By the time the negative consequences of this action show up financially, this CEO will have collected his or her bonus and probably moved on. Firms committed to a long-term perspective ensure that when their managers are compensated with shares or options in the company, these rewards are based on long-term company returns. Some cynics say that this means that the managers never get paid! When Locust managers, including CEOs, rotate every three or four years, this might well be true.

Aligning executives' remuneration with the long-term prosperity of a business is not a problem for Honeybee firms, because they value retaining and developing employees. For example, by 2009 global financial services provider Allianz had been led by only nine CEOs since its founding in 1889.

Retaining senior executives promotes stability. This is because a succession of new CEOs is likely to disrupt long–term strategies and plans as they seek to make their mark through short–term actions. Taking a long-term view allows investment in specialised facilities, including equipment or buildings, and growth strategies that focus on long cycles. For example, ZF Friedrichshafen, a key supplier of components to the auto industry, invested in specially designed facilities for promoting creativity, a project intended to pay off in enhanced innovation down the track.

Anticipating a long tenure, Honeybee CEOs can direct resources to the long-term sustainability of the organisation and to building an enabling culture. During the 23 years Reuben Mark served as CEO of consumer goods manufacturer Colgate, he developed the company culture around its global values. This paid off financially as well. Total shareholder returns following CEO Mark's tenure were 4206 per cent, compared with only 1483 per cent across the S&P 500. Colgate also outperformed its peers over the same period, whose shareholder returns delivered only 3085 per cent according to Colgate's 2007 annual report.

In short, Honeybee enterprises value the long term, whether it concerns stakeholder relationships, planning, financial or other performance measures, innovation, managing staff or their own investment plans. By contrast, many Locust-led firms stand accused of mortgaging their futures to produce short–term profits. Which is the more sustainable? In Box 3–8, read about BMW's long-term plans to revolutionise the car industry. This company pursued its long-term vision over two decades, even in difficult times.

Box 3–8: Long-term planning at BMW

A good example of long-term strategic planning comes from BMW. Despite its success with conventional fuel technology, BMW has pursued a long-term vision for a world in which cars are driven by hydrogen. After decades of development, the hydrogen car is ready but an adequate network of hydrogen filling stations could be another twenty years away.[104] Meanwhile, the company has developed innovative technologies to support its Efficient Dynamics program, which is aimed at making all BMW vehicles both highly fuel efficient and high in performance as part of the 'sheer driving pleasure' the company promises its customers. For 2020, BMW's vision is to be the leading provider of premium products and premium services for individual mobility. BMW clearly takes a long-term perspective backed by long-term resource planning and innovation.

Evidence that the long-term approach pays off

Research shows that companies focused on the long term generally outperform those that are bound to the short term.[105] For example, as a group, long-tenure CEOs produce greater total shareholder returns than short-term CEOs.[106] This is not surprising given other research revealing that senior executives' behaviour has little measurable effect on the short-term financial performance of an enterprise.[107] Short-term results can be better explained by events that are beyond a CEO's control. Linking leaders' remuneration to short-term performance, whether positive or negative, is therefore quite irrational. Long-term thinking also permits long-term investment in expensive facilities, processes, projects, innovation and people development.

> *. . . companies focused on the long term generally outperform those that are bound to the short term.*

Focusing on the long term is a foundation element in the Sustainable Leadership Pyramid because it can be introduced at any time of management's choosing. Decisions based on the long term underpin Honeybee leadership and support other practices. Among others, a long-term focus allows serious investment in training and development, succession planning, retaining staff in difficult times, stakeholder relationships, planning and managing change and pursuing a vision. Long-term preparation is needed to create key performance drivers of innovation, staff engagement and quality. Similarly, it takes time to develop devolved decision-making, trust, effective teamwork, an enabling culture, a self-managing workforce and to share knowledge. Thus, a long-term view is essential to achieving the higher-level practices and the key performance drivers shown in the Sustainable Leadership Pyramid.

Organisational change

Management guru Peter Drucker[108] argued that change and continuous innovation – whether within markets, globalisation or other competitive challenges – should be viewed as opportunities rather than as threats. But this can be hard to practise when organisations are experiencing unprecedented levels of change, to which the people in them have to adapt. Part of the need for so much change has come from globalisation, which brings more competition and opportunities. Globalisation requires developing new skills, such as dealing with intercultural differences. Many other external factors are also pressuring organisations to adapt, including rapid changes in technologies, customer needs and processes.

Irrespective of the reasons for change, Locust managers in particular are under continuous pressure to improve short-term performance, to avoid being the target of takeovers, sackings or the firm going out of business.[109] Often managers – as well as many academic researchers – view change as isolated events without considering the effects of the changes and their implementation on daily operations.[110] They underestimate the disruptive effects that introducing major change can have on the organisational system as a whole. Furthermore, managers often do not have the skills to cope with this much change. Many complain that training and support are lacking during times of turbulent change – when they are most needed.[111]

Not all change is turbulent and demanding, and different levels of change can be distinguished. At a basic level, organisations are continually developing and adapting to new situations as they and the people within them learn. Typically, these evolutionary adaptations are quite small and localised in particular parts of a firm. At other times change is quite deliberate and on-going via incremental continuous improvement processes. A third kind of change can be revolutionary through external events or when certain stakeholders decide to alter the status quo in a major way.[112]

Honeybee leadership minimises revolutionary upheaval, preferring incremental change. When major change is required in Honeybee enterprises, it is a planned and managed process whenever possible. In times of relative stability, changes can be carefully planned to make sure new processes and behaviour are compatible with the existing system – unless, of course, the whole system requires modification. However, altering an entire system is expensive and challenging. For various reasons discussed in Chapter 1, people often resist major change.

Research shows that successfully managed change is rather rare.[113] If you think of an organisation as a system, this finding is not very surprising. It is unrealistic to expect major change to occur just because leaders want it to happen. After all, employees' behaviours must also adapt, and they need compelling reasons for doing so. Here a shared vision of the future is an essential roadmap for action.

Change becomes impossible to manage when everything is shifting and there is no constant point of reference. In dynamic operating environments, some changes may happen so quickly that planning is not possible. To avoid organisational shutdown, a firm's systems need to be balanced. Systems need to be sufficiently dynamic to be able to cope with unpredictable change, but stable enough to be able to cope with occasional disruption.

Honeybee leadership encourages and rewards continuous improvement, but this does not mean that new fads are mindlessly adopted. Chopping and changing to the latest fad thwarts the evolution of a clear sense of purpose and identity. Rather, under Honeybee philosophy major change is a considered, systematic process whenever possible. Honeybee leadership is concerned about reinforcing and protecting the firm's strong culture and reputation.

However, in a dynamic and competitive marketplace major change is inevitable, especially for long-established firms. Change need not involve the entire organisation but can be required at different times and in particular parts of a business for strategic purposes. Box 3–9 illustrates the strategic nature of change over a decade for wealth manager UBS.

Box 3–9: UBS – master of strategic change

UBS's motto of 'global leadership through corporate trans-formation' drove the strategy behind the many acquisitions and mergers during the 1990s in this then highly profitable wealth management firm. For more than a decade, UBS carefully acquired businesses that contributed to the group's strategy.[114] In the process, the culture of each added organisation was evaluated to see how it fitted with the mother company. Lessons from this sequence of acquisitions and mergers include the need to adopt a systematic, analytical approach. However, using intuition in responding to opportunities is also important. The bank learned that it was essential to have a strong unwavering commitment to its vision. It was vital to balance the need for continuity of top management with the need to adapt the management as the organisation changed. To benefit from the acquired firms, UBS needed to value their often different capabilities and cultures.

UBS adopted varying strategies for integrating the different companies it acquired. In some cases, newcomers were speedily incorporated into the existing culture. Sometimes cultures were left unchanged. At other times, the differences were exploited to change the culture at headquarters. An instance of reverse 'takeover' arose with the acquisition of O'Connor & Associates from the US. O'Connor is a risk management firm whose culture is very egalitarian, open in its thinking and focused on teamwork. Head office deliberately used the O'Connor group's different style to influence the more conservative Swiss bankers. Apart from bringing in technical expertise that the bank had previously lacked, the O'Connor acquisition changed UBS fundamentally. The company went from measuring itself just against Swiss competitors to benchmarking itself against the rest of the world. This supported UBS's strategic move from being a Swiss bank to a global player. A few conservative bankers were no doubt shocked at first!

A cultural challenge for UBS that has had severe repercussions emerged from the strategic takeover of US-based Paine Webber in 2000. How would the Locust leadership philosophy of the US company blend with the Honeybee philosophy of UBS's Swiss headquarters? Initially, UBS decided not to interfere with the Paine Webber formula, and the Locusts appear to have dominated. In 2007, UBS shut down its in-house Dillon Read Capital Management division because this hedge fund had lost US$384 million from overexposure to the US subprime mortgage market. Huge financial losses continued in 2008 and 2009. The Swiss-based CEO had to resign, and UBS was investigated by the Internal Revenue Service for allegedly assisting US clients to evade taxes. Poor risk management, misaligned incentive programs and a short-term focus on making quick returns shook the foundations of this organisation in 2007–08. In 2009 litigation with the US tax authorities was settled, but the Swiss government withdrew its investment in UBS and losses continued. Time will tell how things pan out for this master of strategic change.

Evidence that considered change pays off

Research into the relationship between change and organisational performance is surprisingly thin.[115] However, some research demonstrates that carefully staged change is generally more effective than jumping on to the latest management fad.[116] The wisdom of taking a considered approach to change is also endorsed by Professor Jim Collins' research into 1435 successful US companies that have been on the *Fortune* 500 list since 1965. Findings suggest that successful change comes by building up breakthrough momentum towards achieving a shared vision. This is preferable to lurching back and forth trying various radical change programs and restructurings. Only 11 'good' companies were recognised as achieving greatness in Collins' study.[117] In each of these 'great' companies, the approach to change was systematic and considered. For example, 'great' companies did not jump on technology bandwagons, but made bold investments in carefully selected technologies that were linked to achieving their goals. Management ensured that key people had room within their roles to make the required changes.

> *It is unrealistic to expect major change to occur just because leaders want it to happen.*

Research into the savings and loan industry in California suggests that most technological, regulatory and economic changes that these banks experienced improved even their short-term financial performance.[118] This was particularly so where the changes built on established routines and competencies. Thus, these changes blended with the existing system and helped the organisation's performance.

Other researchers compared pairs of European firms in four industry sectors. In each case, one member of the pair was performing better than the other. The results showed that the high performers differed from the low performers in the way they led change, managed the environment, treated their employees and took a coherent, strategic approach to change.[119]

Research into the US baseball industry indicates that the effects of change and the ability to plan for changes depend on the operating environment at the time. Change can have positive effects on an organisation when its conditions are relatively stable.[120] However, change has negative effects when it occurs in unstable situations. Unable to plan even if they wanted to, organisational members are likely to mimic competitors rather than seek their own optimal direction. This can reduce growth and team performance, the researchers concluded.

Further research is needed to investigate the relationship between Honeybee approaches to change and business performance. However, the above analysis suggests that a considered approach to managing change realigns the people, systems and strategy without pulling the enterprise in competing directions. Of course, planning and managing change requires the people involved to have the necessary time and resources to do so.

Management can decide to take a considered approach to managing change wherever possible, making this practice a foundation element in the Sustainable Leadership Pyramid. To achieve effective change, managers have to commit to long-term efforts to change people's attitudes and behaviour as well as modify the associated systems and processes. Part of this involves providing an environment in which people can engage in continuous learning and development and develop trust – again showing the interconnectedness of Honeybee elements.

Financial market independence

Finance and accounting outcomes drive much of the business world these days. In a survey of 4500 leaders from about 900 companies, more than a quarter stated that the single action that brings them the most respect is 'bringing in the numbers'.[121] That this was the most frequent response is not surprising given that managers who do not meet their financial targets are not likely to survive in their organisations.[122] This also applies to many Locust-led non-listed, not-for-profit and government departments, where meeting the numbers is the main priority.

Business schools, analysts, ratings agencies, traders and other people behind the financial capital markets have often been blamed for the short-term perspective of the Locust approach. This manifests itself in a fixation on growth and profits over three- or six-monthly reporting periods, and judging how well an enterprise is doing based on fluctuations in the share price.

Interviews with 12 finance professors revealed that they and their peers accept that the financial capital markets create the main game for organisations.[123] Worryingly, these professors claimed that the markets could not be changed or challenged, and must be accepted. No doubt their students also accept that an organisation's activities must be aimed at meeting the requirements set by the capital markets. But how rational and efficient are those markets and their requirements?

Contrary to popular wisdom, short-term variations in share price reflect neither shareholder value nor a company's value. This narrow approach to creating wealth for investors rests on many false economic assumptions. For a start, maximising profits is not the same as maximising the wealth of a firm. Also, between 50–80 per cent of a firm's value can be attributed to non-financial assets, such as human, brand and intellectual capital.[124] Therefore, why the emphasis on a few, potentially peripheral financial measures in evaluating how well an organisation is doing? Is it just because financials are easier to measure than human or intellectual capital?

> *. . . the markets could not be changed or challenged . . .*

Managers also seem worried about the narrow focus on short-term returns. Alarmingly, 38 per cent of CEOs from one thousand leading global companies agreed that the requirements of the capital markets pose the major threat to their corporation's value and brand.[125] Actions that challenge the constraints imposed by the financial markets may be necessary in the long-term interests of an enterprise. However, this is difficult to do when shareholders demand large short-term dividends, which suggests that executives should manage shareholder expectations. Telling the markets that the company is focused on the long term, as Google did when it listed publicly, can attract more patient investors.

Honeybee leadership challenges the financial markets in different ways. Some companies avoid any involvement with those markets. For example, they manage their growth targets by relying on their own resources, Radio and IT communications specialist Rohde & Schwarz has developed several mechanisms for maintaining its independence. First, its own sophisticated forecasting system enables the business to adjust its financial and other processes to avoid having to borrow outside money. By forecasting well in advance, the company has time to protect itself from changing markets. Using its forecasting tools, Rohde & Schwarz was able to predict the end of the dot.com boom and minimise the adverse effect on its business.

Many firms choose to remain in private hands rather than list publicly. About 87 per cent of the more than 10,000 employees at US-based software creator SAS support their CEO's decision to resist public listing. Overwhelmingly, SAS employees value the company's independence from the capital markets.

A closed system of ownership and bank financing has protected many family firms from the influence of the capital markets. Independence can be threatened in such businesses when the family wants to sell out, and outside investors may not be as patient as the family.

However, even publicly listed Honeybee-led firms will stand up to the financial markets or carefully manage their relationships with their financial masters. After all, Wall Street analysts and their demands are not always right, and no outsider understands the enterprise as well as its employees. Two-hundred-year-old Colgate, for instance, disappointed some analysts by continually innovating in small steps, rather than creating the major breakthroughs that analysts like to see in a multi-billion-dollar company. This philosophy of incremental improvement meant that back in 2002 about 38 per cent of Colgate's turnover came from products less than five years old. Today, Colgate persists with its continual renewal strategy, alongside a recently introduced search for 'big hit' new products. Success is evident in Colgate's consistent financial excellence, including the record results achieved in 2006 and continued in the following years.

Munich Re, a publicly listed, professionally managed global player in reinsurance, often challenges the financial markets (read about this in Box 3–10). Sometimes it takes great courage for a middle-sized company to challenge the financial markets.

Automaker Porsche refused to engage in the quarterly reporting demanded by the Frankfurt Stock Exchange. Porsche argued that this short reporting timeframe distracted the company from the more important long term. The stock exchange threw Porsche off the M-DAX index. Porsche remained steadfast and became the most profitable automobile firm in the world in 2004, having established its right to report to its shareholders at intervals of its own choosing. Would Porsche have been as successful without asserting its independence from quarterly reporting?

> *Porsche refused to engage in . . . quarterly reporting . . . and became the most profitable automobile firm in the world in 2004.*

Nordstrom challenged the analysts to rescue itself from Locust leadership. In 1997, this US fashion retailer got into trouble after the family stepped back and handed the firm over to professional management. The new management introduced Locust principles to this traditional Honeybee organisation. Within a couple of years, Nordstrom's famous customer service was besieged with complaints for the first time ever. The share price fell to about $6 and the company's glowing image faded. Major shareholders in this listed company, the Nordstrom family, went against the analysts' wishes and came back into management at senior levels. Within three years the company's prosperity was restored along with its legendary service levels. By 2007, the share price had steadily grown to around $50. In this case, the Nordstrom family had ignored the analysts' disapproval of their action, seized back the reins and returned the company to its profitable Honeybee culture. Four Nordstrom family members joined the management team, including three joining the board in 2007. To ensure transparency, each director stands for election every year.

It is a mistake to think that because Honeybee companies challenge the financial markets, they are not interested in profits. Profitability and good returns to investors help preserve a firm's independence from private equity hedge funds and similar outsiders. One of the stated objectives of Rohde & Schwarz employees is to make so much profit that the family owners of this radio and IT communications company have no rational alternative but to continue to invest in the family business. This protects the firm from outside investors who might otherwise force a short-term perspective, with all the negatives such change is expected to bring.

Many Honeybee companies have an interest in balancing the demands of the share markets with their own sustainability, particularly those involved in the financial services sector. Financial institutions such as Bendigo Bank (Australia) and Munich Re (Germany) are close to the capital markets, if not a direct part of them. Yet they are basically committed to the Honeybee way. So too is Warren Buffett, head of the highly successful investment firm Berkshire Hathaway. Berkshire Hathaway lives from its investment and insurance businesses but uses debt sparingly, refusing to over-leverage its balance sheet. One attitude that the senior executives hold dearly is that they will not sell any good business that they own – Berkshire Hathaway is in there for the long haul. Misleading accounting manoeuvres or smoothing of quarterly results are not part of this company's ethic. These and other financial institutions may well lead the way to a more sustainable future, as we discuss in Chapter 5.

Honeybee firms value their independence from the capital markets and seek to place the needs of the business over the demands of analysts, investors or other 'masters'. The focus of this section has so far been on business firms, but government and not-for-profit organisations are held to account by politicians, their members or other constituents. Therefore, while the financial markets are not relevant for such enterprises, a parallel arises for these organisations in not blindly following these 'political masters'. Honeybee-led government enterprises may risk questioning their political masters in the interests of the organisation, even at a possible cost to themselves.

Box 3–10: Munich Reinsurance challenges the capital markets

As one of the world's largest reinsurers, Munich Re insures more than 4000 primary insurance companies operating globally. Established in 1880, the group now employs about 47,000 people. Employees include researchers from over 80 disciplines who analyse meteorological, geological, medical and other information to improve insurance operations. Reinsurance is a long-term business that requires methodical planning and forecasting using the best information available.

Munich Re occasionally challenges the various stock exchanges on which it is listed directly. For example, in 2005 it argued that formulae used in valuing stock on the New York exchange could be improved. This argument fell on deaf ears. Earlier, Munich Re had mounted a major challenge to the financial markets just before the 2001 terrorist attacks in the US. Before 9/11, analysts had criticised Munich Re for not distributing about US$2 billion in reserves to shareholders. The reinsurer had resisted these demands because its estimates showed that this amount would be needed to cover unknown but anticipated claims. Events like 9/11 were unimaginable until then. But Munich Re had assessed the total value of insurance claims that it would face that year at around US$2 billion.

Immediately after 9/11 and destruction of the twin towers, Wall Street analysts and rating agencies insisted on knowing exactly how high Munich Re's liability would be. Now they doubted that the reinsurer had made sufficient provision for its liabilities. Imagine the situation if Munich Re had heeded the analysts' calls to distribute the reserves just before 9/11.

At that shocking time no insurance company could immediately assess its specific liability, and so the market began to speculate. A 'negative fantasy' was the way the company's annual report described the resulting demolition of its share price.[126] Within 24 hours Munich Re stock tumbled from €285 to €207, eventually wiping about a third off the company's value. The fall in the share price was arrested only when the company started to quantify its losses at 3 pm on 12 September. Interestingly, this reinsurer's liability for 9/11 was around the US$2 billion that its experts had set aside.

Nothing really changed within this company on 9/11, except that its share price was punished because some analysts thought that they knew the reinsurance business better than Munich Re did. The moral of this story is: in the interests of your business, don't slavishly follow the dictates of the capital markets and its less expert minions.

Evidence that independence from the financial markets pays off

Are companies that challenge the financial markets more sustainable than their peers? Some companies are living proof that they can be.

However, because few listed firms openly challenge the financial markets, direct academic evidence is sparse. One reason for not bucking the system is that analysts wield considerable power to punish a company that displeases them. A poor analyst report or rating can damage a firm's standing in the market place. Some rating agencies have reportedly threatened to downgrade firms that refuse to engage the agency to carry out an audit.[127] Another reason for a lack of research evidence on organisations that challenge the capital markets and their associated businesses is the common assumption that the markets are unchallengeable. The supremacy of the financial capital markets was severely weakened in the market collapse in 2008.

One way of retaining independence from the financial markets is to avoid them altogether by remaining under private control. As mentioned in Chapter 1, family firms have been shown to outperform their independently owned and managed peers on the Standard & Poor's index. A study of privately held, high-performing German companies revealed annual revenue growth rates among such companies almost double that of the German DAX stock market index, and nearly three times the average growth of all German companies.[128] This suggests that remaining independent of the financial markets does not hinder financial success.

However, much of the evidence for the effects of challenging the financial markets is indirect, relying largely on the kinds of arguments presented above. As Harvard Professor Clayton Christensen pointed out,[129] financial markets damage organisational performance through the negative impact that short-termism has on other Honeybee elements. These include training, innovation and retaining staff. Similarly, those companies that consider a range of stakeholders' interests outperform those with a narrow focus on shareholders.[130] Furthermore, the actions of some hedge funds in saddling a business with debt can make it unsustainable, as many examples show. No wonder sustainable enterprises prefer to remain independent of the financial markets and make their own business decisions.

How a firm responds to the pressures of the financial capital markets is obviously influenced by many factors. However, top management can take the decision to consider the interests of the firm over the demands of the capital markets at any time. For this reason, the extent to which firms are exposed to the damaging effects of the financial markets is a foundation element in the Sustainable Leadership Pyramid.

Responsibility for the environment

Environmental responsibility is core to Honeybee leadership. This is based on two considerations: one is ethical, the other is pragmatic. The ethical consideration is that people have no right to damage others' health, livelihood or quality of life. No generation has the right to live off what belongs to future generations. This includes the rights to a quality life through their share of clean air, water and other natural resources and to enjoy a healthy, non-toxic environment.

The pragmatic consideration is that degrading the context within which an enterprise operates poses a long-term threat to a firm's own sustainability. Destroying the earth is of no long-term value to an enterprise. The impetus for environmental protection can come from investors, insurers or lenders, customers and staff, regulations or moral concerns, or a need for damage control, public relations and brand protection. Whatever the source of motivation, care for the environment is an important part of sustainable leadership.

Increasing external pressure on all businesses to adhere to environmental protection standards is inevitable given a global concern about declining air, water and land quality. As different forms of cancer and other health problems spread, quality of life diminishes for everyone. Those living on low-lying Pacific islands are threatened by flooding from melting polar ice caps as the globe warms. In places like Australia, many cities and towns are running out of water while the local water authorities waste water by not investing in infrastructure to prevent pipes from bursting and leaking. The need for greater environmental awareness and care is therefore essential at government levels.

However, business also has a contribution to make here. Locust and Honeybee philosophies can be distinguished in their attitudes towards the environment. The Honeybee approach is committed to protecting the environment irrespective of whether or not this is mandated. Honeybee organisations work to strict environmental standards wherever they operate, and they expect their suppliers to do the same.

This contrasts with the Locust philosophy. Many Locust adherents seem convinced that to be competitive compels them to pollute and to consume non-renewable resources at whatever rate appears necessary.[131] The pollution that contributes to those corporate profits has to be cleaned up by the local community. This clearly violates the principle that the 'causer' pays for any damage to non-contracting third parties.

A 2002 survey showed that few US firms had embraced environmental protection. Managers polled were resistant to adopting the international environmental management standard ISO14001. The managers claimed that they could not justify the costs and, in any case, they believed that their existing standards were sufficient.[132]

Locust managers argue erroneously that they cannot control suppliers, particularly foreign ones. Allegedly, because suppliers are independent entrepreneurs, the company has no control over them. However, foreign multinationals in fact exert tremendous control over their suppliers' operations because of their buying power.[133] These arguments reflect Dunphy's sustainability Phases 2 and 3, as discussed in Chapter 1.

By contrast, conforming to ISO14001 or its equivalent is commonplace in Honeybee manufacturing and service enterprises. Honeybee companies publish environmental audit reports. They often hang notices throughout their offices and factories showing progress. Charts track their water and energy savings, waste management, decreasing use of toxic and non-renewable resources and similar indices. Read about what cleaning specialist Kärcher does in Box 3–11.

In many parts of Europe, particularly north of the Alps, governments have enacted a raft of laws designed not only to protect the environment but also where possible to improve it. There, manufacturers of cars, household appliances and other consumer goods have long been required to take their products back at the end of their useful lives for recycling. Rather than adding to costs, designing for disposal has often resulted in simpler and more efficient assembly methods. The pressure for environmental responsibility has also affected retailers. It is in many retailers' interests for goods to be packaged for recycling because some national laws allow customers to leave all the excess packaging from their purchases behind in the stores. In this way, the stores inherit the disposal problem. Retailers in turn can reduce their disposal problem by choosing suppliers who package appropriately.

Honeybee firms, particularly those operating at Dunphy's Phase 6 level of sustainability, are likely to strive to be ahead of the legislation because it is the right thing to do. They apply their stringent environmental standards wherever they go. Marriott International Hotels operates globally, including in locations where environmental laws are slack. Yet a company-wide environmental program guides Marriott associates in conserving wildlife, water and energy wherever they operate. Associates promote clean-air initiatives, manage waste and clean their local communities. Marriott staff plant trees. Company policy is based around the concept of 'reduce/reuse/recycle' as much as possible. Hong Kong still has weak environmental laws, but nonetheless the JW Marriott Hotel in Hong Kong is a leader in environmental measures. Its recycling and other advanced processes for managing waste are imitated by other businesses.

A new source of pressure to respect the environment is coming from the finance industry. Investors and financiers routinely assess company risk profiles. Lenders are placing environmental conditions on loan-seekers. Insurance companies may refuse to insure businesses with poor environmental track records. Potential damage and negligence legal suits raise the risk level of environmentally unfriendly businesses.

Global banks such as HSBC link the pursuit of economic growth to a healthy environment. HSBC incorporates good environmental practices into its own offices, equipment, consumption of energy and other resources. It includes environmental risk assessment in lending decisions and expects borrowers to adhere to legal and regulatory requirements. HSBC supports specific environmental projects and willingly has sent up to 2000 employee volunteers to work on conservation projects worldwide. While doing all this, the HSBC group of companies reported record earnings each year between 2003 and 2007, and recorded pre-tax profits during the global financial crisis. The group outperformed industry benchmarks financially in that period. Thus environmental protection does not have to come at shareholders' expense. It contributes to shareholder value by managing risk and reputation and by raising staff engagement.

Box 3–11: Environmental achievements at Alfred Kärcher GmbH & Co. KG

The company's motto is 'simply clean'. This German-based business provides cleaning and irrigation solutions, services and products. A family-owned business employing more than 6600 people in about 41 countries, Kärcher focuses on the environment in many ways. The first is directly through its cleaning products, solutions and services. Not only do Kärcher's products traditionally clean production sites, offices and homes, in 2005 the company branched out into cleaning drinking water.

'Lifecycle thinking' is incorporated into the design, manu-facture, repair and disposal of all products. The aim is to ensure that at all stages of development a product affects the environment as little as possible. The company is ISO14001 certified at its German, Italian, Chinese and Brazilian manufacturing plants, and certification is underway at other locations. A central team, assisted by others at plant level, manages the worldwide environmental protection system that began in 1996. This includes environmental auditing, emissions control, managing waste and toxic chemicals, and ensuring that harmful materials are not incorporated into products.

Everyone is considered responsible for the environment at Kärcher – including customers, suppliers and employees. For customers, tips on cleaning in an environmentally sustainable way are to be found on Kärcher's web site. Free return and disposal for old electrical machines is now legally prescribed throughout the EU, but Kärcher was already offering this service to customers before the law came in. Suppliers must adhere to Kärcher's stringent materials requirements, which go well beyond EU legal specifications.

In 2004, Kärcher won an award for its many initiatives in getting employees to use green methods of transport in coming to work. For example, employees who cycle to work can participate in a lottery to win attractive prizes such as a top bicycle. The company pays 50 per cent of the train and bus fares for staff using public transport, 75 per cent for apprentices. Costs are further reduced because Kärcher bulk orders annual transport tickets. The company assists those employees who drive with car pooling, and provides drivers with free lessons on how to reduce fuel consumption. Staff using electric cars can recharge the batteries free of charge at work. The company's own buildings use advanced environmental technologies, such as geothermal heating and cooling, solar power, wood chip heating and greened roofs.

This strong focus on the environment does not come at the expense of profits; rather, it occurs while Kärcher makes record profits. In 2006 the business grew by more than 13 per cent, selling 6.07 million products and increasing revenues to a record €1254 million. This was the best business result in the company's 70-year history – but then they said that about the results in previous years as well! As the firm's management stated in the 2007 Environmental Report,[134] 'customers respond well to environmentally friendly businesses'. Judging by the 2007 turnover, which increased to €1380 million spread fairly evenly across products and regions, and the €1401 million achieved in 2008, this may well be true.

Evidence that commitment to environmental responsibility pays off

Often environmental protection policies are viewed as part of corporate social responsibility. However, research shows that a focus on the environment as a separate stakeholder can pay off in many ways. First, relating the market value of firms in the Standard & Poor's index to their environmental performance is revealing. Not caring for the environment wipes large amounts off firms' market value.[135] Research into 186 industrial companies in Spain provides additional support for a generally positive relationship between proactively caring for the environment and business performance.[136] Specific outcomes depend on the bundle of environmental practices operating in a particular situation.

Caring for the environment can lower production costs, enhance the firm's brand and reputation, appeal to customers and reflect good management practices. On the pragmatic side, IBM discovered that looking after the environment is profitable. IBM invested US$1 billion in environmental measures over five years. After deducting all costs, savings exceeded the costs by a factor of two to one. Back in 2002, this translated into more than US$238 million that IBM saved while helping the environment.

> *. . . IBM discovered that looking after the*
> *environment is profitable.*

Businesses that care for the environment also make their enterprise more sustainable by managing risk. This brings benefits by limiting potential legal claims for damage in the event of accidents such as chemical or oil spills. Products can be designed to be more environmentally friendly to produce, operate and dispose of. This can reduce costs, generate savings and so raise profits.[137]

For facilities managers, creating buildings to minimise adverse effects on the environment can save an estimated 250 per cent of the building's up-front costs over an assumed 40-year usable life.[138] The financial savings occur in various ways, including through reduced energy costs, increased market value, lower risks of health liability claims because of better air quality indoors and providing more pleasant working conditions to attract and retain employees. The savings are so substantial that a whole new industry has emerged, referred to as Contingent Performance Contracting. One variant of this is that contractors fund changes to clients' facilities at their own cost and share the savings with the client.[139]

Thus, taking responsibility for minimising a business's environmental footprint benefits organisational performance in many measurable ways, including financially. The decision to become environmentally responsible can be implemented at any time, making this a foundation element in the Sustainable Leadership Pyramid.

Social responsibility

Businesses that contribute positively to society – over and above the employment, investment returns, and services and goods that they provide – are said to demonstrate corporate social responsibility (CSR).[140] Dunphy's six sustainability phases, applied essentially to the environment in Chapter 1, apply equally well to differentiating between firms' adoption of CSR.[141] Locust philosophy characterises the first three phases. Honeybee leadership enters at Phase 4 and culminates at Phase 6, where sustainable practices are seen as the right thing to do.

Some firms might appear to be operating at Phases 5 and 6, but use their CSR initiatives primarily for public relations purposes. This is not genuine Phase 6 behaviour, which views caring for society as an end in itself.

There are many reasons for engaging in corporate social responsibility other than common decency. These include that CSR contributes to business sustainability, that stakeholders will support a good enterprise, and to protect a company's reputation.[142] Furthermore, CSR activities can potentially create a range of competitive advantages for the firm.[143]

CSR activities can take many forms. Some companies focus on philanthropic donations, employ apprentices or sponsor university groups. Others seek to improve community relations by allowing employees to volunteer during working time. Yet others invest in major environmental or humanitarian projects, or establish charitable foundations.

Under Locust leadership philosophy, CSR takes a back seat to short-term profits. The Locust belief is that a company already serves society well by providing jobs and generating wealth for shareholders. The widespread nature of this Locust view in the UK is evident in a study of SMEs employing up to 500 people. British managers were asked to rank ten factors affecting their businesses.[144] Overall, social and environmental responsibility ranked ninth and tenth respectively.

Worse still, many CEOs do not consider sustainability to be very important. Only 6 per cent of CEOs from the world's leading one thousand global companies thought that sustainability was the most important issue for their enterprise in 2004.[145] This is a quite extraordinary result, given that non-sustainable businesses by definition do not have a future.

> *Only 6 per cent of CEOs . . . thought that*
> *sustainability was the most important issue*
> *for their enterprise . . .*

By ignoring the social costs of their actions, managers are not honestly reporting the true costs of doing business. Sacking employees may make the balance sheet of a company look good in the short run. But apart from simply shifting the costs of looking after those who cannot find another job to the taxpayer, it can also undermine the long-term sustainability of the enterprise. Not training apprentices and refusing to employ older people, irrespective of the potential contribution they may be able to make, have similar effects. Unnecessarily passing on costs to others underreports the true cost of doing business. Therefore, decrements to others' well-being or wealth have to be factored into the equation as external costs.[146]

Clearly, large business has more resources to engage in CSR than SMEs. Yet the evidence suggests that family-owned small businesses are also active in their local communities. For example, despite their reputation for giving CSR a low priority, SMEs in the UK often provide business advice to others, volunteer for school and civic bodies, such as local councils or chambers of commerce, and work with local police.[147] British SMEs have been found to contribute about ten times more than large corporations, making a social contribution of about £3 billion annually. However, the activities of SMEs tend to be somewhat fragmented and informal.

How does social responsibility show up in practice? One example comes from the auto industry. BMW seeks to be socially responsible in many ways. It actively sponsors cultural and sporting events, strives to act as a good neighbour and citizen wherever it operates, and safeguards and creates jobs for people from the local communities. These are just a few examples of social responsibility which, along with BMW's commitment to the environment and its people, have earned it a leading place in various sustainability indices. These include the Dow Jones Sustainability Group, FTSE4Good and the Swiss-based SAM Sustainability Group.

Publishing sustainability reports holds firms accountable to internal and external stakeholders for the enterprise's performance in moving towards sustainable development. Within some industries, commitment to CSR reporting is highly inconsistent. For example, sustainability reporting varies substantially in quality among the world's top ten mining companies. Researchers into the mining industry distinguish 'mature reporters' such as Anglo American, BHP Billiton and Rio Tinto from five others described as 'adolescents'. Then there is the third group, euphemistically called the 'latecomers' to social reporting. Thus, even among major players in an industry where corporate social responsibility ought to play a significant role and where suitable role models exist, engagement is highly variable. Furthermore, confidence is not high in how reliable this reporting is.[148]

Latecomers can also be helped via the Global Reporting Initiative (GRI). The GRI offers guidelines for organisations wanting to measure and report on its sustainability efforts in a transparent and comprehensive way. According to the GRI,[149] sustainability reports should provide a 'balanced and reasonable representation of the sustainability performance of a reporting organisation'. The reports should include negative as well as positive contributions.

An important question is how far a business should go in its focus on social issues. Which social issues should be considered? Clearly, if a leader becomes excessively focused on social issues and ignores the needs and expectations of other key stakeholders, problems can arise. This was alleged in the case of the Body Shop whose founder, the late Anita Roddick, used the business to finance her passion for social issues. Some say she went too far and neglected the business side of her enterprise to follow her social conscience. Read more about Anita Roddick in Box 3–12.

Box 3–12: Corporate social responsibility at Anita Roddick's Body Shop

Anita Roddick, famous founder of the Body Shop, wrote about herself:

> The Body Shop and I have always been closely identified in the public mind. Undoubtedly, because it is impossible to separate the company values from my own personal values, and the issues that I care passionately about – social responsibility, respect for human rights, the environment and animal protection, and an absolute belief in community trade.[150]

Roddick believed that businesses should use their power to do good, so she used her stores to promote social and environmental change. The Body Shop worked with Greenpeace. It took credit for getting Shell to act in a more community-spirited way than it had in the past. Roddick set up trading relationships with economically impoverished Amazonian tribes and Mexican farmers. The Body Shop paid fair prices to farmers for nuts, seeds and other natural cosmetic materials. In 2005, the business had 42 of these projects running in 26 countries. Roddick spent much of her time sourcing new products and fighting for humane causes. Through the operators of nearly 2000 Body Shop stores, Roddick multiplied her capacity to do good by harnessing the efforts of thousands of people in pursuing the goals and values they shared.

In 2006 the Body Shop was sold to L'Oreal, a Paris-based global firm. A major question is whether the new owner will continue the focus on social responsibility. If so, will this succeed without Roddick's own passion for bringing values into an industry that is not known for its community approach? What will happen to the franchisees who joined Roddick because of her quest? Sadly, Anita Roddick died in 2007 in the midst of fighting for the causes she believed in.

Evidence that commitment to social responsibility pays off

Analysing the effects of CSR on financial performance is complex because CSR is a broad concept with many different dimensions to it. Furthermore, CSR initiatives have been reported on any scale for only a limited time, and assessing the effects on firm performance normally requires a long-term perspective. However, research from around the world already indicates that being socially responsible can add to, and certainly does not damage, a firm's reputation or financial performance. For a start, it helps attract talented employees.[151]

Socially responsible firms can perform very well on the stock market. Research conducted between 2000 and 2003 shows that the share prices of firms ranked as best in class outperformed their competitors by 23.39 per cent.[152] Best in class in this case means best socially, environmentally and in terms of employee focus. An Australian study found that companies with higher corporate social responsibility ratings outperformed the local index by more than 3 per cent over periods of four and ten years.[153]

In Europe, the UK and the US, socially responsible firms generally match or outperform their less responsible counterparts financially. Any fears of losing out financially because of social engagement are therefore unwarranted when the process is properly managed.[154] In fact, the relationship between CSR and financial performance may be a dynamic one. Good returns provide the funding for engaging in socially responsible activities that enhance the firm's image and brand, thereby indirectly contributing to the bottom line.[155]

Current research into the relationship between CSR and business performance is probably overly simplistic. Most scholars simply distinguish between firms that are socially responsible and those that are not. The nature of a complex concept such as CSR needs to be examined in more depth. An analysis of 61 socially responsible investment funds between 1972 and 2000 suggests that the relationship between CSR and financial performance could well be curvilinear.[156] This means that too much or too little CSR can negatively affect business performance, the optimum probably lying somewhere between those extremes. The outcome also depends on the criteria for choosing the companies to include in a fund and the way financial performance is measured.

The nature of the CSR activities themselves can affect reputation.[157] Interestingly, how socially responsible a firm is may have a stronger effect on employees' identifying with the enterprise than on perceived market and financial performance, at least according to Israeli CEOs.[158] Identifying with the firm is advantageous because it enhances employees' work outcomes and job performance.

> *. . . socially responsible firms generally match*
> *or outperform their less responsible*
> *counterparts financially.*

Thus, the current evidence suggests that being a socially responsible enterprise can pay off for investors. In addition to the potential financial benefits mentioned above, intangible benefits accrue to socially responsible firms. To the extent that an excellent business reputation and attracting and motivating talented staff are advantageous, socially responsible enterprises have the edge over their less responsible peers.[159] Furthermore, a reputation for being socially responsible may protect firms during stock declines.[160] Used strategically, corporate social responsibility can benefit a business according to US strategy guru Professor Michael Porter. It can provide a 'source of opportunity, innovation, and competitive advantage'.[161]

Again, a management decision to become more socially responsible can be taken immediately, making this a foundation element in the Sustainable Leadership Pyramid. Engaging with the community, considering social impacts in weighing up decisions and producing a public report on CSR activities do not depend on other foundation elements being in place first.

Stakeholder consideration

The stakeholder approach actively promotes the interests of a wide range of individuals and groups inside and outside an enterprise. Sometimes CSR is considered part of the stakeholder approach but, given the prominence that CSR is currently receiving in government and corporate circles, we treat it as a separate foundation element.

A major difference between the Locust and Honeybee leadership philosophies lies in the perceptions about who has obligations to whom, whose interests the enterprise's actions impinge upon, and how these obligations and interests can be reconciled in a mutually beneficial way.

Locust philosophy has it that shareholders and owners of enterprises have one interest and one interest only; namely, to get a good return on their money. Therefore, under this simplistic view the only obligation the enterprise has is to ensure healthy quarterly returns for the shareholders.

In stark contrast to this, the Honeybee view is that the interests of shareholders and owners can best be met when the interests of all those who need to contribute to the task of enriching the shareholders are simultaneously taken care of. This includes employees, customers, suppliers, managers, board members, patrons, the media, governments and politicians, regulators, alliance and other partners and even future generations. Few organisations will recognise or give the same weighting to all these potential stakeholders, but Honeybee enterprises consider a far wider range of stakeholder interests than Locust leadership.

Part of the rationale for the singular focus of the Locust approach on the shareholder is the belief that the shareholders' contribution to the firm in the form of equity far outweighs the contribution that anyone else makes. Therefore, the sole obligation of the enterprise is to meet the expectations of the shareholders.

In Table 3–1 we explore the question whose investment matters more: the shareholders' or the employees'? Under the Locust view, only the shareholders' investments count. Others' substantial investment in the firm, such as that of a long-term employee, is routinely ignored or dismissed. Honeybee leadership accepts that many groups contribute to the success of a firm. Hence many people may have legitimate interests in a business as well as a personal and emotional stake in it.

The Locust emphasis on shareholders in measuring enterprise performance is rather surprising, considering that shareholders are likely to have little interest in the actual business of a publicly listed company, just in improving the value of their share portfolio. Many share traders therefore take a short-term view at the expense of long-term sustainability. When executives are also shareholders in the business and part of their remuneration depends on the short-term share price, there is clearly a conflict of interest. As

Table 3–1: Whose investment matters more?

	Shareholder	Employee
Contribution (value creation)	capital (N.B. in public corporations, shareholders own the shares but not the corporation's assets or liabilities)	labour, know-how, skills, ideas, entrepreneurship, cultural fit
Fungibility	complete	low
Entitlement	residual cash flow	wages, perhaps bonuses
Expectations	residual cash flow	wages, other rewards, personal growth, fulfilment
Risk exposure	low to high (risk can be managed or spread, can get out at any time and quickly)	high (risk difficult to manage, cannot spread risk, cannot withdraw labour easily)
Catastrophic loss	loss of capital (can be offset against gains elsewhere)	loss of job, back-wages, superannuation or pensions (no offsetting)
Extraordinary gain	shareholder is the major beneficiary	some employees may derive modest to large benefits depending on shareholding/options

executives, they should be pursuing the long-term interest of the firm. As shareholders, they may be tempted by short-term gains.

No doubt managing stakeholder relationships is complex and challenging, but sometimes business activities can also affect small numbers of people very directly. A classic story told of W.L. Gore & Associates (makers of Gore-Tex® and other products) is that one of its factories closed for a few days after a neighbour complained that pollution disturbed her cows' milk production. The plant remained closed until Gore had fixed the pollution problem for this individual stakeholder.

Time can play an important role in managing Honeybee stakeholder relationships. However, not all stakeholders need attention all the time.[162] Sometimes the interests of one group, such as shareholders, appear to be made subservient to those of other groups, such as employees. This may well promote longer-term benefits for shareholders, for example by reinvesting dividends in the business.

> *Honeybee leadership accepts that many*
> *groups contribute to the success of a firm.*

Taking a stakeholder approach can be justified in terms of its benefits to shareholders. For example, protecting the environment is a form of risk management at chemical and mining companies. It also leads to cost savings as the environmental reports issued by firms such as WACKER (chemicals), ZF (automobile components) and IBM (services) illustrate.

Talented people often like to work for good companies. In Hong Kong, associates stay longer at Marriott International Hotels because Marriott treats its employees better than local competitors do. These and other benefits flow from a concern about diverse stakeholders.

Another way of looking at the importance of stakeholders is to consider the effect of not taking stakeholders' interests into account. What if there are no resources left for a high quality of life for our children and grandchildren? What if they could not breathe the air or drink fresh water? Would customers remain loyal if banks reduced service branches? How will suppliers treat customers who mistreat them? Read about how Locust firms treat suppliers in Box 3–13.

Box 3–13: How (not) to treat auto suppliers

One difference between Locust and Honeybee businesses is revealed in the way they treat suppliers. Honeybee leadership seeks a respectful, close partnership with a limited number of long-term, trusted suppliers. Locust leadership typically searches for the cheapest tender rather than valuing its relationships with suppliers. According to an article in the *Harvard Business Review*, many suppliers do not trust their Locust customers' unethical practices and lack of respect.[163] Here are some contrasting examples reported on page 104 of the article:

- The CEO of a supplier to Ford, GM, Chrysler and Honda said: 'Honda is a demanding customer, but it is loyal to us. American automakers have us work on drawings, ask other suppliers to bid on them, and give the job to the lowest bidder. Honda never does that.'
- A senior executive from a Ford supplier: 'In my opinion, Ford seems to send its people to "hate school" so that they learn how to hate suppliers. The company is extremely confrontational. After dealing with Ford, I decided not to buy its cars.'

The same authors point out how US car manufacturers focus solely on costs in supplier relationships. For example, GM can get out of its supplier contracts immediately a cheaper alternative comes up. However, the US operations of more Honeybee-oriented companies such as Honda and Toyota value the innovation that comes from close working relationships with a small number of suppliers. This involves trust and respect for these stakeholders.

Of course, not all companies operating in North America demonstrate hatred and disdain towards their suppliers! Like their counterparts in Japan, Honeybee enterprises build a closely knit network of suppliers wherever they are based. They involve suppliers in mutual learning, and improving and developing knowledge that reinforces the partnership. This does not mean that Honeybee-led firms do not seek low prices from their suppliers, but they also value the innovation, goodwill and other benefits stemming from long-term relationships.[164]

Evidence that considering multiple stakeholders pays off

Traditional organisational performance measures generally improve under stakeholder policies, and shareholders benefit financially when the needs of multiple stakeholders are met in both the long and the short term.[165] Taking care of multiple stakeholders can affect intangible business assets positively as well. These include forming alliances with other firms and intensifying relationships with customers and long-term experienced employees.[166] In addition, addressing the perceptions and needs of different stakeholder groups affects a company's name and bottom line, as a study of the airline industry demonstrated.[167] How customers, employees, capital providers, labour representatives, investors and local communities are treated affects both reputation and company performance. Knowledge that adds to a firm's competitiveness is also derived from working with stakeholders, as is innovation.[168]

At a minimum, three major stakeholders are considered in Honeybee organisations: customers, shareholders and employees. Research suggests that there is indeed a link between these three interest groups. For example, staff satisfaction and customer satisfaction become mutually reinforcing.[169] A study of service firms in China concluded that simultaneously focusing on customers, employees and competitors increases a company's chances of enhancing its performance, compared with focusing on just one of these stakeholder groups.[170] These researchers measured financial, market and corporate social responsibility performance.

Customers remain a major stakeholder group for successful enterprises. Numerous studies show that high levels of customer satisfaction enhance financial returns.[171] An interesting UK project demonstrated this by examining the costs of improving customer service in the privatised water industry. Addressing customer needs raised the actual service costs, but the improvements increased shareholder value overall.[172]

A Swiss investigation into relationships between 137 buyers and OEM suppliers showed that collaborating with suppliers has a positive effect on the performance of the buyer firm.[173] The buyers' innovative capacity increased through trust and collaboration with their suppliers – and buyers experienced better financial results.

Thus, research supports the link between the broad Honeybee stakeholder focus and better business performance on various measures. Considering the interests of a range of stakeholders is a foundation element in the Sustainable Leadership Pyramid, because management can decide to embrace this practice at any time.

Vision

Vision is difficult to define. Academics and practitioners often use the words 'vision', 'mission', 'purpose', 'dream', 'direction', 'big idea' and the like interchangeably. Sorting out these differences is beyond the scope of this book, but for us vision refers to whatever provides a clear direction or higher-order purpose for an organisation's future. A compelling and plausible vision is widely regarded as essential to leadership activities such as implementing a strategy and directing change.

Honeybee leadership espouses a strong vision that employees are expected to share. For example, Novartis provides its employees with a higher-order purpose through its 'mission' to discover, develop and successfully market innovative pharmaceutical products. These products cure diseases, ease suffering and enhance customers' quality of life. At the same time, Novartis' 'vision' includes remaining a leading and highly respected company. It aims to provide a shareholder return that reflects outstanding performance while adequately rewarding those who invest ideas and work in the company.

The nature of a vision varies in how it is used, its content and the context in which it occurs. Some businesses use formal vision statements or a stated and shared organisational philosophy. In other cases, a company's vision derives more from its brand and reputation than from explicit statements. For example, at automakers BMW and Porsche ideas of quality, continuous improvement and excellence drive the workers rather than formal vision statements. A culture of innovation, quality and excellence is embedded in what employees do every day at these car manufacturers. Nonetheless, a shared vision is important in guiding their futures. A previous chairman of the board, Joachim Milberg, made clear that the CEO at BMW must be someone with vision and the ability to turn this vision into reality, together with his or her team. The slogans 'sheer driving pleasure' and 'efficient dynamics' capture the essence of BMW's vision.

Continental Airlines emphasised the important role of a clear vision in its recovery from the turmoil in the airline industry associated with the 9/11 terrorist attacks in the US. The 2002 annual report states:

> As we have watched our competitors stumble (and sometimes fall) in these difficult times, the importance of operating with a clear, understandable plan, that allows everyone to know what the goals are and how we will measure success, has never been greater.[174]

For Continental, the way ahead is embodied in its 'Go Forward' plan.

> *A compelling and plausible vision is widely regarded as essential to leadership activities such as implementing a strategy and directing change.*

Visionary companies do not necessarily suit every worker. 'Visionary companies are so clear about what they stand for and what they're trying to achieve that they simply don't have room for those unwilling or unable to fit their exacting standards,' according to researchers Collins and Porras.[175] Only those employees who fit extremely well with the core values, beliefs and demanding standards of a visionary company will find it a great place to work. Hence Honeybee enterprises make very sure that their people accept the organisation's vision and that the organisational culture supports achieving the vision. This requires paying attention to recruitment and selection to ensure a good employee fit with the organisation. See how construction firm Seele does this in Box 3–14.

Box 3–14: Seele – 'searching for excellence'

Seele is a small Bavarian construction firm that designs and builds customised façades, roofs and other building elements out of glass and steel – such as the façades and stairs in Apple stores – for a predominantly international clientele. It avoids working on standard projects and claims never to compete just on price. This highly successful firm created a global reputation by building revolutionary designs that appear to defy the laws of physics. Seele has managed to reduce the usual 30kg/sqm of steel and glass structure to 4–5kg/sqm. The less steel, the more expensive the construction is. Quality and profitability make this organisation stand out.

Operating on the vision of 'searching for excellence', Seele attracts creative architects and engineers as customers, suppliers and employees. The Seele employee is carefully chosen from the many applicants for openness, innovation and creativity, teamwork, a solution orientation, liking an open environment and being customer-focused. The focus is on transparency of people, process and product, as well as on quality and creativity. This is reflected not only in the firm's transparent glass buildings and offices but also in the people and the way the business is run as it pursues its vision of excellence.

Evidence that pursuing a shared vision pays off

Considerable research shows that organisations with clearly stated and shared visions perform better on various financial and other measures than similar firms without such visions.[176] Customer and staff satisfaction are enhanced when the employees' vision aligns with the firm's vision.[177]

Evidence is increasing that under visionary leadership business performance is better than under other leadership paradigms,[178] especially in times of uncertainty. A UK study concluded that organisations that follow a vision and are led by values are able to sustain their successful performance over the long term.[179] Enterprises benefit from shared vision and values via increased worker commitment, motivation and job satisfaction, which then combine to enhance performance in visionary organisations through better decision-making, self-management and innovation.

Although vision is widely associated with superior organisational performance, a study of large Australian public sector organisations suggests that not all visions positively affect follower attitudes.[180] Rather, it is important to distinguish between strong and weak visions in assessing how effective a vision is. Honeybee enterprises have strong, clear and widely shared visions guiding staff behaviour. This contrasts with Locust leadership, where achieving a strong vision – apart from a vision of creating short-term shareholder profits – is difficult. In the absence of other foundation practices such as caring for people, retaining and developing staff, amicable labour relations and a long-term perspective, how could it be otherwise?

The decision to introduce a vision as an essential strategic tool can be taken at any time by management. For this reason working with a vision is considered a foundation practice in the Sustainable Leadership Pyramid.

> *Customer and staff satisfaction are enhanced when the employees' vision aligns with the firm's vision.*

Summary

In this chapter we introduced the 14 foundation practices that distinguish Honeybee and Locust leadership philosophies. These form the foundation practices because each can start to be implemented virtually immediately once the decision to pursue it has been made. Having other practices in place is not essential to starting the foundation elements, although other practices contribute to the effectiveness and success of many elements in the Sustainable Leadership Pyramid. We have drawn on a range of case examples to illustrate the different ways in which each principle is implemented in real enterprises, as well as on research evidence for the contribution each element can make to organisational performance.

Research shows that the Honeybee position on the foundation practices is likely to be associated with enhanced organisational performance compared with the corresponding Locust approach. Honeybee firms invest heavily in developing and training staff. Both social and technical capabilities are developed for employees at all levels of the organisation. Under Locust philosophy, the costs of training and development of lower-level workers are borne by these employees on the grounds that they might not stay long with the firm. Only an elite group is trained by the employer. As a result, Locust employees tend to develop general skills rather than specific skills needed by a particular employer.

Honeybee firms show that they value employees' contributions to the firm's success by caring for and treating staff well in many ways – at least compared with Locust leadership. Locust enterprises tend to regard employees as an easily exchangeable resource.

Honeybee leadership expends considerable effort in retaining employees even in difficult economic times. The corresponding action for Locust firms is to shed staff and rehire when times recover.

Honeybee leadership is concerned with continuity through succession planning, and wherever possible promotes employees from within the organisation. Leaders of Locust firms typically assume that new ideas are best found by hiring from outside the business.

Honeybee leadership seeks cooperative relations with unions and other representatives of their employees, whereas antagonistic labour–management relations characterise Locust organisations.

Many of the foundation elements relate to how the organisation is run. We saw that Honeybee leadership works with top teams at the executive level. This contrasts with the 'heroic' individuals whom Locust enterprises hire, often from outside, to manage the tough, ruthless, asocial and profit-dominated business.

Honeybee firms are strongly committed to ethical behaviour, whereas Locust leaders regard ethics as a dispensable part of risk management. If Locusts can get away with unethical behaviour they will consider doing so.

Adopting a long- or short-term perspective is another element that distinguishes the two leadership philosophies. Honeybee leadership bases its decisions primarily on the long term, accepting lower short-term results if it means delivering better results down the track. For Locust firms, many factors pressure managers to give priority to the short term at the expense of the long term.

Some of these pressures stem from the financial capital markets or other financial or political masters a firm is beholden to. While Locust corporations respond to the dictates of the financial markets and other masters, Honeybee leadership makes its own decisions. Honeybee enterprises are prepared to challenge pressure coming from analysts and major investors for the sake of the business.

How they approach organisational change also differs between Honeybee and Locust leadership. Locust enterprises are willing to try many new fads, often in an *ad hoc* and unsystematic way. For Honeybee firms continuous improvement is highly valued, but other interference in their well-functioning systems is carefully considered. Major change is therefore planned in detail, considering how various stakeholders and organisational systems will be affected.

A further major difference between the two approaches lies in the number of stakeholders that the firm considers. Honeybee enterprises adopt a wide-ranging stakeholder focus, realising the crucial role that stakeholders can play in furthering the interests of the enterprises. Locust leadership narrowly focuses on the short-term interests of investors and shareholders, regarding anything beyond that as a waste of money.

Honeybee leadership treats the environment as a valuable asset for both pragmatic and ethical reasons – pragmatic because it is the smart thing to do, and ethical because it is the right thing to do. Locust enterprises perceive the environment as little more than a resource that beckons to be exploited.

Honeybee enterprises perceive themselves to be part of a broader community, the survival and well-being of which legitimises and enables its own existence. Locust enterprises perceive themselves as owing allegiance to no one other than their shareholders.

Finally, we saw how an embedded vision drives Honeybee businesses whereas Locust enterprises struggle to develop and share a higher-order purpose – beyond enhancing shareholder profits.

In the next chapter we look at higher-level practices and key performance drivers that emerge from these foundation practices.

notes

1   Hewitt Associates, 2001
2   Levitan and Werneke, 1984
3   The contents of this box were derived from information available in the public arena, including the company web site http://www.huawei.com; accessed 20 February 2006, 31 January 2007, 14 July 2009
4   Aguinis and Kraiger, 2009; Becker *et al.,* 1997; Jacobs and Washington, 2003; OECD, 2001
5   Bassi and McMurrer, 2004
6   OECD, 2001
7   For example Carmeli and Tishler, 2004a; Ghoshal, Bartlett and Moran, 1999
8   Ewing and Wunnava, 2004; Hofstede, 1993
9   Ichniowski and Shaw, 1999
10   Pfau and Cohen, 2003
11   Goerke and Pannenberg, 2004

12 Levitan and Werneke, 1984; Weihrich, 1999
13 Danford *et al.,* 2005
14 Lane, 2000
15 http://www.continental.com/web/en-US/content/company/history/2001-2010.aspx?SID=4953A9FEEF8E4F95B1232F649BED656D; accessed 8 September 2007
16 Gittell, von Nordenflycht and Kochan, 2004
17 Alexiou and Tsaliki, 2009
18 For example Bronars, Deere and Tracy, 1994
19 Laroche, 2004
20 Martinez and Norman, 2004
21 Michie and Sheehan-Quinn, 2001
22 Danford *et al.,* 2005
23 Gittell, von Nordenflycht and Kochan, 2004
24 Morishima, 1991
25 Carmeli and Tishler, 2004b
26 McNabb and Whitfield, 1997
27 Rousseau and Batt, 2007
28 Hodges and Woolcock, 1993
29 For example Holm and Hovland, 1999; Michie and Sheehan-Quinn, 2001
30 Chatman, 1991
31 Kristof-Brown, Zimmerman and Johnson, 2005
32 Larsson *et al.,* 2007
33 Cascio, 2002; Holm and Hovland, 1999
34 Hillmer, Hillmer and McRoberts, 2004; Ramsay-Smith, 2004
35 Sheridan, 1992
36 Dess and Shaw, 2001
37 Pfeifer, 2005
38 Ichniowski, Shaw and Prennushi, 1997; Pfau and Cohen, 2003
39 Cascio, 2002; D'Souza *et al.,* 2005
40 Yu and Park, 2006
41 Pfau and Cohen, 2003
42 Djordjević and Djukić, 2008; Love and Kraatz, 2005
43 Reisel, Chia and Maloles, 2005
44 Zatzick and Iverson, 2006
45 Gevity Institute, 2006
46 Collins and Porras, 1994
47 http://www.investors.ups.com; accessed 14 February 2010
48 http://www.sustainability.ups.com/sustainability/index.html; accessed 14 February 2010
49 Purcell *et al.,* 2003
50 Bernthal and Wellins, 2006
51 Clutterbuck, 1998; Collins and Porras, 1994
52 Booz Allen Hamilton, 2003
53 Boeker and Goodstein, 1993
54 Bernthal and Wellins, 2006
55 Van Herpen, Van Praag and Cools, 2005
56 Tzafrir, 2005
57 Hutton, 2002
58 For example Pfeffer, Hatano and Santalainen, 1995
59 Addison and Belfield, 2000; 2001
60 Pfeffer, Hatano and Santalainen, 1995; Wood, 1996
61 Heath, 1999
62 See Continental Airlines 2002 and 2003 annual reports
63 Florida and Goodnight, 2005
64 Florida and Goodnight, 2005
65 Cropanzano and Wright, 2001; Huselid, 1995; Huselid and Becker, 2000; Schneider *et al.,* 2003; Vogus and Welbourne, 2003

66 Chan, Gee and Steiner, 2000; Fulmer, Gerhart and Scott, 2003; Romero and McFarlin, 2004; Van Marrewijk, 2004
67 Levering, 2000
68 Becker *et al.*, 1997; Pfau and Cohen, 2003
69 Rauch, Frese and Utsch, 2005
70 Pfau and Cohen, 2003
71 Kinnie, Hutchinson and Purcell, 2000
72 Kinnie, Hutchinson and Purcell, 2000
73 Wall and Wood, 2005
74 Montgomery and Ramus, 2007
75 Bianco *et al.*, 2000
76 Dönch and Frank, 2006, p. 209
77 For example Hubbard *et al.*, 2002
78 For example Bennis, 2003; Nadler and Tushman, 1990
79 Flood *et al.*, 2000
80 Lardner, 2002
81 Business Leader Online, November 1999, http://www.businessleader.com/bl/nov99/cover.html
82 Carpenter, Geletkanycz and Sanders, 2004
83 Certo *et al.*, 2006
84 Finkelstein and Hambrick, 1996
85 Collins, 2001b
86 Ling and Jaw, 2006
87 Hubbard *et al.*, 2002
88 Carmeli and Tishler, 2004a
89 Flood *et al.*, 2000; Lucier, Spiegel and Schuyt, 2002
90 Edmondson, Roberto and Watkins, 2003
91 Harris and Bromiley, 2007
92 Bennis, 2003
93 Jose and Thibodeaux, 1999
94 Cameron, 2006
95 Verschoor, 2004
96 Cameron, Bright and Caza, 2004
97 Jones, 1995
98 Trevino *et al.*, 1999
99 Eberl and Schwaiger, 2004
100 Montgomery and Ramus, 2007
101 Recardo, 2000
102 For example Marchington and Zagelmeyer, 2005
103 Kennedy, 2000
104 Dönch and Frank, 2006, p. 209
105 See Mitchell, 2001; Sethi, 2005
106 Booz Allen Hamilton, 2003
107 Hart and Quinn, 1993
108 Drucker, 2003
109 Hambrick, Finkelstein and Mooney, 2005
110 Meyer and Stensacker, 2006
111 Longenecker, Neubert and Fink, 2007
112 Van Aken, 2007
113 House and Aditya, 1997; Waldman, Javidan and Varella, 2004
114 UBS, c. 2004
115 Pettigrew, Woodman and Cameron, 2001
116 Ghoshal and Bartlett, 1996
117 Collins, 2001b
118 Haveman, 1992
119 Pettigrew and Whipp, 1991
120 Wezel and Saka-Helmhout, 2006

121 Bernthal and Wellins, 2006
122 Longenecker, Neubert and Fink, 2007
123 Parker, 2007
124 Goldenberg, 2000
125 World Economic Forum, 2004
126 Munich Re Group, annual report, 2001
127 Klein, 2004
128 Venohr and Meyer, 2007
129 Nelson, 2005
130 For example Sethi, 2005
131 For example Bansal, 2002; Ladd, 1970
132 Bansal, 2002
133 Sethi, 2002
134 Available at: http://www.karcher.com/int/about_karcher/Environment; accessed 14 February 2010
135 Konar and Cohen, 2001
136 González-Benito and González-Benito, 2005
137 Dunphy, 2003
138 Von Paumgarten, 2003
139 Bazerman and Gillespie, 1999
140 Amalric and Hauser, 2005
141 Dunphy, 2003
142 Porter and Kramer, 2006
143 Dennis *et al.*, 2008
144 *Management Services*, 2002
145 World Economic Forum, 2004
146 Ghoshal, Bartlett and Moran, 1999
147 Nicholls, 2005
148 Jenkins and Yakevleva, 2006
149 http://www.globalreporting.org/NR/rdonlyres/ED9E9B36-AB54-4DE1-BFF2-5F735235CA44/0/G3_GuidelinesENU.pdf
150 Available at www.anitaroddick.com; accessed 20 December 2005
151 Montgomery and Ramus, 2007
152 oekom research and Morgan Stanley Private Wealth Management, 2004
153 Rey and Nguyen, 2005
154 Vermeier, van de Velde and Corten, 2005
155 Orlitzky, 2005; Orlitzky, Schmidt and Rynes, 2003
156 Barnett and Salomon, 2006
157 Brammer and Pavelin, 2006
158 Carmeli, Gilat and Waldman, 2007
159 Orlitzky, 2005
160 Schnietz and Epstein, 2005
161 Porter and Kramer, 2006, p. 80
162 Connolly, Conlon and Deutsch, 1980
163 Liker and Choi, 2004
164 Sako, 1992
165 For example Berman *et al.*, 1999; Jones, 1995; Ruf *et al.*, 2001
166 Dyer and Singh, 1998; Leana and Rousseau, 2000; Preston and Donaldson, 1999
167 Martinez and Norman, 2004
168 Harrison, Bosse and Phillips, 2010
169 For example Vora, 2004
170 Chung-Leung *et al.*, 2005
171 For example Anderson, Fornell and Lehmann, 1994; Babakus, Bienstock and Van Scotter, 2004; Bernhardt, Donthu and Kennett, 2000
172 Ogden and Watson, 1999
173 Corsten and Felde, 2005
174 Continental Airlines annual report 2002, p. 4
175 Collins and Porras, 1994, p. 9

176 For example Baum, Locke and Kirkpatrick, 1998; Hamel and Prahalad, 1989; Kantabutra and Avery, 2003; Oswald, Stanwick and LaTour, 1997

177 Kantabutra and Avery, 2007; 2005

178 For example Barling, Weber and Kelloway, 1996; DeGroot, Kiker and Cross, 2000; Hewitt Associates, 2004; House, Woycke and Fodor, 1988; Jing, 2009; Lowe and Galen Kroeck, 1996; McColl-Kennedy and Anderson, 2002; Ogbonna and Harris, 2000; O'Regan and Ghobadian, 2005

179 Purcell *et al.*, 2003

180 Rafferty and Griffin, 2004

4

Higher-level Practices and Key Performance Drivers

How firms decide to proceed on each of the foundation practices described in the previous chapter has consequences for the business and its employees. These consequences occur on two levels that we term 'higher-level practices' and 'key performance drivers'. Managers can decide that they want employees to self-manage, work in teams or be innovative and engaged, but whether this happens usually depends on the necessary foundation practices being in place.

In this chapter, we describe six higher-level practices that emerge from the foundation practices. Then we introduce three key performance drivers that in turn arise from combinations of the higher-level practices. The key performance drivers are distinguished from the higher-level practices in that the performance drivers directly influence customers. We use published research findings to show the likely contribution all these variables can make to organisational performance.

The higher-level practices and key performance drivers interact with some or all of the foundation practices as well as with one another. Therefore, the case studies illustrating this chapter often demonstrate multiple practices.

Higher-level practices

The six higher-level practices relate to devolved and consensual decision-making, self-managing employees, team orientation, the organisational culture, sharing and retaining knowledge, and trust. Each is discussed in turn, accompanied by examples from living organisations and research evidence.

Decision-making

A major difference between Locust and Honeybee leadership philosophy lies in their approaches to decision-making. Under Locust leadership, decision-making power is exercised by designated managers and does not require much if any input from staff. By contrast, Honeybee decision-making tends to be both devolved to the lowest level within an organisation and strives for consensus.

Under Honeybee leadership, strongly participative and devolved decision-making is possible because power tends to be dispersed throughout the enterprise, not concentrated at the top (see Box 4–1 for an example of dispersed decision-making at the Fraunhofer Society). In some cases this can mean that people at the lowest level of the organisation can get involved in decision-making at the highest level of the enterprise. Some Honeybee firms voluntarily include employees on their supervisory boards, enabling them to influence strategic decisions. For example, after financial services provider Allianz was (re)incorporated as a European Union company, CEO Michael Diekmann said: 'We deliberately chose to continue our policy of codetermination because we believe our employees' right to participation is both correct and crucial.'[1]

Typically, participation is pushed down to the lowest operational level in Honeybee organisations. One result is that innovations come from all over an organisation when ordinary people are enabled to make extraordinary things happen, as the late Peter Drucker emphasised.[2] Allowing people to make decisions that affect their work is often referred to as *empowerment*. One form of empowerment comes from the ability of employees to contribute to making important decisions on an on-going basis, rather than just on selected decisions. At automaker BMW, decision-making is typically devolved to the lowest level. An example is that individual workers on the production line are empowered to stop the line if they think this is warranted. This decision can be made after consultation with the team, or independently by a single member. It is important to note that production-line downtime is very expensive and is measured in minutes per month. Allowing individual workers to make such far-reaching decisions demonstrates BMW's trust in its staff.

Consensus involves getting acceptance of a decision within a group, even if the decision is not unanimously agreed to. If those not initially in favour agree to go along with a decision, consensus has been reached. Achieving consensus requires time for people to be heard, and can be frustrating for those seeking an immediate outcome. Notwithstanding this generalisation, consensual decision-making can be very fast in some SMEs that operate on Honeybee principles. For example, at glass and steel construction specialist Seele meetings are informal and can occur anywhere, including in the firm's kitchen. The company's premises are designed to encourage continual communication between designers and implementers, between interacting project team members and between anyone and the joint CEOs. Discussing issues broadly improves quality by sharing knowledge about what does and does not work. Even fast-paced communications and IT companies such as Nokia and SAS seek consensus in decision-making whenever they can, even if decisions take a little longer.

> *. . . ordinary people are enabled to make*
> *extraordinary things happen . . .*

Locust managers can short-circuit this process by simply proclaiming their decisions. However, the seeming advantages of making fast managerial decisions are somewhat illusory. After all, managers still need to gain the acceptance of those who have to implement those decisions. Although individual managers can make decisions faster alone, research shows that joint decisions tend to be of better quality than those made by a single individual.[3] Honeybee leadership encourages collaborative decision-making to enhance, among other things, the quality and acceptance of a decision. Whether the process of achieving consensus is fast or drawn out, making decisions in groups typically leads to higher acceptance of the decision.[4]

As the size of organisations increases, the ability of workers to make independent decisions becomes more difficult but also more important. To quote Samuel Palmisano, CEO of IBM: 'A top-down system can create a smothering bureaucracy that doesn't allow for the speed, the flexibility, the innovation that clients expect today.'[5]

Box 4–1: Devolved decision-making at Fraunhofer institutes

The largest contract research organisation in Europe, the Fraunhofer Society, consists of more than 80 research units, including 57 scientific research institutes at 40 different locations in Germany as well as representative offices abroad. Among the Fraunhofer inventions that have changed the lives of many people is the MP3 player.

Decision-making at Fraunhofer is devolved to the 15,000 employees in the individual institutes, except for a limited range of strategic decisions made at headquarters. The self-managing institutes are responsible for attracting and carrying out commercial research contracts. Annual turnover is about €1.4 billion. Individual institutes make their own operational, scientific and commercial decisions. Individual scientists make decisions on their own projects, enjoying a highly devolved form of decision-making. Given the culture of autonomy enjoyed by the scientists within the various institutes, the extent of the society's president's decision-making is in practical terms restricted to non-scientific matters at headquarters in Munich, such as organisational and human resources policies.

Fraunhofer competes in the open marketplace for talented staff, but its ability to pay high salaries is limited by government regulations to public service levels. Therefore, ways of attracting scientists other than salary become important. Attractions include the freedom for employees to develop their own workgroups, take sabbatical leave and pursue personal development goals. Perhaps one of the most attractive features at Fraunhofer for scientists is the devolved decision-making.

Evidence that devolved, consensual decision-making pays off

A 2008 McKinsey survey of 2327 executives from a wide range of industries, regions and functions investigated whether strong decision-making processes lead to good decisions.[6] Several features of decision-making were found to be strongly associated with good financial and operational outcomes, including increased profits and rapid implementation. According to the executives interviewed, it is important to ensure that people with the right skills and experience are included in the decision-making process, use transparent criteria and reliable facts and have the people responsible for implementing a decision participate in making that decision.

Scholars also assert that empowering employees with goals and the right information, training and resources makes good things happen.[7] That pushing decision-making to the lowest level in an organisation benefits an enterprise is not surprising. It recognises that the people actually doing the work understand the requirements of the job better than those removed from the task. This assumes, of course, that the workers have the required competence, motivation and values.

Being involved in making decisions on a continuing basis enhances worker satisfaction far more than occasionally being consulted.[8] Having satisfied workers in turn is recognised as an important organisational outcome. Research shows that empowering environments enhance performance at the work unit level and encourage individual performance.[9] One estimate suggests that employee involvement programs increase productivity by 2–5 per cent.[10] The same writers noted that employees involved in decision-making report higher levels of loyalty and commitment to their employer, along with increased job satisfaction, compared with their non-involved colleagues.

In teams, devolved and consensual decision-making can improve productivity and make the members more proactive.[11] Empowered teams also tend to display higher levels of customer service, job satisfaction and organisational and team commitment. These outcomes in turn contribute to better business performance, as measured by various financial criteria,[12] thereby providing competitive advantage for the firm.

Sometimes other variables combine to influence the effects of empowerment on organisational performance. For example, researchers found that hotels with empowered employees were able to charge more for their rooms, particularly when employees also shared knowledge and adopted a team orientation.[13] This benefits those hotels' income stream. A study of Korean firms illustrates the importance of the quality of decision-making on organisational performance.[14] These researchers reported a powerful connection between an organisation's commitment to its employees and the employees' ability and willingness to engage in 'useful' decision-making processes. The usefulness of this engagement results from the training and talent that employees bring, their motivation and their willingness to collaborate and work for the good of the organisation.

Thus, consensual and devolved decision-making reinforces several of the other higher-level practices of Honeybee leadership, in addition to financial outcomes and employee satisfaction. These include the ability for teamwork and collaboration, an enabling cohesive culture, employee self-management and the trust that people at all levels of the organisation will make informed and ethical decisions. Together they drive quality, staff engagement and innovation. The evidence shows that involving workers in decision-making has far-reaching consequences with respect to the other higher-level practices and the key performance drivers, and ultimately therefore to organisational performance.

Self-managing employees

How employees are expected to work varies under Locust and Honeybee philosophies, ranging from staff working to specifications when told what to do, to employees performing independently of managers.[15] Employees told what to do are said to be 'externally managed' while the others are 'self-managing' or 'self-leading'. Locust managers are more likely to externally manage staff, whereas Honeybee leadership prefers self-managing employees.

In this book we use the term 'self-managing' to refer to employees who control their own behaviour, initiate and self-lead.[16] Realistically, not everyone is able and willing to be self-managing because of their personal preferences, personality, skills and for other reasons.[17] Some people have a higher need for supervision than others and therefore require more external management.[18] Firms seeking self-managing employees need to build these requirements into their recruiting, selection and induction procedures to ensure that new recruits fit the desired employee profile for self-management. The shadow side of allowing employees to self-manage and make decisions is that managers with a high need for control struggle with, or even resent, the loss of control and are subject to increased uncertainty.[19]

Self-managing employees work towards a direction or shared vision prescribed by leaders and/or by a strong organisational culture. Some may formulate and pursue their own vision. Knowing where they are heading, self-managing employees work out how best to achieve particular goals and targets by using their skills and initiative.[20] Guided by an enabling culture and a compelling vision, these employees determine what to do and how to do it. Self-managing people assess problems, set goals, pursue those goals and reward or sanction themselves for their successes or shortcomings.

Self-managing employees are vital for today's dispersed and networked organisations. Distributed teams and remote, global workers make it much more difficult for managers to retain control, supervise workers and exercise power over people in other locations. The keys to success in the new networked organisation are collaboration and sharing power rather than centralised, directing leadership.[21] As Samuel Palmisano, CEO of IBM said:

> You just can't impose command-and-control mechanisms on a large, highly professional workforce. I'm not only talking about our scientists, engineers, and consultants. More than 200,000 of our employees have college degrees. The CEO can't say to them, 'Get in line and follow me', or 'I've decided what your values are.'[22]

For Honeybee leadership, the focus is not on a few designated individuals who wear the mantle of leader; rather it is on the organisation, with all its members operating as part of a broader system. Under this view, well-educated and skilled workers do not need to be instructed in how to do their work. Employees engaged in work that appeals to them do not need motivating or controlling by a manager.

Furthermore, other elements in the workplace can replace or augment the role of leaders.[23] These so-called *substitutes for leadership* include closely knit teams of highly trained individuals who support and learn from each other. Technology can take over many of a manager's controlling and other functions, such as the computers that monitor and direct behaviour in many call centres. Additional substitutes for leader guidance are found in detailed workbooks, guidelines, policies, explanatory notes, expert systems, training courses and standard operating procedures. Clearly a manager's work is also reduced when employees share a strong vision and set of values. Vision and values help people understand the direction they are heading in and the way to get there. These and other leader substitutes can be built into organisations when they are viewed as entire systems. Working through substitutes for leaders changes the manager's role from sole decision-maker and controller to team-player and facilitator. Substitutes for leaders can also curtail the excesses frequently associated with 'heroic' leadership.

People in Honeybee organisations at all levels can be self-managing. At US retailer Nordstrom, sales assistants are empowered to manage their relationships with customers to ensure maximum customer satisfaction. At W.L. Gore & Associates, famous for Gore-Tex® fabrics, self-management goes further. No one tells anyone else what to do at Gore. Individual workers, called associates, are expected to manage themselves. Guidance from mentors and sponsors is provided, but these people are not bosses. They cannot tell their mentees what to do. This applies from production through to top management, and in every country where the 9000 or so associates work. Interestingly, about 50 per cent of Gore associates claim that they are leaders.[24] Key to Gore's effective self-management is that all associates are selected because they share the Gore vision and values and fit with the firm's culture. Gore displays an extreme form of self-management known as organic leadership.[25] It is difficult to implement, but very powerful when done well.

Autonomy and self-management also apply to teams. As a team becomes more self-managing, the members engage in 'management' activities such as coordinating the team's performance, quality and control systems; generating performance reports; and operating continuous improvement programs.[26] For teams to self-manage, individual members need to have a positive orientation towards the enterprise. They need the appropriate attitudes, skills and behaviour to work in teams. Individuals need to be able to self-manage themselves as individuals and as team members, so that they can fulfil their commitments to their teammates. Introducing a highly participative work system can be difficult if too many individuals are reluctant to accept the required amount of autonomy.[27] This can be clarified at the recruitment stage and developed throughout an employee's career. In Box 4–2, you can read about how many of the elements in Toyota's human resources systems engender autonomous employee behaviour among its Japanese workers.

Under Locust leadership, staff can be expected to self-manage to only a limited extent. This is because self-managing workers need to be committed to the organisation and have developed the appropriate skills.[28] These elements are less characteristic of Locust organisations than of Honeybee firms.

Box 4–2: How Japanese employees self-manage in the Toyota way

Toyota overtook GM as the world's largest car manufacturer for the first time in 2007, and is leading the world in hybrid and other innovations. The company is regarded as a role model in lean production. Part of its success is attributed to the 'Toyota way', derived from the Toyota Production System. The company has developed many systems to ensure that its employees understand and follow the 'Toyota way' in a largely self-managing manner. Masaki Saruta has identified some of the ways in which Toyota's culture shapes this behaviour in Japan.[29]

Basically, the company's personnel management system extends way beyond conventional human resources manage-ment.[30] Via training and other communication techniques, each worker is expected to live and breathe the company's values and ideals. The performance management system partially assesses the extent to which an employee understands the Toyota way. 'Toyota people' comply with the company's expectations for concentrated labour and long working hours – even at the expense of personal goals and family life. (The company provides dormitories for workers who do not make it home!) In this respect, the 'Toyota way' differs radically from Honeybee leadership as practised elsewhere, particularly in Europe where there is a concern for work–life balance. Perhaps in the Japanese context, where long working hours are the norm, Toyota's high-pressure working conditions are acceptable to its staff.

The Toyota person is shaped by a combination of incentives and training. Incentives start with generous wages based on merit rather than seniority. A small work group structure motivates staff to contribute hard work and to avoid being absent. Not wanting to let teammates down encourages members to contribute quality work over long hours. The company also uses job enrichment and enlargement as a motivator for people to attend in-house training programs to develop specialist skills. Everyone who participates in the training is eventually promoted despite large differences in ability. One major function of the training is to spread the Toyota values and way of working.

Employees are given high levels of authority at an early age. Self-motivation derived from an interest in their work is a company expectation – everyone at Toyota is expected to enjoy their work. The company explicitly claims to combine personal motivation with the goals of the organisation, according to Saruta. Quality circles and other mechanisms stimulate original suggestions for improvement and bind teams together. Under the Toyota way, workers strive to improve quality, reduce costs and deliver on time. Waste, defined as anything that is not adding value, is eliminated wherever possible, whether it is a hand movement or a material.

Saruta describes how all these elements combine to drive Toyota employees to contribute long hours of concentrated work and continuously seek improvement – admittedly for a generous wage. If workers actively cooperate with Toyota human resources management, training and other policies they are more likely than their colleagues to be promoted and receive pay increases. Interestingly, if workers make mistakes, management gets blamed. This is because under the Toyota way, it is the manager's job to teach operators the skills so that operators can be self-managing.

Naturally, the organisational culture, processes and systems need to support self-managing employees, guiding them in the appropriate direction. Creating an environment for self-management depends first on establishing some of the 14 foundation practices discussed in Chapter 3 and on support from other higher-level practices. For example, to be successful, self-management requires employees to be empowered to make decisions affecting their work and to share the organisation's vision and values. At W.L. Gore & Associates, employees' behaviour is bound by the firm's four key values. These same factors also favour increased innovation under Honeybee leadership compared with the Locust approach. You can read more about self-management at this innovative organisation in Box 4–3.

In addition to having the right technical skills people also need the right psychological and social profile to self-manage, including being able to initiate, direct and motivate themselves under autonomous conditions.[31] Otherwise, autonomy and self-management are difficult to achieve. Opportunities for career progression via internal promotion and a philosophy of retaining staff can also foster self-managing behaviour.

Evidence that a focus on self-managing employees pays off

Research shows that self-management enhances various organisational effects, including job performance. Numerous researchers have found that, compared with less autonomous workers, those who believe they have high autonomy in their work report more positive experiences. These include more job satisfaction, greater involvement and commitment to the firm, higher motivation and performance and lower levels of stress and depression.[32] Self-managing workers thus bring many benefits to a business, including higher organisational performance stemming from the increased employee motivation and commitment at both the individual and business unit levels. For example, at the individual level researchers found that delegation, which is part of empowering self-managing workers, not only enhanced Chinese employees' commitment to the organisation, it increased job satisfaction and task performance as well.[33]

Improved outcomes depend at least partly on how much the workplace meets the self-esteem needs of individual employees. In addition, an employee's willingness to accept responsibility for delegated activities influences whether or not delegation enhances the workplace. An Australian study of self-managing employees in a manufacturing setting also highlighted the role of job satisfaction in promoting self-management and team performance.[34]

An example of research at the business unit level comes from a study of 68 Hong Kong primary schools, which the researchers treated as business units. They found that the more self-managing schools also contained more self-managing groups and individuals compared with other schools. Furthermore, the self-managing schools performed better on many measures of educational quality, as well as on measures of staff commitment and morale.[35]

Self-managing staff have been linked to higher levels of innovation,[36] although the relationship between autonomy and innovation is complex.[37] Within the framework of the Sustainable Leadership Pyramid (see Figure 2–1) innovation is identified as a key performance driver, and is discussed in more detail in a separate section. However, to underscore the interactive effects of Honeybee practices, we briefly touch on innovation here. Too little autonomy reduces innovation, while high autonomy can expose firms to diverse risks unless worker autonomy is also accompanied by factors designed to ameliorate those risks. This includes ensuring a Honeybee culture of high trust, clear objectives, agreement on fundamental issues and sharing a common vision and values.[38] This demonstrates how both foundation and higher-level practices link into the key performance driver of innovation.

Team orientation

Teamwork and collaboration are increasingly being seen as essential for achieving business goals and developing competitive advantage for a firm.[39] This is particularly so for fast-changing, knowledge-based global enterprises. Teams provide greater flexibility and faster responses to change than do many individuals. They promote innovation and the exchange of knowledge. As a result, employees who can self-manage, communicate with others, work in teams and take responsibility are becoming increasingly valuable. This is particularly so in Honeybee firms where the culture supports teamwork.

Effective teamwork is hard to achieve under the short-term perspective of the Locust model. This is because short-tenure employees in Locust enterprises tend to know each other less well, are less skilled and hence trust each other less. In addition, they are not as bound by a strong corporate vision and culture and may well compete more with each other internally. When team members are pitted against each other, team performance necessarily suffers. Because members are less able to work autonomously, Locust teams tend to be manager-led. Locust teams work under various degrees of supervision depending on the members' skills, trustworthiness and cohesion. Thus, Locust cultures tend to have a limited capacity for teamwork.

This can have negative effects on performance. Among other things a lack of support for, and commitment to, teamwork can foster knowledge hoarding, individual profiling and neglecting team responsibilities. Since teams, particularly self-managing teams, can bear responsibilities that could never be carried out by a group of individuals,[40] cultures not supportive of teams can disadvantage a firm's performance.

By contrast, Honeybee teams can draw on highly skilled individuals who know each other well, are committed to a strong corporate vision and culture, are willing to share information and knowledge and hence are highly trustworthy and trusting of each other. Honeybee teams are likely to have the competence, authority and integrity to solve quality problems on the spot. Therefore, they tend to be empowered to an extent that would be unthinkable in most Locust organisations. Research also shows that high-performing teams tend to be associated with leadership that uses a vision,[41] another Honeybee principle.

> *. . . Locust cultures tend to have a limited*
> *capacity for teamwork.*

Let us look at some examples of how teamwork is employed in Honeybee firms. First, at companies such as BMW, rewards and sanctions are often team-focused *and* individual.[42] BMW requires individual teams to be accountable to other teams for their quality and timeliness. In the event that a team passes on mistakes to the next group, that team has the costs of fixing the errors taken out of their wages or bonuses. This certainly focuses teams on satisfying the needs of internal and external customers! Furthermore, at BMW every worker is expected to demonstrate business 'nous'. This means that employees should understand not only their own jobs but also where the business is heading. BMW teams elect a spokesperson to represent them to the outside, coordinate activities and chair team meetings. However, this person is not a conventional boss or supervisor. The spokesperson needs to exert influence, not authority, to gain consensus in making decisions. At BMW, the production line is stopped to allow regular team meetings; during team meetings in service departments some team members may have to remain available for clients.

Research-based enterprises often use relatively unstructured teams. At Fraunhofer, Germany's leading applied research organisation (see Box 4–1), the concept of 'fractal organisation' has given rise to project teams that self-organise and self-optimise. A fractal team allows members to come and go as their expertise is required on particular projects. These teams can easily adjust to changing customer needs and other circumstances. Similarly, at W.L. Gore & Associates there are no bosses or rigid structures. People organically form project teams in response to market opportunities (see Box 4–3).

Running an airline is the biggest team sport imaginable, according to former Continental Airlines CEO Gordon Bethune. Bethune views the airline business as a collection of self-managing teams – from cockpit to cabin and management teams. These teams need to function as a whole to ensure that the entire enterprise works and is sustainable. Extensive communication about the company's performance is part of the glue that binds associates together. Another part of the glue is commitment to an employer that values its people in many different ways.

Under Marriott's strong team ethic, the rewards for collaborating curb individual self-interest. Not only do associates within a particular hotel cooperate and work in teams, so do the various Marriott hotel brands. The different brands refer business to each other to promote the interests of the entire company.

Box 4–3: Free-flowing organic teamwork at W.L. Gore & Associates, Inc.

Founded in 1958, W.L. Gore & Associates Inc. is one of the 200 largest privately held companies in the USA. Its worldwide sales exceed US$2.5 billion, created by about 9000 associates in more than 45 plants and sales locations worldwide.[43] This highly innovative enterprise has invented many products based on polymer polytetrafluoroethylene (PTFE) and holds in excess of 2000 patents. Gore-Tex® is the most famous of Gore's brands, but its products are also used in electronic signal transmission, fabric laminates, medical implants and in various other industries. More than 25 million Gore medical implants have been used in patients worldwide.

Gore is one of only four companies to appear in every listing of Fortune's annual 100 Best Companies to Work For in America, and on similar lists in Europe, Asia, the Americas and elsewhere. This is largely because of its special culture. Since its inception, Gore has avoided traditional hierarchy. Instead, Gore offers a team-based environment that fosters personal initiative, promotes person-to-person communication among all associates and encourages innovation. Associates believe that the firm's flat structure contributes to staff satisfaction and retention. The company works hard to maximise individual potential. It cultivates an environment where creativity can flourish. A fundamental belief in people and their abilities is key to Gore's success, along with an insistence on product integrity and excellence. Gore prides itself on having the best quality in each market it enters.

At Gore, hands-on innovation is encouraged. Those closest to a project make decisions. Teams organise around opportunities and leaders emerge. There are no chains of command or predetermined channels of communication. Instead, associates communicate directly with each other and are accountable to fellow members of multidisciplinary teams. There are no bosses at Gore, and no one tells anyone else what to do.[44]

Associates are recruited for general work areas and are carefully selected to ensure that they fit the culture. With the guidance of starting sponsors (who are not bosses) and a growing understanding of opportunities and team objectives, associates commit to projects that match their skills. The work environment combines individual freedom with cooperation and autonomy with synergy.

Everyone can quickly earn the credibility to define and drive projects. Sponsors help associates chart a course in the organisation that will offer personal fulfilment while maximising their contribution to the enterprise. Each associate has various kinds of sponsors, but none is a boss.[45] Sometimes leaders are appointed, but they are defined by natural 'followership' whereby they remain leaders as long as people will follow them. More often, leaders emerge naturally because of the special knowledge, skill or experience that they have for advancing a particular business objective.

Despite the free-flowing nature of the culture, Gore is not chaotic and unmanageable. Leadership is 'organic',[46] held together by a shared vision and set of values. Bill Gore, the founder, anchored four guiding principles in the firm's culture that are adhered to around the Gore world. These principles are not defined in great detail but represent broad guidelines to cover many situations. A major principle is to make and keep *commitments* to others. A second one concerns *fairness*, to each other and everyone with whom the business comes in contact. A third principle is *freedom*. This means freedom to encourage, help and allow other associates to grow in knowledge, skill and scope of responsibility. Finally, the *water line* is a metaphor used to manage risk. If a decision is 'below the water line', it has the potential to sink the ship. Then particular processes and specified experts in the firm have to be involved.

Evidence that a team orientation pays off

The weight of evidence shows that teamwork contributes to enhanced organisational performance. For a start, teams foster greater worker satisfaction.[47] In teams people act more in the interests of the business than out of self-interest. Higher productivity, initiative and quality can be achieved, as can higher levels of customer service, job satisfaction and organisational and team commitment.[48] Effective, motivated and trustworthy teams also require less supervision than their counterparts.[49] Yet they can deliver better quality, because they have the skills, motivation and values to deliver superior outcomes. Realistically, managers cannot attain 100 per cent supervision, which makes for inconsistent quality. This means that in companies such as BMW supervisors, who are expensive but actually add little or no value, can be largely dispensed with. All these effects contribute to better organisational performance measured on financial, brand and customer satisfaction criteria.

Research indicates that effective teams are associated with higher financial performance. A nationwide British study collected managers' assessments of their workplace financial performance, and concluded that the benefits of using teamwork outweighed costs.[50] Monetary and time costs can be incurred through developing, maintaining and continually enhancing team skills.

IBM's 2006 global set of interviews with 765 CEOs from different countries supports the conclusion that organisations with a team–based culture are more profitable. In team–based enterprises, researchers found that the average operating margins for the past five years exceeded by nearly three times those of organisations that were individually focused.[51]

Providing rewards for individual contributions in addition to team rewards also pays off. Where individual team members were rewarded, operating margins increased by 2 per cent on average and revenue grew about 3 per cent faster than in organisations not providing individual rewards.[52]

Many other specific performance improvements are associated with teamwork. For example, members of self-managed customer service teams reported significant improvements in service quality, while sales increased by more than 9 per cent.[53] An even greater increase in productivity arose when garment workers adopted teamwork, averaging a 14 per cent increase per team.[54] Teamwork enhanced productivity in small American steel mills by more than $1.4 million in additional output per mill.[55] Productivity rose particularly on the more technologically complex production mill lines. The researchers claim that teams on complex lines that were provided with group-based incentive pay increased their productivity most of all. A study of UK firms identified teamwork as an important factor in a firm's long-term success.[56] Teamwork contributes to continuous improvement within organisations, as well as to the quality of working life.[57] Research also indicates that managers who encourage collaborative work are perceived as performing better and as having followers who put in extra effort.[58] Employees working under highly team–oriented leaders in Chinese firms exhibited significantly higher motivation, commitment and trust compared with their counterparts led by people who were not particularly team-oriented.[59] This occurred even with employees whose values did not fit the organisation well.

In short, the published research evidence suggests that teamwork and collaboration, implemented appropriately, enhance business performance and bring many other organisational benefits. However, research also shows that enhanced business performance through teams is not automatic.[60] There can be many reasons for this. For example, employees may not have the complex coordination skills or other capacity required for teamwork. Alternatively, organisational support for self-managing teams may be lacking. Some research has shown that autonomy is particularly important for effective teamwork, along with how meaningful members find the team experience and a belief that they can affect outcomes.[61]

Teamwork is shown as a higher-level practice in the Sustainable Leadership Pyramid because effective teamwork cannot simply be commanded. It needs to be developed and facilitated by various antecedent foundation practices. Teamwork depends on the foundation practices of retaining staff, training and developing their technical and social skills and letting employees know that they are valued. Other foundation practices that are likely to support effective teamwork include being an ethical enterprise, taking a long-term perspective to allow teams to develop, role-modelling by the top management team rather than a solo heroic CEO, and being a company that values the interests of various stakeholders, including employees. Furthermore, teamwork is supported by knowing that change is a considered process and that teams are not likely to be continually disrupted. Having a clear vision to work towards and not being driven to short-term actions by the financial markets or political pressures also support teamwork.

Working in teams requires support from other higher-level practices, such as a culture that enables people to collaborate and develop trust and an environment in which employees can share knowledge, self-manage and make decisions. Hence, teamwork emerges from the 14 foundation practices and is supported by other higher-level practices. We will see later that teamwork also influences the key performance drivers of staff engagement, innovation and quality.

Culture

The culture of an organisation refers to the informal norms and rules that govern people's behaviour. Culture includes shared feelings, beliefs and values. Enterprises with an enabling culture can clearly state what their values are – whether it is teamwork, trust, innovation, quality, excellence, customer service, managers being more or less important than workers and/or the need for satisfied employees. Honeybee companies are clear about what they stand for and where they are going, even though their cultures differ in detail. As a result of a shared culture, employees may well boast to outsiders about how special their workplace is.

In a Locust enterprise, it is more difficult to foster an enabling culture except perhaps a culture revolving around shareholder profits. This culture might not necessarily be willingly shared at lower levels. Maintaining any kind of culture is a challenge in Locust organisations. There, staff turns over faster than in a Honeybee business, losing the people and their networks needed to develop and maintain the culture. This is a threat to services giant IBM, even though it espouses a Honeybee leadership philosophy in many respects. As discussed in Chapter 3, IBM continually sheds about 20,000 people each year. It is therefore difficult to get people who believe that they are only transient to commit to the future of a firm.

Creating and maintaining a consistent organisational culture takes time, and this requires a long-term perspective. To ensure that newcomers fit the culture, recruiters in Honeybee firms will seek people whose values match those in that organisation's culture. As such, many recruiters emphasise attitude and social skills over technical competencies. For example, surgical instrument producer Aesculap places social skills, teamwork and communication ahead of technical skills. Aesculap prefers to appoint candidates with good people skills even if they have low (but developable) technical skills in preference to people with excellent technical skills but an inappropriate attitude. This is because it is nearly impossible to change people's basic beliefs, values and attitudes so that they are right for a particular organisation.[62] Technical skills can be acquired more easily provided, of course, there is the necessary level of aptitude, training and resources.

> *. . . employees may well boast to outsiders about how special their workplace is.*

Preserving an enabling culture also requires that external appointees are socialised into their new employer's ways. By selecting staff for cultural fit, Honeybee employers exclude people from their workforce who clearly fail to share common values. Socialisation can increase cultural fit further where the values do not conflict with an employee's deeply held personal values. Some companies provide extensive induction programs for new recruits, often rotating young employees between departments to build their experience. At W.L. Gore & Associates special starting sponsors mentor newcomers to help ease them into the company culture (see Box 4–3).

It is important to note that recruiting for shared values does not mean that organisations have to lack diversity. However, certain core values, such as treating others with respect and behaving ethically, are non-negotiable. These values play a key role in recruiting, training and promoting employees under Honeybee leadership. Automobile supplier ZF Friedrichshafen spends considerable time interviewing potential employees, often for a whole day, to make sure the 'chemistry' is right.

Some commentators perceive an enabling culture as a disadvantage and an impediment to necessary change. This risk is addressed in Honeybee organisations by their emphasis on innovation and continuous improvement. Box 4–4 describes how these values work together in the strong culture at Marriott International Hotels.

However, it is important that managers are consistent in the culture that they espouse to different stakeholders. For example, when the corporate values declared to customers and the actual values and culture experienced by employees differ substantially, employees' attitudes can be adversely affected. This starts a downward spiral. The workers do not strongly support the 'lie' and their ambivalence is transmitted to customers, who then begin to mistrust the company brand. Recruiting staff for cultural fit helps here. Employees selected because their values align with the values underpinning the brand are more likely to perceive the organisation as supporting those values. In turn, this positively affects customer perceptions of the brand and raises trust in it.[63]

Box 4–4: Marriott's organisational culture[64]

Marriott International Hotels is headquartered in Washington DC but operates globally. In 2008, Marriott International's sales reached almost US$13 billion. Marriott strives to provide exceptional customer service, opportunities for employees to grow and attractive shareholder returns. Long-term shareholders would have received an annual return of more than 16 per cent on their investment over a 52-year period. Apart from its financial success, Marriott is consistently ranked by *Fortune* magazine as the lodging industry's most admired company and one of the best places to work. The company takes its social and environmental responsibilities as seriously abroad as it does in the US – even though legally this is not always required. The US Environmental Protection Agency awarded Marriott the 2008 Sustained Excellence Award.

Like many Honeybee businesses, Marriott's vision, values and people practices are similar wherever its approximately 146,000 employees (as of 2008) operate. Employees are driven by the vision of making people who are away from home feel among friends when staying at a Marriott facility. The company's core values centre on integrity, taking responsibility, fairness and ensuring consistency between words and actions. Other aspects of the culture include a commitment to continuous improvement, overcoming adversity, hard work and fun. The business pursues the highest possible quality and consistency in service. Achieving this involves relentless change, improvement and renewal. Managers keep close to both staff and customers by walking around and talking to people. However, managers do not do all the work! The company recognises and celebrates all its associates' contributions.

Marriott's philosophy is based on the notion that if its associates are confident and happy, this positive attitude will be reflected in whatever they do and will make customers happy. In addition to being provided with a wide range of social benefits, associates are well trained and supported by systems that ensure consistency. These include 66 steps for cleaning hotel rooms, 39 steps to ensure food quality and a 20-day process for reinforcing the Marriott values (whereby a different value is practised by all employees each day). As part of strengthening the values, employees are briefed on the particular value being practised at that day's associates' meeting. This could, for example, involve exceeding customer expectations or anticipating customer needs.

A strong teamwork ethic is infused throughout Marriott's culture. In this basically egalitarian culture, the rewards for working together outweigh those of self-interest. Outrageous incentive packages are not used to keep talented people from leaving because a culture of teamwork depends on collaboration, not competition. In these and many other ways, Marriott International Hotels has adapted its systems to support

> its strong culture. Although associates are very loyal and support the vision and core values, they can be critical when necessary.[65]

Evidence that having an enabling culture pays off

An enabling organisational culture and a set of shared values characterise Honeybee leadership philosophy. For well over two decades now, scholars have demonstrated that a strong, widely shared culture is associated with enhanced organisational performance in both government and private enterprises.[66] The benefits of a strong culture are particularly marked in relatively stable environments compared with when conditions are volatile.[67] However, many studies have shown that the effects of culture on performance endure. Early findings from 34 large US companies revealed that over a five-year period firms with a participative culture displayed returns on investment that averaged twice as much as the other firms in the sample.[68] Later research into 150 US publicly traded companies showed that enterprises with a defined culture significantly outperformed their weak-cultured counterparts over a six-year period.[69] This study found that having a strong culture alone can be a handicap in turbulent times by preventing firms from adapting to new conditions.

Thus, cultures need to be not only strong and widely shared, but also flexible enough to enable the firm to adapt when necessary. In another sample of 207 large US companies, those that focused on building strong corporate cultures outperformed the stock market by a factor of 15.[70] This was not a short-lived coincidence. The same firms outperformed their competitors on various financial criteria over an 11-year period, enjoying revenues that were four times as high as competitors who failed to manage their cultures as well. Other researchers have concluded that cultural beliefs, attitudes and tasks are significantly associated with financial performance on many measures.[71]

Other scholars have demonstrated that organisational culture affects different factors relating to organisational performance. These include staff satisfaction and commitment, intentions to stay with the employer, morale and teamwork. For example, branches of a US bank differed in level of staff turnover and productivity, depending on the culture in the branch.[72] Where workers held less favourable attitudes employee turnover was higher, sales lower and growth reduced – compared with branches where workers held more favourable attitudes. The researchers found that those branches characterised by less favourable attitudes were more likely to close down.

Another consideration is that the internal culture of a firm influences the impression that the entity makes on people outside the organisation. In other words, organisational culture can affect brand and reputation. A Canadian study showed that clients' perception of a fitness organisation's culture significantly influenced their satisfaction and intention to stay with that provider.[73]

Many positive links have been uncovered between organisational culture and various indicators of business performance. Developing and maintaining the adaptive and enabling culture required in Honeybee enterprises is influenced by most of the 14 foundation practices, starting with vision and values, training and development, being ethical and retaining staff for the long term. An organisation's unique culture emerges from how these and other practices are implemented. Furthermore, the Honeybee foundation practice of making major change in a planned and considered way can support the benefits of an enabling culture by providing relative stability inside the enterprise. Culture is a higher-level practice that emerges from many of the foundation elements, supported by other higher-level practices.

Knowledge-sharing and retention

Increasingly, enterprises everywhere are becoming more dependent on the ability and willingness of their workers to share their knowledge and hence promote learning in the enterprise. This applies to both Honeybee and Locust organisations.

Originally, information and communication technology (ICT) was expected to be the mainstay of knowledge-sharing. For example, salespeople would enter their client details and feedback into a database each day for others to see and learn from. Experts would dump their knowledge into a computer system for others to access. Retirees would be brought back to ensure that their knowledge was captured in some ICT system within the firm.

Despite some successes with the technology, it quickly became evident that employees in many businesses could not be commanded to share their knowledge. People felt especially uncomfortable doing so through ICT systems. Nor could people be forced to regularly update their knowledge by consulting ICT systems. Rather, knowledge-sharing depends on promoting quality relationships.[74] This shifts the focus of managing and creating knowledge from systems to humans. Increasingly, managers and academics are realising that real value for corporations and society is created when people relate to one another informally. Relying on formally structured communication channels is particularly unhelpful in global organisations with high diversity and complexity.[75] Instead, relationships need to be fostered on a human scale.

To do this, many firms are creating communication environments that encourage people to share knowledge in informal ways. Examples include informal meetings in coffee shops and staff kitchens or attendance at company seminars, road shows and other corporate learning events. Professor Karl-Erik Sveiby reports on how managing knowledge reduced patient fear and added value in a Norwegian private hospital.[76] Nurses in the hospital wanted to reduce the fear that patients experienced before going into surgery. Despite some scepticism from the doctors, the nurses experimented by inviting previous patients to join new patients over coffee and cake. Naturally they discussed their operations. Afterwards, the surgeons and nurses agreed that the initiative was a great success because the new patients' fear had indeed been reduced. But looking more closely at what had happened was revealing. Both surgeons and nurses stated that the new patients asked fewer questions and needed fewer relaxation drugs before their operations. The patients were learning from each other as knowledge of what happens during surgery was being transferred from the old patients to the new ones. This transfer of knowledge resulted in time savings and other benefits for hospital staff. In the end, the surgeons' resistance was overcome and medical staff began to share their new knowledge with other colleagues. Although cost savings arose directly from needing fewer relaxation drugs, Sveiby concludes that most of the value added by knowledge-sharing was intangible through savings in time, enjoyment and creating structural capital in new policies and procedures. More complex knowledge-sharing environments involve communities of interest where people with similar interests meet, either in person or online, to exchange ideas. These fluid communities can change membership, disband and re-form as needed. Read about how Holcim in Switzerland approaches knowledge-sharing in Box 4–5.

For Munich Re knowledge is at the heart of its reinsurance business, which is based on risk. Knowledge stems from employee experience and expertise, innovation, learning from clients and other partners and conducting its own research. To stimulate knowledge-sharing and communication, Munich Re has developed a culture whereby employees meet a different colleague from the organisation for lunch each day. The staff cafeteria has been fitted out with two-seater tables to support this tradition.

Capturing and stimulating knowledge exchanges can be particularly challenging for global businesses. Colgate's collaborative culture is supported by systematically sharing recipes for success. This is reinforced by considerable travel, conference attendance and email exchange in a culture of open communication. A strong organisational culture allows people to share experiences and values with colleagues. In turn, widespread communication and shared goals can support continuous improvement in service or product quality. Combining these practices and effects indirectly influences financial performance through increased efficiency and sustains the organisation by exploiting its shared knowledge.[77]

An ambitious approach to fostering informal communications among people can be seen at global Swiss pharmaceutical corporation Novartis. Novartis has been trying for many years to address a knowledge conundrum that it expressed thus: 'If Novartis only knew what Novartis knows.' In the 1990s a formal knowledge manager role was established. This position was abolished in 2006 after about a decade of experimenting with knowledge-sharing. This was not because the experiments had failed; quite the contrary. By then, knowledge-sharing was embedded in the organisational culture. In 2005, Novartis began to convert its Basel campus into a knowledge city designed to promote communication, learning and innovation. The knowledge city houses researchers and other employees in a university-like campus with open-plan spaces, as well as providing childcare facilities, restaurants, cafés and shops. The idea is that as associates go about their daily lives, chance encounters with their colleagues will stimulate communication and learning.

> *. . . knowledge-sharing depends on promoting*
> *quality relationships.*

Both Locust and Honeybee leadership benefit from sharing knowledge, but knowledge is more difficult to manage in the transient workforces characterising Locust enterprises. Sharing knowledge is made easier for Honeybee enterprises because of their long-term focus on retaining and valuing their staff; continual staff development; a high-trust culture, where chatting in a cafeteria is encouraged rather than frowned upon; a focus on teamwork; and minimising internal competition that encourages knowledge hoarding. Innovation systems deeply embedded throughout the organisation tap into the knowledge that many stakeholders hold. Retaining relationships with ex-employees and suppliers, another Honeybee characteristic, helps keep knowledge in an organisation. High employee turnover may bring fresh knowledge from outside the firm, but it does so at the cost of losing internal knowledge to competitors. The challenge is to continually update resident knowledge and promote its sharing while preventing unwanted outsiders from getting their hands on it.

Box 4–5: How Holcim nurtures knowledge[78]

For Zürich-based building materials supplier Holcim, knowledge management is fundamental and is expected to happen globally. In encouraging stakeholders to share knowledge, the company developed a framework consisting of five elements: information content, people, ways of creating and disseminating knowledge, and ways of exchanging data and information services. These four elements are clustered around a fifth critical element, namely, *structuring knowledge*. Recognising that simply using IT databases is not effective for sharing knowledge, the company developed a web of knowledge islands to structure its knowledge. The islands are clustered into specialised areas, such as mill operators or IT. The purpose is for the islands to share knowledge among about 40 communities of practice. This reflects the firm's belief that corporate knowledge is best managed by the people who own, need, create and use it.

Communities of practice bring the *people* and *content* elements of the model together. Community members engage in a *managed process* for creating, sharing and reusing knowledge, supported by appropriate *infrastructure*. The fluid communities of practice provide the day-to-day social context in which knowledge can actually be shared. The groups can form and disband to meet the need for them to share knowledge at a particular time.

Holcim uses various other devices to create and share knowledge, including staging corporate learning events. The firm collects experience accumulated over the past 20 years of managing projects. Debriefings highlight the lessons learned from current projects. Before starting a new project, people are expected to consult the debriefed lessons.

Evidence that knowledge-sharing and retention pay off

Recognising that sharing and retaining knowledge contribute to organisational performance is relatively new, and remains difficult to define and quantify.[79] Some research findings are inconsistent. For example, the effects of managing knowledge did not show up on purely financial measures in a 2003 study of *Fortune* 500 firms said to manage their knowledge well.[80] Yet in the same year, another study concluded that applying knowledge did enhance the performance of 208 manufacturers.[81]

Overall, research across many different industries and countries indicates that sharing knowledge and hence promoting organisational learning is important to business performance. Comparing a selected global group of learning companies with competitors revealed that organisations that learn gain competitive advantage and that this shows up in superior long-term financial and market performance.[82] Similarly, an Australian study of 200 enterprises concluded that being a learning organisation is related to better organisational performance.[83] In this investigation, performance was measured in terms of knowledge, financial results and customer satisfaction. Sharing knowledge across divisions enhanced the profitability of 250 *Fortune* 1000 firms, particularly when the process was supported by appropriate IT systems.[84] In Spanish companies, learning and knowledge integration were also linked to better business performance.[85] A study of Chinese high-tech enterprises revealed that these firms' innovation capacity is significantly related to knowledge acquisition, and in turn is positively related to long-term corporate growth.[86] Finally, research into hotels concluded that knowledge-sharing among employees was related to organisational performance.[87]

Knowledge-sharing qualifies as a higher-level practice in the Sustainable Leadership Pyramid because it is dependent on certain foundation practices. These include taking a long-term view, providing training and development and retaining people. Other higher-level practices such as team orientation, trust and an enabling culture reinforce the practice of retaining and sharing knowledge. The resulting bundle of higher-level practices in turn leads to high staff engagement, including the retention of those who have the knowledge.[88] These effects also play important roles in innovation, improving business processes and quality, and ultimately in creating competitive advantage.

Trust

Two major approaches to trust distinguish Locust and Honeybee leadership.[89] These are similar to Sako's 'arm's-length contractual relationships' (low trust) and 'obligational contractual relationships' (high trust).

To regulate obligations, arm's-length contractual relationships (ACR) rely heavily on written contracts or agreements, on the more general rules and regulations governing how business is done, as well as on relevant standards. For example, suppliers are judged by universal expectations that they will perform to certain quality or professional standards. In return suppliers can expect to be paid once they have delivered their goods and services. This form of trust requires acceptance that promises will be honoured. Relying on trust from arm's-length contractual relationships allows partners to pursue their own interests. They can change partners or the nature of their interests at any time. This is an individualistic approach that depends on a strong ethical code about keeping promises. Where no explicit promises are made, individual partners are free to improve their own position without regard to its effect on others. They can pursue cheaper options, for example. This is based on the assumption that the 'untempered exercise of bargaining power in commercial negotiation is fair'.[90] Loyalty is not a consideration under ACR trust, which characterises Locust leadership.

A second kind of trust, obligational contractual relationships (OCR), relies on goodwill rather than contracts, regulations and standards. OCR assumes that parties in a relationship will mutually commit to work together, and be willing to do more than they have contractually agreed to do. OCR partners regard each other as dependable, and can be relied on not to take advantage of the other. Judging a party dependable or not is largely a function of reputation and the experiences one has had with the other party. This approach to trust is favoured by Honeybee leadership.

In practice, these basic types of trust are likely to be present to varying degrees in business relationships, whether with employees, suppliers, investors or other stakeholders.[91] Under OCR trust, goodwill towards the relationship arises. This is evident at Continental Airlines. Even in difficult financial times the company has funded, and intends to continue funding, employee retirement benefits at a higher level than the law requires.[92] Fulfilling promises such as these is essential in maintaining employee trust in management.

OCR trust is consistent with Honeybee leadership in various ways. This is because OCR trust takes a long-term view of relationships. At Locust enterprises supplier contracts may be regularly put out to tender for the lowest price at short intervals, or the process may even be subject to bribery and other forms of unethical behaviour.[93]

Trust is complex and difficult to measure, and can operate in different directions. For example, a worker might trust other co-workers but not management or the organisation as a whole. Or management might not trust employees. Implicit messages contained in organisational processes provide one way to gauge management's trust in employees.[94] Provision of training and other professional development programs can signal an organisation's commitment to, and trust in, its people. Similarly, sharing information with employees about how the company is performing financially indicates trust. Naturally, merely trusting others is not sufficient by itself. These others need to be trustworthy. The prerequisites for trustworthiness are essentially the same as for trust.

The antithesis of trust is control and fear. Control comes in for considerable criticism. At its most benign, conventional control practices result in mere compliance. In bureaucratic and controlling cultures, workers essentially engage in routine behaviour. They are less likely to initiate without first referring to a supervisor or manager, since they will generally not be empowered to make decisions or take risks. This undermines the ability of an enterprise to innovate and be creative. However, control may be essential when the workforce has low skill or work morale is poor.[95]

At a more dysfunctional level, control produces behaviour such as resistance, less risk-taking and false reporting, reduced collaboration among associates, stifled initiative, diminished creativity and increased dependency.[96] If control leads to punishing mistakes, fear of punishment can make people cover up mistakes and be reluctant to innovate. Researchers have since confirmed many of the pitfalls of control theory that Gouldner identified in his 1954 book *Patterns of Industrial Bureaucracy*.[97]

Under Locust leadership, employees have to be controlled and closely supervised rather than trusted to do the right thing. Here, ACR agreements and control govern relationships, not goodwill. Locust enterprises often use fear, particularly job insecurity, in the hope that it will energise people. However, while material and symbolic rewards constitute excellent motivators, fear is destructive and demotivating. Not only does fear emotionally upset people but it may also result in the wrong things being learned and people becoming more risk-averse.[98] This can stifle innovation and change, because although people know what should be done they are afraid to take action. A particularly insidious aspect of fear induced by job insecurity is that it is generalised fear, which staff can do little to fix.

> *Locust enterprises often use fear, particularly job insecurity, in the hope that it will energise people.*

An extreme example of fear and control occurred under Harold Geneen's presidency at ITT in the 1970s.[99] On the positive side, Geneen rapidly turned an ailing US$766 million telecommunications business into a multibillion dollar, multinational conglomerate.

However, this was not sustained. Towards the end of his 17-year tenure, ITT began to crumble. The dismantling of this conglomerate continued under Geneen's successor, but what remains is the ITT Corporation today. Geneen essentially did not trust his staff, requiring up to 1500 executives globally to report to him on every major issue. One of the stories about Geneen is that he had a dozen or more attaché cases lined up in his office, each stuffed with plans, memos and reports so that he could keep a close eye on his managers. Fear and distrust were everywhere. Individuals were afraid of being caught uninformed, humiliated in meetings or punished. In such an atmosphere of fear and distrust, thinking laterally and trying new things had little place – ITT lacked the collaborative culture needed to promote innovation. Yet paradoxically Geneen believed that the key element in successful management was 'emotional attitude', a feeling that makes a manager the person he (or she) is.[100] Without much if any trust, the emotion most prevalent at ITT was fear.

By contrast, OCR trust based on goodwill is more flexible, agile and adaptive than compliance forced by formal policies and procedures.[101] US Professor Lawrence Mitchell argues that Locust firms should drop the hire–and–fire mentality and ideas that workers have to be controlled.[102] Instead, managers should use trust. Both trust and control are forms of risk management, and neither can eliminate all risk. Those who trust and those who control are equally exposed to the possibility of employee deceit. However, in so far as controlling manager behaviour signals distrust, it can generate resentment, deceit and other negative reactions.

Managers in Locust organisations tend not to be greatly trusted themselves. As a consequence they labour under ever-growing legal requirements. At the same time calls are increasing for Locust managers to be trusted to do the decent thing, and to be relieved of some of the current heavy legal restraints and monitoring.[103] This paradox is not surprising given the ambivalent attitude of the Locust approach to ethics. The legislature does not trust managers to do the right thing, managers do not trust their employees and employees do not trust managers. This is not a healthy situation, and trust needs to be revived as soon as practicable.

Companies that work on trust and respect do not need so many rules and procedures to control them. At Rohde & Schwarz (radio and IT communication and measuring equipment) and W.L. Gore & Associates (e.g. Gore-Tex®), employees contribute to the company's development without being boxed in by formal job descriptions. They are trusted to know what needs to be done.

Size is no obstacle to trust. Even a global giant like IBM recognises the importance of trust. IBM has made trust and personal responsibility central values. Instead of wielding heavy controls, IBM emphasises the importance of trusting its approximately 255,000 people to make decisions and act consistently in line with the firm's values. Samuel Palmisano, IBM's CEO, believes that trust, respect and shared values ultimately determine an enterprise's competitiveness.

> *IBM has made trust and personal*
> *responsibility central values.*

Trust creates loyalty, which benefits an enterprise in various ways, too. For example, when Continental Airlines was in trouble after the 9/11 attacks on New York and Washington, management appealed to the staff to stand by the company. And the employees did (see Box 3–2). During difficult times at WACKER Chemie employees across the board took a 5 per cent pay cut with only a verbal promise of being paid back. The company honoured its promise a few years later. Thus, employee trust was reinforced at these Honeybee companies. Read about how trust and confidence are critical to technology group Giesecke & Devrient in Box 4–6.

Box 4–6: Trust underpins success and sustainability at Giesecke & Devrient

Munich-based Giesecke & Devrient is a global technology group more than 150 years old that serves many governments and major corporate clients. Over the years it has made several strategic changes to its business, expanding from printing banknotes to producing and selling the machines that check the authenticity of banknotes. Then it added software and chip production to make credit and smart cards. More recently, the firm has expanded into digital security for wireless and other technology. Of course, high security is built into many of Giesecke & Devrient's products and operations – as visitors experience when having to hand over their passports to gain access to company offices.

The company vision is 'technologies that inspire confidence worldwide'. Confidence in the company and its products is vital because this firm prints money for more than 80 countries. It generated record revenues of €1.69 billion with nearly 10,000 staff in 2008. With more than 50 subsidiaries and joint ventures, Giesecke & Devrient is present in about 30 countries.

To achieve its vision Giesecke & Devrient relies heavily on promoting trust, which it regards as fundamental to its sustainability. All internal interactions and external business relationships are based on a strict corporate code of conduct. Trust starts with employees, who share the company values. Trust extends beyond employer–employee relationships to embrace customers and suppliers.

Trust works in several ways. Being sustainable and having a long track record are prerequisites for developing customer trust in the Giesecke & Devrient brand. It strives to be the trusted partner in a range of security technologies. In turn, being sustainable is an outcome of customers' trust. Governments must be able to protect the security of their borders and currencies. Corporations (as well as individuals) need to have confidence in the security of their data.

Staying in private hands is also very much a strategic decision to preserve confidence in the Giesecke & Devrient brand. Executives believe that listing publicly would destroy this trust. The company's goal is long-term sustainability, which centres heavily on being known as a trusted brand.

Evidence that trust pays off

Research shows that OCR trust with suppliers is associated with achieving superior performance.[104] One reason for this is that OCR trust saves on transaction costs such as continually looking for new partners and inducting them into the firms' needs. Relationships are based on goodwill. Once OCR partners have been chosen, they tend to be retained. Further savings arise in not having to continuously engage in detailed negotiating or in monitoring compliance. Lower levels of inventory are needed because of the responsiveness and goodwill of OCR partners if delivery dates or quantities change. Monitoring costs are also lower because partners can be relied upon to deliver the desired quality. Should problems arise, communication is so good that the issues can be relatively easily dealt with.

The evidence shows that fostering employee trust with its associated components of respect, credibility, pride and fairness pays off in many ways.[105] Trust facilitates cooperation, loyalty, relationships, organisational commitment and the likelihood that employees will innovate. Job satisfaction and accountability are also related to trust, as is how employees cope with organisational change. In situations where employees perceive that they have little control over change, trust in their supervisor increases commitment to the organisation. Trust also has links to customer satisfaction, loyalty and a firm's brand.

Various researchers have found that a culture of trust is associated with higher financial and operational performance and lower employee turnover, including in restaurants and local government settings.[106] Trust is also a major element for employers designated Great Places to Work – firms that also generally outperform their competitors.[107] Managers who were more or less trusted by their staff were perceived differently in terms of their ability, benevolence and integrity.[108] Part of the increase in performance where trust is high has been attributed to the effect trust has on risk-taking. Researchers looking into the relationship between organisational trust and risk-taking have concluded that trust has an advantage over other forms of risk management.[109]

Overall, therefore, research indicates that the effects of trust on organisational performance are positive. Trust in the workplace is more advantageous to business performance than lack of trust and reliance on control. Trust clearly forms a higher-order outcome of the 14 foundation practices. Creating a trusting culture cannot be decreed by management. Rather, it depends on the decisions that management makes about certain foundation practices. Employees tend to trust management more when the company signals its desire to keep staff for the long term (job security), the performance management system is fair,[110] and insiders have a chance to apply for management positions. Trust in management and the organisation can also be strengthened when employees see that other stakeholders are being treated well, including the environment and the community.

Employees of Honeybee-led firms are expected to assume individual responsibility and to organise themselves, often within teams. To do this, workers need to understand the business and their own contribution towards it. This requires an open communication policy so that employees understand the overall strategy. Openness in turn involves trust. These relationships are based on the belief that both parties are working towards a common purpose or vision. Common sense indicates that stakeholders are more likely to trust and be loyal to an ethical enterprise than an unethical one. Making change a considered process and involving all levels of employees in major decisions are other foundation practices likely to engender trust. Practices of this kind help generate the trust that Honeybee firms require of their long-term, highly skilled employees. Locust organisations are generally not in a position to depend on their employees' trust.

In this section we have discussed six higher-level variables and seen that their emergence requires an appropriate organisational environment. Self-managing employees able to make decisions require foundation elements in place, such as a clear vision and developed skills. Neither an enabling culture nor trusting employees can be brought about by command. Similarly, employees cannot be forced to share their knowledge or collaborate in teams, even if management orders them to do so. To occur these higher-level practices require foundations in a long-term perspective, ethical behaviour, a sense of job security achieved by retaining and developing staff, having succession planned, people feeling that they are valued and sharing a vision. Job security is also reflected in trust, which in turn is facilitated by retaining and developing staff.

The six higher-level practices then give rise to three key performance drivers, discussed next.

Key performance drivers

Three key performance drivers are described in this section, namely innovation, engaged staff and quality. These drivers emerge from the interactive effects of the 14 foundation practices and the six higher-level practices already outlined. They lie behind what customers experience in terms of product and service. Customers are affected by quality and innovative products and services and positive staff engagement, particularly where service is involved.

Innovation

IBM surveyed 756 chief executives in following up on its 2006 Global CEO Study.[111] The CEOs said that pressures to achieve profitable growth were forcing them to focus on innovation. Two-thirds of these CEOs indicated that major, radical changes were needed in their organisations over the next two years to cope with growth pressures. These findings suggest that many organisations will have to innovate seriously to survive, whether led by Locust or Honeybee philosophy. Worryingly, only about half the CEOs interviewed claim to have successfully handled changes of this magnitude before.

British political economist Will Hutton acclaimed the success of the Honeybee model at the end of the 20th century.[112] He attributed this success largely to its innovativeness and higher productivity growth compared with Locust firms. The lauded capacity of Locust leadership to shed staff rapidly has the advantage of enabling it to change direction quickly and support radical innovation.[113] However, the long-term benefits of this approach are dubious. Yes, an enterprise can simply buy the new skills it needs, but such change comes at a price. Among other things it prevents management from creating and supporting the deep, systemic innovation culture needed to increase the long-term wealth of a firm.[114]

Systemic innovation in product, service, process and management is core to Honeybee leadership.[115] Innovation is a strategic tool – a widespread capacity inside a business. Often innovation is incremental, particularly in process and management, rather than radical. Under Honeybee leadership, new ideas originate at all levels – from the shop floor, customers, suppliers and various other stakeholders. New ideas come from new media as well, including from wikis and blogs. The resulting ideas are evaluated through formal processes rather than being left to chance. In some cases, innovation systems have led to 'know-how' profit centres being established. This can create additional value for the enterprise from spin-off ventures centred on its innovative services. For example, Porsche has turned innovative product and process know-how into a separate profit centre employing more than 3000 researchers.

However, creating an environment in which employees can continuously improve their activities is complex. It is not just a matter of throwing money at R&D, as a Booz Allen Hamilton study of the one thousand largest spending corporations on R&D showed.[116] The study found no correlation between amounts specifically allocated to R&D and financial performance. This is not surprising because other research suggests that all employees, not just a few R&D workers, need the opportunity, skills and incentives to continuously generate ideas to add value to a business.[117]

A long time horizon is important in innovation for various reasons. First, embedding innovation processes in the organisational culture takes time. Second, a short-term focus prevents firms from investing in innovations that do not show immediate benefits, especially in difficult economic times.[118] Popular measures such as offering employees and contractors short-term contracts work against being innovative.[119] A short-term approach hinders innovation designed to improve business processes and change the business model, as well as decreasing the chances of making radically new discoveries. Recognising this, even in hard times, Honeybee companies – small and large – continue to innovate and rarely cut their R&D budgets.

Experts such as US professor Clayton Christensen and his colleagues claim that some commonly used financial analysis tools work against making sensible decisions to invest in innovation.[120] This is because of the short-term focus that tools such as the use of discounted cash flow bring to evaluating investments in innovation. Similarly, using earnings per share as the measure of shareholder value creation encourages managers to avoid investing in projects where the payoff will take some time.

The importance of innovation to Honeybee enterprises is easy to see in practice. For construction firm Seele every building project is unique, requiring extensive innovation and customisation on every job. Kärcher is justifiably proud of its consistent record of developing more than 80 per cent of its cleaning products, systems and solutions in the previous five years.

Not surprisingly, many Honeybee enterprises have formal innovation processes. New ideas are requested from employees, who are often rewarded for ideas that save the company money or generate new solutions and opportunities. At surgical supplier Aesculap, the company receives 600–700 ideas annually. The people with the best suggestions receive about €2000 at a gala celebration. At BMW, rewards of up to €15,000 are available for creative ideas. Marriott is continually improving its hotel services and processes. This Honeybee company favours an informal method of getting new ideas for running its hotels without using monetary rewards. Marriott managers walk around the business talking to hotel staff and customers. This provides many easy opportunities for associates to put forward ideas and for hotel customers to provide feedback to improve the business.

> *At BMW, rewards of up to €15,000 are available for creative ideas.*

Many Honeybee companies adopt a highly strategic approach to innovation. For example, American global services giant IBM regards innovation as more than the 3000–4000 patents it generates annually. This is because invention alone does not deliver value unless it is applied to new developments and provides solutions. At IBM, innovation involves creating customer solutions out of inventions. Swedish Atlas Copco once promoted itself as the 125–year-old construction equipment supplier with brand-new ideas for helping its customers achieve results. Not surprisingly, then, Atlas Copco regards innovation as the ultimate driver of long-term growth and profits in its global operations. One of Finland-based Nokia's four corporate values is 'renewal' – a continuous willingness to change, a passion for innovation and searching for new ideas and ways of working. Australian-based Bendigo Bank focuses on the needs of its stakeholders in generating its innovative community banking products and strategies (see Box 4–7).

At many Honeybee firms, customer feedback and ideas are integrated into future solutions. For example, the innovation system at US-based software developer SAS requires that every customer suggestion has to be recorded and sent to software user groups for evaluation. The top ten suggestions emerging from this process are nearly always implemented. Clearly, SAS values close relationships with its customers as part of its innovation process.

Directing financial and people resources towards innovation reinforces this strategic approach. SAS reinvests about 24 per cent of revenues in R&D, nearly twice the average of its major software competitors.

Innovation is also valued at Honeybee companies like Rohde & Schwarz (radio and communications technology) and WACKER (chemical products). Even in tough economic times, both these companies maintain their R&D allocation. This expenditure is over and above the systemic innovation processes that are an integral part of their organisational culture. For example, in 2006 at WACKER more than half the 3800 staff suggestions were implemented, saving the company €3.8 million.[121] The employees submitting the suggestions received bonuses as rewards.

Box 4–7: The Bendigo and Adelaide Bank innovates to meet social needs

Australia's Bendigo Bank started life in 1858 as a conventional building society. It registered as a bank in 1995, distinguishing itself markedly from its competitors at the time with its strong focus on customers. By 2008 Bendigo Bank had grown into a highly successful business, merging with Adelaide Bank late in 2007 and hence changing its name. The new group employed about 5500 people in more than 430 locations nationally in 2009, managed assets and deposits worth more than A$47 billion and serviced about 1.4 million customers.[122] The bank is owned by around 82,000 shareholders. Bendigo Bank declared an after-tax profit of $121.8 million in 2006–07, and continued to be profitable in 2008. The year 2009 brought a 26 per cent drop in profits to $173 million, although revenues had increased over 2008. Interestingly, even during the depressions of 1890 and 1930 and the global financial crisis of 2008-09, this organisation declared a profit. What can we learn from Bendigo Bank?

The bank's overall strategy is to generate sustainable value for all stakeholders, and to be particularly close to customers and the local communities in which it operates. The bank consistently ranks number 1 for customer satisfaction among banks in Australia. To achieve this, it invests long-term in people, skills, systems and structures to find ways of improving the future for its customers and communities. The strategy involves positioning the brand in unique niches, such as by franchising its Community Bank®.

A Community Bank® returns banking to the community by enabling and empowering local people to set up and manage their own banking. The Community Bank® concept resulted from the closure of more than 2000 bank branches in rural Australia by other large banks that left many rural communities without banking facilities. Public outcry was huge. Across all banks in Australia, the number of branches tumbled by about 29 per cent in seven years.

By setting up a local, publicly owned company, communities can own and operate a franchised Community Bank®. Local investors contribute A$400,000–500,000 to start a branch in their town. Bendigo Bank provides the necessary infrastructure and support. Revenue is shared between the community branch and the bank. The local company retains any surplus after paying its branch running costs. A reasonable return is paid to shareholders – between 4 and 10 per cent, according to the bank. The rest of the surplus is available for community purposes, to improve the quality of life of local citizens. By the end of 2009 Bendigo Bank had opened more than 237 community-owned branches, many of which were making sustainable profits. Branch numbers are set to grow further.

The innovative Community Bank® strategy illustrates how improving its contribution to the community enables an enterprise to generate strong demand for its services.[123] This strategy adopts a whole-of-community solution to help sustain and grow its customer base. Thus, even short-term profit is improved by looking after stakeholders. Stakeholders benefit in various ways, starting with innovative banking services, employment and benefits to the community from the profits.

Innovation continues at Bendigo Bank. It is developing similar models to meet other community needs, from improving telecommunications services in rural Australia through to cooperative commercial activities. Here, innovation goes hand in hand with meeting customer needs.

Evidence that systemic and strategic innovation pays off

Research consistently shows that an organisation's progress and growth depend on innovation.[124] Investing in and nurturing the capacity to innovate in new products, services and processes is an essential capability for driving business success. Innovation is possibly the only strategy for survival in a global, interconnected and highly competitive world. It is frequently linked to customer satisfaction.[125]

For firms whose CEOs participated in IBM's 2006 CEO study,[126] innovation in flexible business processes and collaboration showed the clearest correlation with financial performance. This was evident across various financial measures including revenue growth, operating margin growth and average profitability over time. Support for the critical role of innovation driving financial performance comes from a study comparing 20 strong innovators with the rest of the French stock market. The researchers concluded that over ten years the innovative sample strongly outperformed the top 120 public companies.[127] Another study concluded that stock markets respond positively to companies that announce innovations.[128]

Innovation seems to pay off for firms in terms of their reputation and brand as well. Having a reputation as an innovator may ease access to financing, contracts, grants and subsidies, and help attract the best researchers and R&D collaboration partners.[129] Openly publishing and sharing knowledge is one way of letting potential partners know about a firm's expertise. Openness may risk competitiveness in the short term, but is likely to pay off in the longer term in financial and reputational ways.

Major innovation is probably easier for large organisations to fund and implement. However, research shows that incremental innovation also provides competitive advantage to SMEs, enabling them to be profitable and compete successfully with large firms.[130] Thus, innovating affects business performance in many ways and on different scales.

Wealth creation through innovation can be supported in seven ways: vision and strategy, employee competencies, organisational intelligence, creativity and idea management, organisational structures and systems, culture and climate, and managing technology.[131] An orientation towards learning also supports innovation. When its people learn, an organisation becomes more innovative.[132] Furthermore, a study of not-for-profit enterprises concluded that support for learning and innovation encourages empowerment of employees, who often respond with increased trust and commitment to the organisation.[133] Under these conditions, employees also perceive service quality as higher.

Innovation takes many different forms in Honeybee businesses, and is highly valued as a core competency. We have seen that innovation depends on the implementation of many of the 14 foundation practices. These include taking a long-term perspective underpinned by a strong vision, and retaining, skilling and valuing employees. Supportive foundation practices in turn foster the six higher-level practices on which systemic innovation depends. Innovation is stimulated by having an appropriate culture to support innovation, effective teamwork and collaboration, and self-managing employees willing to initiate ideas, make autonomous decisions and share knowledge. Trust supports the long-term perspective required for systemic innovation to work. Obviously, innovation and staff engagement reinforce one another. Engaged staff are more innovative, and a highly innovative culture boosts staff identification with the organisation. This in turn boosts engagement. Hence, one of many virtuous circles that Honeybee practices engender is created.

Engaged staff

Staff engagement is a key performance driver relating to staff motivation and satisfaction. The term 'engagement' is somewhat confused in the literature. There appears to be general agreement that engagement is not a unitary concept, but consists of various components. It reflects the extent to which workers are emotionally committed to their workplace, intend to stay with that employer and are motivated to perform the best they can.[134] One applied view is that engagement is evident in three factors: whether employees *say* positive things about their employer, express an intention to *stay* with that employer and *strive* to achieve organisational goals.[135] To this extent engagement reflects staff loyalty and commitment to an employer.

Honeybee enterprises strive to engage their staff emotionally with the workplace, whereas Locust leadership requires only that employees relate at a cognitive and rational level to the workplace. According to research conducted among more than four million employees worldwide, about half of all employees are disengaged at work.[136] This alarming finding means that inside many companies employee morale is low and readiness to leave high. This is a costly prospect both financially and in terms of potentially lost knowledge and skills.

Empowerment, or rather feelings of being empowered, can contribute to staff engagement. Here a model proposed by Seibert and his colleagues is useful.[137] They distinguish empowering people at an organisational level from the feeling of empowerment that individuals experience.[138] Structures, systems and processes at the organisational level create an empowerment climate that affects the performance of individual work units. People in those work units share perceptions about how empowering the culture is. Devolved decision-making and self-management, both of which characterise Honeybee workplaces, are components of empowerment. Feeling empowered in turn contributes to staff engagement[139] and to the degree to which an employee is satisfied with his or her job and working conditions.

Staff satisfaction, sometimes linked to staff engagement, is considered important because it is closely correlated with customer satisfaction, a major performance outcome.[140] Several reasons have been given for this close relationship. One reason is that customer satisfaction is affected by how employees treat customers; that is, satisfied staff members transfer their positive mood to customers. Research has also shown that employee satisfaction influences product or service quality, which in turn links to how satisfied customers are.[141] The above explanation has been referred to as the 'service–profit chain'.[142] Positive staff attitudes increase customer satisfaction and retention, whereas negative employee attitudes can discourage customers from patronising the business. Therefore, staff satisfaction appears to influence employee engagement, an important contributor to organisational success and viability.

Staff attitudes and behaviour are influenced by the work environment created by the combination of many foundation and higher-order practices operating in a given workplace. Learning which factors drive employee satisfaction in a particular firm is often done through employee surveys, particularly in larger enterprises. Such surveys revealed factors related to employee satisfaction in 18 UK firms: rewards and recognition, communication and work–life balance.[143] However, satisfaction factors will vary with organisational culture, national culture and the local context, as Box 4–8 shows. Thailand's Sa Paper Preservation House engages staff in specifically local ways. Similarly, different factors are linked to commitment among different groups within the same organisation, such as between professionals, line managers and workers.[144] Therefore, it is important to tailor organisational practices, particularly human resources practices, to the needs of different employees in order to engage staff.

Box 4–8: Sa Paper Preservation House – engaged staff[145]

Sa is paper hand-made from the fibre of mulberry trees. It is widely produced in Asian countries with labour-intensive economies. A leader in this industry, Sa Paper Preservation House (SPPH) has operated in Chiang Mai, Thailand, for more than 40 years. The many existing competitors and continual new entrants make surviving in this industry challenging. Starting from a small household business with three family members, the business gradually expanded to 500 employees. Unlike many of its competitors, SPPH products are handmade and of high quality, as evidenced by many awards for product excellence. From small beginnings the business has expanded and survived a number of economic and social crises, including the 1997 Asian economic crisis. It has exported 80 per cent of its products for more than 25 years.

The managing director's philosophy stresses happiness among her employees, believing that unhappy employees are less creative, and therefore that happiness is key to innovation. She treats staff as if they were family members. Of course, creating happy staff also means investing in their development. Staff members are trained in work-related skills and, more importantly, in ethics. The SPPH manager says she would never consider replacing people with machines or other technologies because her employees are a competitive weapon.

Financial arrangements help keep staff happy too. Wages are paid punctually – this is not always the case among SPPH's competitors. Employees are offered interest-free loans and participation in savings programs. Furthermore, SPPH realises that its employees form part of a wider community that has to be considered. If their husbands, wives and children do not have a good quality of life, employees will not be happy. Therefore, the company hires staff and suppliers from the local community and allows employees to work at home to be with their families if they prefer. It treats local suppliers well, particularly in settling bills quickly and sometimes paying more than mulberry pickers ask for. In all these ways, the managing director of SPPH strives to engage her staff by ensuring that employees are satisfied and have sufficient skills to enable her to empower them.

Evidence that an engaged staff pays off for an enterprise

Research shows that both staff engagement and staff satisfaction affect organisational performance, including measures of enhanced team performance, trust, self-managing employee behaviour, customer satisfaction and financial performance such as profits.[146] A Watson Wyatt research paper concluded that increased employee engagement can enhance financial performance, partly because engaged employees tend to be high performers who stay with the company.[147] In Watson Wyatt's 2008–09 survey of 14,000 employees in 11 European countries and across different industry sectors, about 60 per cent of engaged employees tended to exceed or far exceed performance expectations. Similarly, in Watson Wyatt's WorkUSA 2008–09 survey,[148] 89 per cent of highly engaged employees worked for employers that encourage knowledge-sharing across the company. This compares with only 7 per cent of employees with low engagement. Thus, staff engagement affects many sustainable leadership elements and performance outcomes.

An empowering organisational culture has been found essential to fostering individual responsibility and commitment.[149] In Hong Kong, a study of primary schools found that where self-management was strong among groups of staff and individuals, the schools were able to provide a better quality education than their peers.[150] In addition, staff commitment and morale were high at these schools.

In another study, Israeli researchers found that employees held positive emotions towards their workplace when they believed that competitors and customers had a positive image of the employer.[151] An employer's outside reputation appears to affect staff attitudes to the workplace in terms of commitment or 'love', and 'joy' in being part of the organisation.

One of the measures used in studies of firms rated as best employers or among the 100 Best Companies to Work For is staff engagement. 'Best' companies are found to have better relationships with their staff and greater staff engagement than their competitors.

Part of the good news is that staff engagement tends to be stable over time at best employers. Financial, accounting and market measures show that 'best' firms outperform enterprises that are not on the 'best' lists, including in their share prices.[152] Furthermore, employee-friendly companies are more likely to attract talented people, who are then more creative and committed than their less talented peers.

Disengagement, especially among top-performing employees, costs businesses directly in the form of high staff turnover and lost productivity. Less engaged employees are less likely to seek internal training, support and dialogue with their managers and are focused more on activities outside the firm.

Clearly, being an employer of choice reflects on the brand and reputation of an enterprise. Perceptions of a company's quality of work-life affect its growth and profitability. Fifty-eight Best Companies to Work For in the US and 88 Standard & Poor's Top 100 companies were compared in terms of sales growth, asset growth, return on equity and return on assets. The comparison showed that companies with high quality of work life also enjoyed exceptional growth and profitability.[153]

Staff engagement results from many of the foundation practices discussed in Chapter 3, but more particularly emerges from the higher-level practices of devolved and consensual decision-making, self-management, team orientation, an enabling culture, knowledge-sharing and trust. Highly engaged workers are likely to participate in feedback sessions, training and development activities, and other initiatives that reinforce their engagement. An engaged staff also influences customers, forming a basis for enhancing customer satisfaction and through that increased financial performance, as discussed in Chapter 2.[154]

Quality

Interestingly, 27 per cent of CEOs from one thousand leading companies considered quality of services and products the most important measure of business success.[155] Achieving the highest quality possible and promoting excellence is core to the organi-sational culture in Honeybee companies. For a Honeybee-led enterprise, quality is not a matter for debate but for doing.[156]

But what is quality? Various approaches can be identified including product-, customer- and manufacturing-oriented approaches as well as value for money. In some service sectors, such as in education, additional definitions and measures of quality may apply.[157] The value for money aspect of quality is particularly important, because it links in closely with customer satisfaction. Value for money has to do with quality relative to the cost of purchase, and this in turn relates to the cost of producing the services or goods. Whether value for money is achieved can be difficult to measure and therefore is often subjective. For customers, value for money often resides in the return on investment and not necessarily on a low initial purchase price.

A certain level of production and service quality can be facilitated through formal systems and controls, such as total quality management (TQM) or ISO9001. Among *Fortune* 1000 companies, larger enterprises are more likely to adopt formal quality processes such as TQM than smaller firms.[158] However, high quality can also be achieved in small businesses, and without formal accreditation. Honeybee businesses often develop their own additional quality systems, and Box 4–9 provides one such example from the chemical industry.

Systems alone do not guarantee quality. Rather, the approach to quality forms part of a firm's culture and leadership philosophy.[159] The basic principles of TQM reflect that achieving high quality requires involving and empowering people throughout an organisation, engaging in teamwork, focusing on customers and developing widespread processes for continuous improvement.[160] Ensuring quality requires the support of senior executives who control the resources needed to support the desired level of quality. However, to achieve high-quality products and services, and ultimately provide value for money, it is not enough to rely on supervisors. People at all levels of an organisation need to be involved.

High quality is easier to achieve in Honeybee enterprises than in Locust-led firms. Many of the elements required to create a quality culture are basic to Honeybee leadership, including top management support, a focus on people and having a strong culture.[161] In addition to the elements mentioned above that support quality, a long-term perspective is important. Taking a long-term view encourages retaining, developing, investing in employees and valuing them. Loyal, skilled employees with long-term interests in a firm are likely to want to enhance quality. After all, dealing with customer complaints and reworking production errors are not usually very fulfilling tasks for highly skilled workers. Long-term employees are likely to share the company values, and peer pressure from teammates will also enhance quality. Long-tenured workers have come to know and trust others, and are more likely to share their knowledge.

> *. . . SAS constantly puts its quality to the test each year when customers are asked to renew their software licences.*

Thus, many elements of Honeybee leadership culture support high-quality products and services. Observers focused on efficiency tend to be puzzled about the lengths a Honeybee company will go to in achieving excellence.

By contrast, high quality becomes more difficult to achieve under Locust leadership, which relies on supervisors to control and monitor processes. However, as 100 per cent supervision is unrealistic and Locust workers are less skilled and engaged, mistakes will continue to happen. Quality can also be managed through systems and automation but, surprising to some managers, automation is not always the way to achieve high quality. Sometimes the human being is more accurate. For a long while, Porsche used humans to insert windscreens in its cars by hand because older-generation robots were not sufficiently precise in fitting this component. Aesculap's fine surgical scissors are hand-finished to achieve the desired precision. Thus, management cannot always eliminate the human element in striving for high quality. In some industries, such as the service industry, automation is not always an option.

In the service industry, quality takes different forms. US-based software producer SAS constantly puts its quality to the test each year when customers are asked to renew their software licences. This provides users with an opportunity to choose to leave the relationship if they are dissatisfied. It also indicates the high level of confidence that

SAS places in its quality. At US fashion retailer Nordstrom the end goal is satisfying customers, but this starts with the company valuing its own staff. Nordstrom's motivated employees are encouraged to feel passionate about the business, and to use their talents and best judgement in the customers' interests. Staff members are empowered to accept responsibility and be creative in achieving the company's legendary service quality. Similarly, international hotelier Marriott is devoted to providing excellent customer service. Formal systems, which all employees in that part of the business understand, help associates achieve excellence in the hotel business. But high quality requires skilled, engaged and ethical employees.

Box 4–9: World quality at WACKER

Munich-based WACKER is a leader in the chemical and semiconductor sectors, developing a wide range of chemical products and processes used in key industries. Many products are still based around silicon and the modern silicones that the company began producing more than 50 years ago. The group is organised into five divisions: siltronics for producing silicon, the silicone division, polymers (binders and additives), biosolutions for tailored food and life science solutions, and polysilicon (supplying wafers for chips and solar-cell companies).

Believing that 'there is always room for improvement', WACKER values high quality and innovative products. The company has developed an Integrated Management System (IMS) to maintain sustainable business practices, particularly in quality, health, safety and environmental protection. WACKER's IMS regulates workflows, process responsibility and accountability within the framework of the company's productivity, quality, health, safety and environmental principles. The IMS is built around the existing certified management systems used in business divisions and corporate departments, particularly ISO9001 and ISO14001. The company's avowed aim is to ensure satisfied customers, shareholders, employees and a worldwide public.

Evidence that commitment to quality pays off

Companies benefit through increased customer satisfaction as well as financial returns from improving and maintaining high quality.[162] In particular, being ISO9000 registered is related to enhanced operating and business performance.[163] However, the ISO9000 process is not necessarily the *cause* of the better business performance. Rather, research shows that those firms that pursue ISO9000 accreditation already exhibit higher quality than their competitors before seeking accreditation.[164] Thus, it is the overall pursuit of quality that enhances financial performance rather than any particular accreditation system. Winning quality achievement awards such as the Malcolm Baldridge National Quality Award has been found to generate significant value for the winners' shareholders.[165]

Enhancing quality pays off in both production and service enterprises. By embarking on a rigorous quality improvement program, Hyundai USA was able to reduce its vehicle warranty provisions from 5.7 per cent to 1.8 per cent of revenue.[166] Applying this warranty provision reduction to Hyundai's then worldwide revenue of just over £26 billion represents a potential global saving of £1 billion.[167] This shows that the pursuit of quality does not cost more, and can actually save money.

Locust managers often fear that an increase in quality will decrease productivity and raise costs. This is not necessarily so. Studies show that even technologically simple steel production lines can gain in both productivity and quality when self-managed teamwork and other sophisticated human resources approaches are used. In quantifying the gains for steel production, economists estimated conservatively that 1 per cent more working time on a single steel mill line represents about $30,000 gain per month.[168]

Research from the services industry is consistent with this. For example, continuous quality improvement in hospitals typically leads to enhancements in financial and cost performance as well as in customer service.[169] Quality in services and products is also linked to customers' perceptions of a firm's brand and reputation.[170] Researchers claim that improvements in service quality that reduce customer defections by as little as 5 per cent can boost profits by almost 100 per cent.[171] Enhancing quality therefore pays off in all kinds of ways.

Pursuit of quality does not usually occur in isolation. High-performing Spanish firms certified in TQM also tended to implement the people side of quality management more than their competitors.[172] Quality organisations strive for excellence by pursuing cooperation, teamwork, a focus on customers and employees and continuous learning and improvement.[173] These are essential components of Honeybee leadership. Where the elements for achieving high quality are not part of the culture, control and supervision are all that is left. Extra supervisors cost money, thereby incurring costs for activities that are not needed in Honeybee cultures.

Clearly, achieving the high quality that Honeybee leadership strives for depends on implementing many of the 14 foundation and six higher-level practices. Necessary antecedent foundation practices include taking a long-term view, valuing and retaining staff and developing employee skills. All six higher-level practices are required for a quality enterprise: devolved decision-making, teamwork, self-managing employees, trust, opportunities to share and retain knowledge and an appropriate enabling culture. Quality emerges from the interplay of all these factors, and hence is deemed a key performance driver. It is reinforced by the other key performance drivers, whereby engaged staff can be expected to drive continuous improvement, be innovative, help raise quality and hence please the customer.

Summary

In this chapter, we have looked at nine aspects of Honeybee leadership that emerge from the 14 foundation practices described in Chapter 3. These effects include devolved and consensual decision-making, self-managing employees and a team orientation as well as engendering an enabling organisational culture, sharing and retaining knowledge and developing high levels of trust. Under Honeybee leadership, the effects of the 14 foundation practices and six higher-level practices in turn produce three key performance drivers: strategic and systemic innovation, staff engagement and the pursuit of high quality.

We have discussed what each effect refers to, and how companies use and interpret them in practice. Research has shown that the six higher-level practices and the three key performance drivers are linked to higher organisational performance under Honeybee leadership principles. The Locust philosophy does not foster sustainability on these variables over time.

A firm's position on any of the key performance drivers can reflect either the Honeybee or Locust leadership philosophy. The resulting leadership behaviour depends in the first instance on the nature of the 14 foundation practices adopted, and second on the higher-level practices that result. Foundation-level decisions whether to adopt a long- or short-term perspective, an ethical stance, how to manage change and so on feed into the higher-level practices. Whether or not trust is high will be affected by what those foundation practices look like. In other words, a cascading series of foundation and higher-level practices, as well as three key performance drivers, taken together, influence important organisational performance outcomes. These outcomes include reputation and brand, customer satisfaction, financial performance, long-term shareholder value and ultimately sustainability and its companion, value for all stakeholders. These relationships are investigated further in Chapter 5.

notes

1 http://www.allianz.com/en/allianz_group/press_center/news_dossiers/allianz_se/news_2007-05-02.html; accessed 4 September 2007
2 Drucker, 2006
3 Flood *et al.*, 2000
4 Ettling and Jago, 1988
5 Hemp and Stewart, 2004
6 http://www.mckinseyquarterly.com/Strategy/Strategic_Thinking/How_companies_make_good_decisions_McKinsey_Global_Survey_Results_2282; accessed 14 February 2010
7 For example Meindl, 1998; Ogbonna and Harris, 2000
8 Miller and Monge, 1988
9 Seibert, Silver and Randolph, 2004
10 Freeman and Rogers, 1999
11 Kirkman and Rosen, 1999
12 Hung, 2006
13 Srivastava, Barrol and Locke, 2006
14 Miller and Lee, 2001
15 Avery, 2004; Lord and Maher, 1991; Manz, 1986
16 Neck and Houghton, 2006
17 Liu *et al.*, 2003
18 DeVries *et al.*, 1998
19 Kanter, 1989
20 Burla *et al.*, 1994
21 Hirschhorn, 1997
22 Hemp and Stewart, 2004
23 Howell *et al.*, 1990
24 Bell, 2004
25 Avery, 2004

26 Cooney, 2004
27 Manz, Mossholder and Luthans, 1987
28 Manz, 1996
29 Saruta, 2006
30 Saruta, 2006
31 Manz, Mossholder and Luthans, 1987; Manz and Sims, 1986
32 Chen and Aryee, 2007; Hodson, 2004; Lapidus, Roberts and Chonko, 1997; Spector, 1986; Wilhelm *et al.*, 2004
33 Chen and Aryee, 2007
34 Politis, 2006
35 Cheng and Cheung, 2004
36 Carmeli, Meitar and Weisberg, 2006
37 Gebert, Boerner and Lanwehr, 2003
38 Gebert, Boerner and Lanwehr, 2003; Mumford *et al.*, 2002
39 For example Power and Waddell, 2004; IBM Global CEO Study, 2006
40 De Leede, Nijhof and Fisscher, 1999, p. 203
41 Wang, Chou and Jiang, 2005
42 Avery, 2005
43 http://www.gore.com; accessed 14 February 2010
44 Bell, 2004
45 Bell, 2004
46 Avery, 2004
47 Miller and Monge, 1988
48 Hung, 2006; Ichniowski and Shaw, 1999; Kirkman and Rosen, 1999; Kochan, Gittell and Lautsch, 1995
49 Manz, 1990, p. 276
50 DeVaro, 2006
51 IBM Global CEO Study, 2006
52 IBM Global CEO Study, 2006
53 Batt, 1999
54 Hamilton, Nickerson and Owan, 2003
55 Boning, Ichinowski and Shaw, 2001
56 Purcell *et al.*, 2003
57 Kuipers and de Witte, 2005
58 Sosik, 2005
59 Li, 2006
60 Allen and Hecht, 2004; DeVaro, 2006; Power and Waddell, 2004
61 Kirkman and Rosen, 1999
62 Collins, 2001a
63 Yaniv and Farkas, 2005
64 Avery, 2005
65 Marriott and Brown, 1997
66 For example Balthazard, Cooke and Potter, 2006; Safford, 1988
67 Sorensen, 2002
68 Denison, 1984
69 Sorensen, 2002
70 Kotter and Heskett, 1992
71 Marcoulides and Heck, 1993
72 Bartel *et al.*, 2004
73 MacIntosh and Doherty, 2007
74 Wheatley, 2003
75 Nasrallah, Levitt and Glynn, 2003
76 Based on Sveiby, 2007
77 Evans and Davis, 2005
78 Based on Avery, 2005
79 Robinson *et al.*, 2004
80 Castillo, 2003
81 Dröge, Claycomb and Germain, 2003

82 Goh and Ryan, 2008
83 Power and Waddell, 2004
84 Tanriverdi, 2005
85 Lopez, Peon and Ordas, 2005; Prieto and Revilla, 2006
86 Yang, Rui and Wang, 2006
87 Srivastava, Bartol and Locke, 2006
88 Janz and Prasarnphanich, 2003
89 Sako, 1992
90 Sako, 1992, p. 239
91 Caldwell and Karri, 2005; Sako, 1992
92 Continental Airlines, 2007, letter to shareholders
93 Liker and Choi, 2004
94 McCauley and Kuhnert, 1992
95 Lämsä and Pučetaitė, 2006
96 Dose and Klimoski, 1995; Ferris *et al.*, 1995
97 Dose and Klimoski, 1995; Ferris *et al.*, 1995
98 Fessler, 2001; Lerner and Tetlock, 1999; Lewis, 1999; Müller and Hurter, 1999; Scarnati, 1998
99 Pascale and Athos, 1981
100 Geneen, 2000
101 McLain and Hackman, 1999, p. 171
102 Mitchell, 2001
103 Mitchell, 2001
104 Sako, 1992
105 Chun and Davies, 2006; Deepak, Singh and Sabol, 2002; Hubbell and Chory-Assad, 2005; Neves and Caetano, 2006; Thoms, Dose and Scott, 2002; van Marrewijk, 2004
106 Davis *et al.*, 2000; Gevity Institute, 2006; Gould-Williams, 2003; Tzafrir, 2005
107 Levering, 2000
108 Davis *et al.*, 2000
109 McLain and Hackman, 1999, p. 152
110 Hubbell and Chory-Assad, 2005; Mayer and Davis, 1999
111 IBM Global Services, 2007
112 Hutton, 2002
113 Hodges and Woolcock, 1993
114 For example Hamel, 2006
115 Hamel, 2003; 2006
116 Jaruzelski, Dehoff and Bordia, 2006
117 Ichniowski and Shaw, 2003
118 Perel, 2005
119 Michie and Sheehan-Quinn, 2001
120 Christensen, Kaufman and Shih, 2008
121 WACKER 2006 annual report, p. 56
122 2009 annual report, Bendigo and Adelaide Bank Ltd. Available at www.bendigoadelaide.com. au/public/shareholders/financial_results.asp; accessed 14 February 2010
123 Bendigo Bank 2001–02 annual report
124 Batory, Neese and Heineman, 2005; Lawson and Samson, 2001
125 For example Tontini, 2007
126 IBM Global Services, 2007
127 Odo Securities, 2008
128 Sood and Tellis, 2008
129 Muller and Pénin, 2006
130 Bhaskaran, 2006
131 Lawson and Samson, 2001
132 Hult, Hurley and Knight, 2004
133 Latting *et al.*, 2004
134 Allen and Meyer, 1990
135 Hewitt Associates, 2001
136 Gandossy and Kao, 2004
137 Seibert, Silver and Randolph, 2004

138 Quinn and Spreitzer, 1997; Seibert, Silver and Randolph, 2004
139 Seibert, Silver and Randolph, 2004
140 Atchison, 1999; Medley and Larochelle, 1995; Hausfeld *et al.*, 1994
141 Hoffmann and Koop, 2004
142 Heskett *et al.*, 1994
143 Kinnie *et al.*, 2005
144 Kinnie *et al.*, 2005
145 Assistant Professor Sooksan Kantabutra, Mahidol University, Bangkok, personal communication
146 Bakker *et al.*, 2008; Harter, Schmidt and Hayes, 2002; Neck and Houghton, 2006; Politis, 2006; Thoms, Dose and Scott, 2002
147 http://www.watsonwyatt.com/research/resrender.asp?id=2007-US-0298&page=1; accessed 22 September 2008
148 http://www.watsonwyatt.com/research/resrender.asp?id=2008-US-0232&page=1; accessed 15 February 2009
149 Seibert, Silver and Randolph, 2004
150 Cheng and Cheung, 2004
151 Carmeli, Gilat and Weisberg, 2006
152 For example Fulmer, Gerhart and Scott, 2003
153 Lau and May, 1998
154 Loveman, 1998
155 World Economic Forum, 2004
156 Albert, 1992
157 Van Kemenade, Pupius and Hardjono, 2008
158 Lawler, Mohrman and Ledford, 1995
159 Naor *et al.*, 2008
160 Lakshman, 2006
161 Naor *et al.*, 2008
162 For example Anderson, Fornell and Lehman, 1994; Lawler, Mohrman and Ledford, 1995
163 For example Corbett, Montes-Sancho and Kirsch, 2005; Mokhtar, Karbhari and Naser, 2005; Naveh and Marcus, 2005; Tarí and Sabater, 2006
164 Heras, Dick and Casadesús, 2002
165 Balasubramanian, Mathur and Thakur, 2005
166 Hyundai Motor, 2005
167 Calculated viz: £26 billion x 3.9% = £1 billion
168 Ichniowski and Shaw, 1999
169 Alexander, Weiner and Griffith, 2006; Scotti, Harmon and Behson, 2007
170 For example Mitra and Golder, 2006
171 Reichheld and Sasser, 1990
172 Tarí and Sabater, 2006
173 Lakshman, 2006; Perry, 2005

5

Performance Outcomes as Leadership Practices Interact

The core message of this book is that on the input side sustainable leadership involves a wide range of practices. We have identified 23 such 'leadership' practices and explained how they affect organisational performance, depending on whether Honeybee or Locust principles are adopted. On the outcome side, sustainable leadership involves far more than simply being profitable, green or socially responsible, although those goals make a good start. To be sustainable also requires enhancing customer satisfaction, brand and reputation and long-term stakeholder value.

By referring to published research we have demonstrated that Honeybee practices are likely to produce better financial outcomes, customer satisfaction, brand and reputation and shareholder value, ultimately adding to long-term stakeholder value. In other words, academic research shows that management practices that encourage superior organisational performance and sustainability are more likely to be based on Honeybee principles than on their Locust counterparts. This underpins the business case for sustainable leadership.

It has been convenient to examine the practices individually in Chapters 3 and 4. But in reality the 23 elements contributing to sustainable leadership do not occur in isolation. Most operate concurrently across all kinds of organisations. In this chapter, we show how the practices can work together to create sustainable leadership so that organisations remain financially healthy, meet (or exceed) customer expectations, enjoy a good name and thereby increase value for stakeholders (including investors).

We start this chapter by elaborating on how the performance measures and practices are linked – both directly and indirectly – and on the dynamics of the Sustainable Leadership Pyramid. The pyramid can be interpreted in terms of bottom up, top down and lateral influences and effects. It also allows for diverse issues facing an individual enterprise. The pyramid helps identify which foundation practices to start with, or how to improve higher-level practices. Having shown how the practices interact to drive performance, we discuss the power of the Honeybee approach when individual practices are combined or 'bundled'. We also describe how major companies have successfully embedded sustainable practices into their daily activities or are on the way to doing so.

We present evidence showing that it is possible for organisations to change to more sustainable practices. However, there are many paths to success. The case examples used in this book highlight some of those paths for specific organisations. Clearly, challenges face Honeybee leadership, but we conclude with an optimistic view of the future for creating more sustainable enterprises.

Direct and indirect effects of sustainable leadership practices

Relationships between various sustainable leadership practices and organisational outcomes can be direct, indirect or at times both direct and indirect. Let us examine these concepts.

Direct relationships arise where practices drive specific performance outcomes. One example is developing people, which is associated with increased financial performance and shareholder value.

Indirect relationships arise when one practice enhances another practice, which in turn contributes to one of the performance outcomes. For example, having a strong, shared vision contributes to self-management, which is known to contribute to staff engagement. For two of the practices, research suggests that their contribution to organisational performance is essentially indirect. *Independence from the financial markets* benefits firms indirectly by allowing a long-term perspective to be adopted towards innovation and major investments (even if this negatively influences the next reporting period) and retaining tighter control of proprietary know-how. The other practice not linked directly to measures of organisational performance is employee *self-management*. Instead, it has been linked to quality, innovation, motivation, higher job performance, job satisfaction and commitment to the firm, the last four of these being components of staff engagement. Therefore employee self-management indirectly drives organisational performance via all three key performance drivers.

Many effects are *both* direct and indirect. For example, environmental protection measures can lead to direct cost savings through using less energy and water, enhancing manufacturing processes and reducing the need for remedial work. These savings directly influence the bottom line. Environmental friendliness can also directly improve, or at least protect, corporate reputation by preventing damaging accidents and other scandals that can tarnish a brand. An indirect effect of caring for the environment can come from a competitive advantage in attracting talented employees. Talented people contribute to quality and innovation, both of which drive performance. As already noted, staff development has been directly linked to financial performance. However, it also operates indirectly on the performance outcomes by influencing self-management (a higher-level practice) and staff engagement (a key performance driver).

Another example concerns the direct and indirect benefits that can flow from long-term CEOs, who have been shown to outperform their short-term counterparts as measured by the share price. Direct savings occur from fewer expensive searches for replacement CEOs. Indirect benefits arise because long-term CEOs provide better continuity of leadership (this protects the culture). They are less driven by short-term performance than CEOs appointed for three years and so can take a long-term perspective. These and other effects stemming from long-term CEOs contribute indirectly to various foundation and higher-level practices, ultimately therefore driving value for investors and other stakeholders.

Already it is becoming evident that the Sustainable Leadership Pyramid represents a dynamic system, described further in the next section.

Sustainable Leadership Pyramid in action

The Sustainable Leadership Pyramid provides a framework for examining an organisation's current practices. It depicts a system in which the elements can and do influence each other in different directions.

Although we originally intended to show a 'neutral' pyramid that could apply to both Honeybee and Locust leadership, the pyramid does not lend itself to this. Instead, readers can contrast the Honeybee and Locust principles by examining Table 2–1. Each cell or building block of the Sustainable Leadership Pyramid reflects the Honeybee approach to leadership. Introducing 'neutral' terms for the practices would obscure the self-reinforcing nature of the system. For example, without a long-term perspective it is difficult to create the other Honeybee elements. The underlying rationale for the Sustainable Leadership Pyramid collapses completely when Locust elements are introduced because each layer of the pyramid depends on the presence of the supporting layer. Removing the supporting elements renders the overall structure of the system meaningless.

Managers seeking to introduce sustainable leadership should initially view the pyramid bottom up, focusing on getting the foundation units in place. However, another useful way of looking at the pyramid is to view it in terms of achieving the desired organisational performance outcomes shown at the top of the pyramid and asking: What are the antecedent conditions necessary to achieve specific outcomes, and which ones are weak or missing?

For example, if customer satisfaction is a desired performance outcome, which practices are necessary to generate it? Consulting the pyramid suggests that innovation, quality and staff engagement are all essential, especially in service industries. Research shows that many customers look for *innovative products and services* that meet their *quality* requirements relative to price. In service industries, *staff engagement* influences customer satisfaction as staff attitudes are transmitted to customers. Staff engagement may seem less important for employees who do not face the customer. However, to the extent that staff engagement influences quality and innovation, it is important to all businesses. Innovation, quality and staff engagement are the three key performance drivers on the pyramid. In order to create these drivers all higher-level practices are required, and they in turn are supported by all the foundation practices. Hence, the 23 practices are either essential for, or contribute to, creating customer satisfaction.

> *. . . if customer satisfaction is a desired performance outcome, which practices are necessary to generate it?*

How does this happen? In Chapter 4 we saw that high levels of innovation and quality are most effectively achieved by organisations with trusted and loyal team members capable of self-management, supported by an appropriate organisational culture. Taking just one of these higher-level practices – trust – a further question is: what fosters trust in employees at all levels of the organisation? Again, the research findings described in Chapters 3 and 4 indicate that trust can be expected in the presence of certain other higher-level practices: empowered decision-making and enabling culture. Many foundation practices contribute to creating and maintaining trust as well: amicable labour relations, developing people, long-term retention of staff and caring for people, ethics, long-term perspective, environmental and social responsibility, a stakeholder approach and a shared vision. A similar path can be traced for staff engagement. Hence, firms seeking to enhance customer satisfaction should focus initially on staff engagement, quality and innovation to ascertain where the greatest potential for improvement lies, and then work their way down the pyramid to identify areas of weakness.

The limitations of the Locust approach become apparent by subjecting it to this kind of analysis. Locust organisations find it difficult to create high quality, be innovative and engage staff. To this extent, the pyramid also represents an idealistic framework against which organisations can evaluate themselves. How would your enterprise score on these sustainable leadership practices? The Sustainable Leadership Questionnaire provides a survey instrument for assessing a firm's practices (see Appendix A).

A cursory look at the pyramid might suggest that the effects are essentially in one direction: foundation practices at the bottom of the pyramid cause effects higher up. An example of such a simple one-way causation is when the introduction of a bundle of environmentally friendly recycling practices increases financial performance. However, an equally valid view is reverse causation, whereby a profitable manufacturer decides to spend some of the surplus on introducing processes for reducing toxic waste by recycling. Here, financial success kicks off the environmentally friendly initiative. As it happens, research shows that firms that perform well financially invest more in corporate social responsibility than underperforming firms.[1] It would be wrong to conclude from this, however, that only rich firms can afford environmental and social responsibility. Likewise, training people leads to superior financial performance, but training is also more likely to occur when firms are financially well off.

Thus, the elements in the pyramid influence each other in multiple directions. The Sustainable Leadership Pyramid reflects a hierarchy of practices that build on each other and that involve increasing levels of sophistication and complexity. At each level of the pyramid the practices reinforce, and are reinforced by, other practices at that level. For example, devolved decision-making (level 2 of the pyramid) reinforces other higher-level practices such as self-management, teamwork, an enabling culture, trust and knowledge-sharing. This mutual reinforcing occurs at all levels of the pyramid including at the highest level, namely performance outcomes. For example, shareholder value is created when the brand is protected and customers and investors are satisfied.

Relationships in both directions are also illustrated by studies of job security (related to retaining staff on the Sustainable Leadership

Pyramid) and organisational performance. In one study, job security predicted positive financial performance, but job security itself was also predicted when a firm achieved good financial results.[2] This kind of positive boomerang effect puts businesses that practise sustainable leadership on a virtuous spiral, under the motto 'success breeds success'. Employees of successful companies become more committed to the firm and try harder. This in turn pays off in the business results, which continues the virtuous spiral. More is invested in innovation processes and CSR, and so the spiral continues. The link between a firm's practices and performance can therefore go in either or both directions, or interact in complex ways.

> *This kind of positive boomerang effect puts businesses that practise sustainable leadership on a virtuous spiral, under the motto 'success breeds success'.*

Sometimes, however, multidirectional causation does not appear to hold. A study concluded that profitability was likely to produce a higher rate of job satisfaction, but not the other way around. In other words, increased job satisfaction did not consistently produce high rates of profits.[3] There is considerable corroborating evidence for the first finding, as mentioned in Chapters 3 and 4. For example, employee participation leads to improved job satisfaction, productivity and enhanced financial performance.[4] Employees at the 100 Best Companies to Work for in America experience high job satisfaction, receive extraordinary benefits, have fun at work and have opportunities to balance their personal lives and work. Sharing a common vision and values increases job satisfaction, motivation and employees' commitment to the organisation. Empowered teams display higher levels of job satisfaction, customer service and organisational and team commitment. These outcomes in turn contribute to better organisational performance.[5]

Mostly the elements influence each other in both directions, provided appropriate measures are chosen. The reason that the relationship with job satisfaction need not necessarily work in the reverse is that employees may be highly satisfied with their jobs because benefits are obtained for little or no input. Many practitioners have therefore moved their focus from staff or job satisfaction to staff engagement or commitment.

Self-management is another practice that demonstrates these dynamic processes well. Figure 5–1 highlights some of the foundation practices that an organisation would need to examine, and possibly improve, in moving towards employee self-management. These include developing people continuously, amicable labour relations, long-term retention of staff, valuing people, top team leadership, ethical behaviour and sharing a vision. With respect to the higher-level practices, self-management is supported and reinforced by autonomous teams, devolved decision-making and trust. Going up the pyramid, self-management directly contributes to staff engagement, innovation and quality. To the extent that self-management decreases the need for expensive and non-value-adding supervisors, it directly affects financial performance and long-term shareholder value. It indirectly affects brand and reputation and customer satisfaction. Therefore self-management demonstrably plays a crucial role in sustainable organisations. It is facilitated – or, indeed, enabled – by certain foundation practices, and supported and reinforced by particular higher-level practices. Self-management in turn influences all three key performance drivers, and they then affect the organisation's performance.

Importantly, the Sustainable Leadership Pyramid highlights the fact that removing self-management from the pyramid, apart from leaving an obvious blank in the block of higher-level practices, removes all the linkages to the other practices. Notwithstanding its crucial role, there are two possible reasons why Locust managers hesitate or prefer not to embrace self-management. These can also be explained using the pyramid. First, in a typical Locust organisation, employees do not have deep skills, are probably caught up in an antagonistic management–labour relations climate, see the firm as only a temporary 'home', do not feel particularly valued, are not necessarily motivated, do not know or care for the corporate vision and may have to compromise ethical standards. They are not considered trustworthy enough to be able to self-manage. Under Locust management, only those practices that are perceived as directly influencing organisational performance are likely to be attended to. Practices that are perceived (rightly or wrongly) as not directly enhancing performance, such as valuing people, trust or social responsibility, are off the radar.

Figure 5–1 shows all of these linkages and in doing so reveals that self-management does not directly influence the performance outcomes. Instead, it operates through the three key performance drivers. This is consistent with the research evidence. Figure 5–1 graphically highlights the complex direct relationships that just one of the practices, self-management, has with many of the other practices. If indirect linkages were added, for example self-management > trust > staff engagement, complexity increases still further. A similar story could be written for each of the other practices.

If we tried to show all linkages for all practices for which we have found evidence, the diagram would be unreadable. The content would be obscured by too many criss-crossing lines. Hence, it would serve no useful purpose other than, perhaps, highlighting the extraordinary complexity of interactions and interdependencies among the practices. It may well be that this very complexity contributes to the core culture and sustainability of a firm. This allows Toyota, for example, to invite visitors (including direct competitors) into its production plants, show them everything there is to see, yet leave them with little appreciation of the secret to Toyota's success. The secret lies in the hidden interconnections between the 23 elements. In 2010, serious quality problems struck many of Toyota's brands, forcing global recalls of millions of cars. Time will tell where the source of this failure in this essentially Honeybee firm lies.

How connections between the elements show up in practice is likely to differ enterprise-by-enterprise. This generates diverse and unique cultures in businesses operating on basically similar Honeybee principles. Nonetheless, the underlying Honeybee leadership philosophy is discernible across enterprises.

Figure 5–1: Self-management's place in the Sustainable Leadership Pyramid

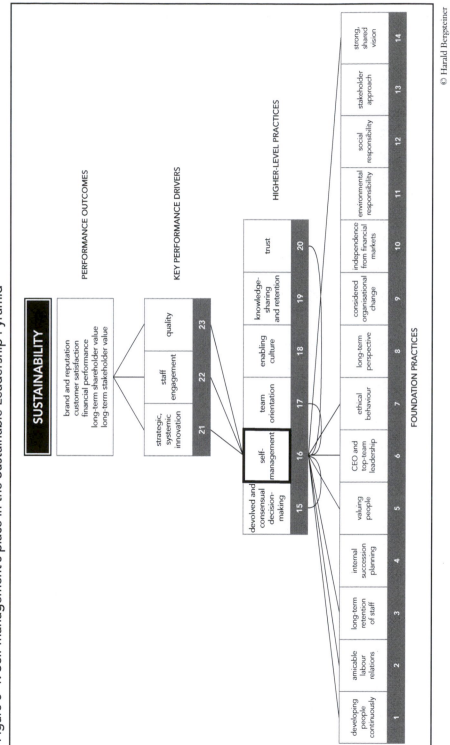

© Harald Bergsteiner

Honeybee elements linked to performance outcomes

As the Toyota example shows, organisational practices not only relate to each other but also drive organisational performance. While quality was high, customer satisfaction, brand and reputation, financial performance and shareholder value were all high. As multiple quality problems emerged at Toyota customer satisfaction and brand and reputation all suffered, which in turn drove down financial performance and shareholder returns.

Table 5–1 below shows the linkages to Honeybee practices that we have been able to ascertain from published research studies investigating organisational performance. This table shows which of the 23 elements are directly associated with each of the four main performance outcomes: financial performance, shareholder value, customer satisfaction and brand and reputation. Note that no studies reported on stakeholder value directly, except in so far as customers (through customer satisfaction) and employees (via staff engagement) are two key groups of stakeholders. It is clear that all Honeybee practices have some association with each of these outcomes.

Several things are evident from Table 5–1:

1. *Financial outcomes*: Except for self-management, research studies link all Honeybee practices directly to financial performance or the equivalent. (In the case of self-management, the research was undertaken in government schools where the measure was educational quality, a key performance driver, because financial metrics were not relevant.) That 22 of the 23 Honeybee practices link directly to financial outcomes is important given the strong pressures that most managers experience to improve financial performance. Thus, research suggests that each element individually contributes to financial success where such measures are relevant to organisational performance.

2. *Brand and reputation*: The second outcome measure most frequently reported by researchers investigating the effects of Honeybee leadership is brand and reputation. Here, we found research evidence directly linking 16 of the 23 Honeybee practices to enhancing brand and reputation. The exceptions were CEO

Table 5–1: Performance outcomes directly supported by Honeybee practices

	Financial performance	Shareholder value	Customer satisfaction	Brand and reputation
Foundation practices				
1. Developing people all the time	✓	✓		✓
2. Amicable labour relations	✓			✓
3. Retaining staff over long term	✓	✓	✓	✓
4. Internal succession planning	✓			✓
5. Valuing people	✓	✓	✓	✓
6. CEO and top team	✓	✓		
7. Ethics as a core value	✓			✓
8. Long-term perspective	✓	✓		
9. Considered organisational change	✓			
10. Independence from financial markets	✓			✓
11. Environmental responsibility	✓	✓	✓	✓
12. Social responsibility	✓	✓		✓
13. Broad spectrum of stakeholders	✓	✓	✓	✓
14. Strong and shared vision	✓		✓	✓
Higher-level practices				
15. Devolved/consensual decision-making	✓			
16. Self-management				
17. Team orientation	✓		✓	
18. Enabling culture	✓		✓	✓
19. Knowledge-sharing and retaining	✓		✓	
20. Trust	✓		✓	✓
Key-performance drivers				
21. Innovation	✓	✓	✓	✓
22. Staff engagement	✓	✓	✓	✓
23. Quality	✓	✓	✓	✓
Performance outcomes				
FP (financial performance)		✓	✓	✓
SV (shareholder value)	✓		✓	✓
CS (customer satisfaction)	✓	✓		✓
BR (brand and reputation)	✓	✓	✓	

and top team, long-term perspective, considered organisational change, decision-making, self-management, team orientation and knowledge management. Since these are primarily internally focused elements, it is not altogether surprising that they do not appear to influence brand and reputation directly.

3. *Customer satisfaction*: Researchers have directly linked customer satisfaction to 12 Honeybee practices. Again the elements not connected to outcomes mostly affect internal organisational behaviour and are not necessarily noticed by customers, except for ethical behaviour.

4. *Shareholder value*: Shareholder value is difficult and controversial to measure and rather removed from a firm's actions. This may account for why researchers have not often reported on this outcome. Also, many factors unrelated to a listed enterprise's activities are likely to combine to influence shareholder value. Nonetheless, the published research shows that 11 Honeybee practices link directly to this outcome measure.

In addition, other interesting observations can be made about Table 5–1. For a start, the three key performance drivers of innovation, staff engagement and quality all relate to the four primary outcome measures used in the literature: brand and reputation, customer satisfaction, financial performance and shareholder value. In other words, these three practices contribute to all performance measures, as the name 'key performance drivers' suggests they should.

Several foundation practices contribute directly to all four performance outcomes as well. These are retaining staff over the long term, valuing people, being environmentally responsible and having a focus on a broad spectrum of stakeholders. Two other foundation practices contribute to three of the four performance variables, namely social responsibility and vision.

Among the higher-level practices, an enabling culture and trust contributed to financial performance, customer satisfaction and the firm's brand and reputation.

As summarised in Chapters 3 and 4, other research studies have uncovered complex relationships among many of the Honeybee practices themselves. For example, developing and training people continuously assists in the long-term retention of staff; conversely, long-term retention of staff makes it sensible to invest substantial resources in staff development. Clearly this represents a mutual interdependency where the various elements influence each other.

Notably, a high concentration of mutual effects occurs at the levels of the key performance drivers and organisational performance. Each key performance driver influences every other key performance driver, and each organisational performance measure influences every other performance measure.

The fact that a cell in Table 5–1 is blank does not mean that there is necessarily no relationship. It simply means that evidence for it has not emerged and might not even have been looked for yet. The table helps identify future research projects. For example, a major study is needed that investigates the effects of all 23 practices on business performance – in the one context and using consistent performance measures. This would enable researchers to evaluate the relative contribution of each practice to business performance.

The evidence to date has had to be assembled from very different small–scale research studies. However, the results indicate which of these 23 practices and performance drivers individually influence which organisational performance outcomes. The research already provides support for making the business case that Honeybee practices relate to enhanced financial performance, customer satisfaction, brand and reputation and shareholder value. Although value for all stakeholders is the ultimate goal of an organisation, or should be, researchers have yet to measure this performance outcome in a comprehensive way.

Clearly, the practices do not operate in isolation but interact in complex ways. We explore the theme of combining or bundling practices in the next section.

The power of bundling practices

We have seen that whether or not an enterprise becomes high performing depends on many practices, on how well they are implemented, and on how these practices and their effects interact. To simplify their research, scholars typically analyse the effects of single variables. However, in the broad reality of a manager's world, individual elements in the Sustainable Leadership Pyramid do not operate in isolation. Observations and practice lead to the conclusion that most business outcomes are actually generated by a number of practices working together. These are referred to as 'bundles of practices'.

Research supports the effectiveness of bundling various elements. A McKinsey study of 230 global organisations found that where combinations of carefully selected initiatives were used rather than individual practices, the business performed better.[6] For example, although making employees accountable, setting goals and priorities, or establishing a performance culture improved business performance, best results were achieved by implementing all three measures at the same time. The combined effect of the bundle outperformed its individual practices.

A study of business models actually used in major US corporations shows how organisations employ multiple leadership and organisational practices to enhance business outcomes. For example, innovative human resources practices are related to improved service quality, cost and financial performance, and are strongly associated with employee and customer satisfaction.[7] Similarly, the Malcolm Baldridge National Quality Award assesses data sourced from different functional parts of an organisation: leadership, strategy, customer and market focus, information analysis, human resources, process management and business results. Kaplan and Norton's Balanced Scorecard framework also combines various kinds of measures.[8] Thus, these approaches support the idea that sustainable leadership requires an integrated approach to managing an enterprise.

Bundled, both Honeybee and Locust practices interact and appear to reinforce one another. In Locust organisations, bundling destructive practices puts an enterprise on a downward spiral. However, for Honeybee leadership, bundling creates a potentially powerful set of practices that can provide competitive advantage and contribute to organisational performance. Exactly how this is done still requires further research, but researchers offer several explanations for better business performance under Honeybee leadership. One reason is that companies that focus on sustainability generally have better management. This alone is likely to lead to better performance. By measuring performance against many criteria, management is better informed in making decisions. Better decisions also set in motion a virtuous spiral.

A more compelling reason is that the various practices gain added potency because they constitute a mutually reinforcing bundle of practices. The sum is greater than the individual parts. Indeed, the individual elements in the bundle sometimes mutually strengthen each other to such an extent that they appear not only interactive but also interdependent. Another way to explain this is to recognise that two variable relationships (for example, training and financial performance) can only take direct effects into account. All indirect effects are necessarily ignored. However, when multiple practices are studied, indirect effects can be captured. Figure 5.2. shows how this works.

Figure 5–2: How indirect effects influence organisational performance

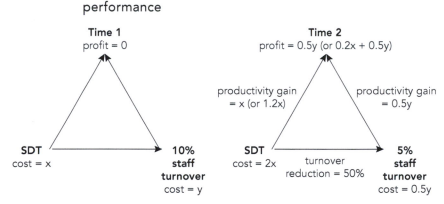

Consider an enterprise at Time 1 and Time 2. At Time 1, the enterprise invests 'x' amount in staff development and training (SDT) and has a staff turnover rate of 10 per cent, which imposes a cost of 'y' on the enterprise. The enterprise at Time 1 is not making a profit and decides to introduce changes; in particular it decides to double the SDT budget to '2x'.

One year further on (Time 2) the enterprise finds that a productivity gain has contributed precisely an additional amount 'x' to the bottom line. Therefore, at Time 2 SDT costs are '2x' increased productivity is worth 'x', leaving the enterprise with net costs of 'x' (2x – x = x). In other words, the extra productivity gain has been eaten up by the extra training costs. Therefore, on this measure alone the intervention seems unwarranted.

However, at Time 2 not only is there a gain in productivity, but because of the introduction of the additional SDT employee turnover has been reduced from the original 10 per cent to 5 per cent, which reduces the costs of managing this turnover rate from 'y' to '0.5y'. This is a net gain. Therefore the indirect net gain at Time 2, that is the indirect profit, is '0.5y'.

In fact, the situation is likely to be better than that because we know from research that the benefits of SDT exceed its costs. Therefore, the productivity improvement achieved as a result of the additional SDT investment is not merely 'x' but, say, '1.2x'. Therefore, from the introduction of the additional SDT the enterprise has reduced its net costs from the original 'x' to '0.8x' (2x − 1.2x = 0.8x), which represents a direct gain of '0.2x'. In other words, on these two factors alone the enterprise derives direct and indirect gains respectively of 0.2x + 0.5y. However, even this is not the whole story because SDT is also known to have beneficial effects on several of the foundation practices, the higher-level practices and on the key performance drivers.

This kind of multiplier effect explains why US public companies that invest extraordinary amounts in training and developing can outperform the Standard & Poor's stock index by between 17 and 35 per cent.[9] Ultimately, a mathematical model that captures this complexity needs to be developed that allows predictions to be made about the likely benefits that any particular intervention could make.

Again, exactly how these interactions occur and whether some practices are effective only when applied in association with other practices needs further investigation. However, convincing evidence of the effectiveness of certain bundled practices comes from investigations into so-called innovative human resources practices, discussed in Box 5–1. Overall, the weight of evidence suggests that implementing employee-oriented human resources practices is not only a good thing to do – because it increases staff satisfaction and engagement – but it also enhances business performance.[10]

A Korean example shows that bundling several Honeybee elements together enhances decision-making. In these businesses, decision-making was of higher quality when conducted by capable and motivated employees. Korean firms in which training, care

Box 5–1: Bundles of high-involvement work practices
         improve performance

High-involvement human resources practices are also known as high-commitment management practices or innovative human resources practices. They represent a systematic approach towards developing the skill, motivation and commitment of the workforce. Unfortunately, the nature of these human resources practices is not defined consistently in the literature, which makes comparing findings from different studies difficult. Practices often regarded as innovative include using teams to solve problems and providing staff induction processes, extensive training and information-sharing, job rotation, profit-sharing and job security.[11] These practices are common in Honeybee enterprises, except for profit-sharing, which researchers generally consider the least essential of these practices.[12]

Research among *Fortune* 1000 firms shows that innovative human resources practices are associated with higher productivity, quality and employee and customer satisfaction, as well as yielding better market and financial performance.[13] In the US health industry, each health facility surveyed saved more than US$1.2 million despite the costs of implementing the high-involvement practices. Outcomes included more satisfied employees, less organisational turmoil and lower service delivery costs.[14]

These and other findings reinforce the view that it is the combination of multiple practices that drives performance, not individual practices alone. Research into adopting teamwork and other innovative human resources systems in American steel mills highlights this. The researchers found increases of nearly 7 per cent in productivity when the bundle of practices was applied compared with traditional systems. This represented an increase of $240,000 per production line each month.[15] Importantly, the same workers were used in both situations, so the enhanced productivity could not be attributed to a change of workforce. Other researchers report a positive relationship between a bundle of human resources practices, trust and the outcomes for individuals and the organisation itself.[16] In banks, organisational climate coupled with appropriate human resources practices was associated with improved business performance.[17] Thus the evidence is mounting that bundles of human resources practices can be more effective than individual applications under a range of industrial conditions.

What is not yet certain is the right combination of practices required to enhance performance in particular industries.[18] The inability to identify the correct bundle of human resources practices for all situations is not greatly surprising. This research is new and complex, needing to take many factors at different levels into account and over time.[19] It is also to be expected that how well, and to what extent, these practices are implemented in a particular enterprise will affect the research results.[20] In some cases their introduction could be just a token gesture rather than a fundamental intervention.

for staff and employee involvement in decision-making occurred demonstrated a higher return on assets than their peers who did not embrace these practices.[21]

Similarly, an analysis of Best Companies to Work For found bundles of elements operating in these cultures: Honeybee elements of trust, valuing a range of stakeholders and relying on employees' contribution to knowledge and innovation.[22] Research also shows that when implemented as a bundle, customer focus, corporate citizenship, performance standards, organisational communication and the extent to which employees identify with the business, influence a firm's financial performance, directly and indirectly.[23]

> *. . . companies that focus on sustainability*
> *generally have better management.*

Bundling appears to work in small businesses too. In small legal firms, bundled Honeybee practices such as providing training and development, selecting employees for cultural fit and potential rather than current skills and knowledge and emphasising long-term career prospects had positive effects on both financial and operational performance.[24] Quality in products and services was highest among small firms where employees also displayed high levels of trust in management. When layoffs are unavoidable, those firms that maintained their bundled high-involvement human resources practices were able to avoid productivity losses.[25]

Larger corporations also bundle practices consistent with Honeybee philosophy. For example, six factors combine to make BMW 'special', according to a previous CEO.[26] These are:

- Vision: 'Premium brand products and services'
- Innovation: 'We are more innovative than others'
- Efficiency: 'We are more efficient than others'
- People: 'Our company has the best brain pool because we are considered the most popular employer, particularly by young professionals'
- Culture/teamwork: 'In our company, there is a very strong We feeling and the shared goal to get ahead of competition as one strong, high-performance team'
- Independence: 'We are independent and therefore we do not have to make any compromises'.

Clearly, the relationship between the Honeybee practices is not always straightforward. This became apparent in a research project examining the effect that a bundle of employee-autonomy practices had on innovation. The practices included decentralised self-management and decision-making, enabling autonomy and empowerment and participative leadership. All are consistent with Honeybee leadership, which strives to maximise employee autonomy and self-management. While these practices benefit innovation, research has shown that they can harbour certain unplanned effects, including coordination problems. The researchers concluded that these risks could be countered by underpinning autonomy with a clear vision, consensus decision-making and trust.[27] Again, these are Honeybee practices that interact in complex ways. Under *ad hoc* worker control, without these constraints innovation actually declined. Thus, bundling practices is important.

A further demonstration of the power of combining Honeybee criteria comes from research looking at the relationship between innovation, quality, growth, profitability and the market value of a business.[28] The results suggest that a firm's capacity for innovation, while maintaining quality, drives growth and profitability. This in turn increases its market value. However, these variables are interlinked in complex ways. Innovativeness influences growth and profitability; quality mediates between innovation and profitability; innovation and quality both affect market value, as do growth and profitability.

We are not alone in pointing out the interrelatedness of Honeybee practices. In a recent study, two researchers proposed 'that every process and procedure in a firm is embedded in a set of other processes . . . From a hierarchical perspective, at the foundation are a firm's specialised knowledge and resources, which are combined to generate lower-order capabilities; these, in turn, are combined to generate higher-order capabilities.'[29] This reflects our notions of foundation and higher-level practices. These researchers showed empirically that certain hierarchical and interconnected capabilities provide competitive advantage that is difficult to imitate when they are embedded in the 'organisational sociocultural fabric'. This is what we have also found in our research. Their approach differs substantially from ours in detail because they focused on functional capabilities such as operations, R&D, marketing, new product development, store management and merchandising capabilities.

However, in their report these researchers refer to many of the Honeybee practices that we have identified. These practices include knowledge management and sharing, strong customer relationships, top-notch training at all levels in the firm, empowerment, trust, innovation, low employee turnover and strong organisational culture. Unfortunately these researchers did not clarify how individual practices contribute to the functional capabilities and hence organisational performance. Interestingly, the researchers concluded that they expected that embedding the capabilities would contribute to firm performance over and above the benefits to be obtained from the individual capabilities.

Future scholars will need to determine whether and when the effect of bundling is additive, multiplicative or even more complex. We know, however, that certain smaller bundles of Honeybee practices in areas such as human resource management practices, innovation, teamwork, quality and trust are more effective when implemented as a bundle rather than individually. This and the accumulating evidence for sustainable leadership practices raises the question of why Honeybee principles are not more widely adopted. This is discussed next.

Institutional and cultural influences on Honeybee leadership

In Chapter 1, we noted various reasons why managers might be reluctant to change to Honeybee practices. These were primarily psychological and organisational reasons. However, external pressures also affect a business, encouraging managers to behave in certain ways. These external influences are often referred to as 'institutional factors'.

Institutional factors include the regulatory framework in which a business operates; taxation and general economic conditions; what competitors and other firms are doing; and the expectations of important professional organisations, society, social activists and a range of other stakeholders. Values inherent in the local culture also influence how a business is likely to operate. For example, high-involvement human resources practices appear to be more effective in some countries than in others. Researchers found that high-performance human resources practices enhanced organisational performance more among Irish than among Dutch firms.[30] The specific practices examined in nearly 400 enterprises included provision of incentive systems, training, guidance and selective recruitment. The combined effect of these practices exceeded the sum of the individual effects in Ireland but not in the Netherlands.

What are the broader effects of national culture on Honeybee practices? Do Honeybee enterprises operate better in Central European, South African or Scandinavian countries where the national culture is supportive of this kind of leadership? Certainly, it sounds easier to pursue Honeybee leadership principles when other CEOs (some of whom may sit on the firm's board), society, regulatory authorities and similar institutional factors support them than when most others regard Locust leadership as the only way to go.

However, research has shown that being innovative and having a strong organisational culture do not depend on the country in which a business is based. High-performing firms transcend differences in national culture. Instead, they develop common patterns of Honeybee practices that drive their success.[31]

Therefore, the evidence from both practice and academic studies suggests that Honeybee practices can be, and have been, adopted in different cultures with broadly similar results. This is also evident from many of the examples in this book, where firms operate globally under Honeybee leadership.

Challenges for Honeybee leadership

Institutional preferences outside the firm do not rule out adopting a Honeybee philosophy inside a business, but they do not necessarily make it easy either. Indeed, the pressures on enterprises to succumb to short-term performance, particularly by chasing quarterly targets, are immense. Among other factors, these pressures include:

- most business schools teach it[32]
- professors bow to conventional wisdom[33]
- many academic journals support it[34]
- US government policies require it[35]
- much of the media, including the financial media, proselytise it[36]
- most managers are tied into it via self-interest[37]
- financial markets drive it[38]
- therefore, many major investment funds are locked into it, and
- given the above, many managers do not know of alternatives.

Irrespective of the advantages of Honeybee practices, market factors, the general business environment and personal prejudices can affect the extent to which managers embrace Honeybee leadership. In addition to these generalised pressures from wide sections of the global community, some highly destructive pressures are coming from particular operators who have learned how to use others' exposure to their one–sided advantage.

Taking Germany as an example, Honeybee leadership has been the traditional model in that country. Now groups of investors, which a prominent German politician referred to as 'locusts', are buying up privately held businesses under the pretence of making them more efficient. Essentially, two locust models are employed. The first is known as a 'private equity transaction', which typically saddles the target firms with huge, at times unserviceable, debts. In these transactions traditional companies are bought up using large amounts of debt, then their operations are 'overhauled' to 'improve' short-term figures. This usually means sacking employees, reshuffling management, reducing working capital and improving cash flow to service the debt. Ultimately either the business is split up or some or all of it is sold.[39]

A second model that locusts use involves raiders buying companies' debt from their banks. The raiders then call in the debt at the first opportunity and swap it for stock. Having obtained control, they restructure, 'filet' and cash in.[40] A variation on this practice is when unscrupulous banks lend money to a small firm then quickly recall the loan. This can lead to the borrower company having to register bankruptcy or surrender the business as collateral to the banks.

In these examples, so-called locusts accept the loss of thousands of work places as simply collateral damage while serving their own financial and other interests. This is clearly contrary to many Honeybee leadership principles, not the least being its concern for the long-term and retaining its independence from the financial and other masters. Many of these private equity wheelers and dealers are aggressive proponents of the Anglo/US form of capitalism and Locust leadership.

That companies may need to defend themselves from outside investors and the capital markets to ensure their sustainability is driven home by various horror stories about the destruction of value. For instance, companies considered to be well managed and profitable came under the influence of outside investors when the family owners sold out. The firms were broken up for shareholder profit and saddled with huge debts that drove them towards insolvency. Did this benefit shareholders? The honest answer to this question is – yes. The original family shareholders benefited and the locusts benefited. But in the process value can be destroyed and damage inflicted on various stakeholders, not the least of these being the employees, the local community and suppliers. Stories like this validate the Honeybee philosophy of standing up to the capital markets and outside investors seeking short-term profits.

Rather than labelling all private equity groups as 'locusts' or 'vulture investors', it is useful to distinguish operators of this kind from traditional buyout and turnaround investors. [41] Traditional investors provide fresh equity and take a controlling interest in ailing or no-growth businesses so that they can influence management directly. They try to enhance their returns by restructuring operations, finances and strategic plans. Similarly, not all private equity activities destroy businesses. A World Economic Forum analysis of over 21,000 private equity transactions between 1970 and 2007 concluded that, overall, private equity groups take a long-term participation in their companies, innovation continues and employment does not decrease. [42] This was borne out on a national level, where 3700 French firms backed by private equity generated an estimated 39,000 new jobs. [43] Private equity can therefore enable firms to continue after their founding families sell out. However, even well-intentioned investors can drive an enterprise into ruin by importing inferior leadership practices.

The firms were broken up for shareholder profit and saddled with huge debts that drove them towards insolvency.

Is the financial power of locusts described here heralding the end of Honeybee leadership? You might well ask. In the following section we look at what is likely to happen next, with surprising opportunities for the finance industry to lead the way. Whether this industry chooses the Honeybee path is another matter.

Will financial institutions lead the way?

Both the financial sector, such as banks and insurance companies, and the stock markets have been blamed for the prevalence of the Locust model. Criticism arises particularly from the short-term perspective that analysts and other players in the financial world impose on the corporate sector. In 2004, the World Business Council for Sustainable Development and the United Nations Finance Initiative scathingly described the state of the financial markets: 'If anything, the current crisis is leading to a bunker or herd mentality – less innovation, less risk-taking, and a greater tendency to cluster around the same conclusions.'[44] These criticisms may well apply to the financial capital markets, if not to the financial services sector more generally as well.

The World Economic Forum asked financial market practitioners about this in roundtable discussions. The outcome showed that it was not the personal values of the fund trustees, portfolio managers and analysts interviewed that accounted for why socially responsible investment is not yet mainstream.[45] Instead, the problem is systemic. It lies in industry customs, structures, regulations and the incentives under which financial market players work. Everyone started blaming everyone else in these discussions. The fund managers blamed their clients – mainly pension fund trustees – and their short-term performance demands. Analysts in turn blamed their clients, that is fund managers, for focusing on short-term performance and market valuations.

A further concern about the financial markets is that analysts typically do not consider broad sustainability criteria when assessing the companies they track. A study of *Fortune* 1000 firms revealed that professional analysts consistently underestimated the earnings of companies that used high-involvement human resources practices.[46] Most analysts did not have, or use, information about these practices when issuing their earnings forecasts. This habit of overlooking these and other sustainability criteria is not set to improve. Findings from research into the views of young financial analysts are reported in Box 5–2. They suggest that a generational change is not in sight in this important industry. Youth is not at the vanguard of promoting sustainability.

Box 5–2: Do financial analysts value sustainable leadership criteria?

Financial analysts' views are vital to sustainability because this profession produces forecasts, valuations and opinions about the companies they monitor. Investors, asset managers and rating agencies rely on this information. Therefore how much analysts take account of sustainable practices in their evaluations can determine the extent to which companies are endorsed or penalised by the markets. Both investors and the companies themselves are likely to adjust their decisions on the basis of these analyses. If the analysts reward only short-term actions and performance, then the broadly accepted longer-term business value under sustainable leadership may well be sacrificed to please the analysts.

The World Business Council for Sustainable Development and the UN Environment Program Finance Initiative joined forces to interview analysts younger than 35. They concluded that young analysts do not see any need to include sustainable business practices in their assessments, despite their being closely involved in research.[47] Respondents were not convinced that clients would value this information. Young analysts appear not to be convinced that environmental, social and governance issues have a material effect on business.

Part of their reluctance to consider these factors could be because analysts lack information, training or tools, the joint report concludes. For example, investment professionals say they lack reliable information about environmental performance, and are uncertain about how to compare environmental and financial performance meaningfully.[48]

Worse still, the analysts surveyed indicated that they were largely unwilling to change if it might conflict with their remuneration, career progression or culture. This is surprising in some respects and not surprising in others. It is not surprising in the light of other research suggesting that brokerage houses and policy-makers place little emphasis on environmental and social criteria in assessing a company's past or anticipated performance.[49] Perhaps they really do not know that the two are linked. It is surprising, given that analysts are supposed to be expert at being able to identify, analyse and recommend outstanding performers for their clients. Clearly, it will require a systemic shift of culture, remuneration and goals for these young analysts to change their priorities. It is also surprising given that analysts have a reputation for being driven by greed. If this is true, they should be doing what famous investment guru Warren Buffett does, namely investing in and recommending sustainable enterprises because they deliver better results.

The financial markets sector has a choice. It can continue to emphasise under-performing short-termism at the expense of long-term performance and create havoc around the world. Alternatively, it can exercise its power and lead the charge towards adopting long-term sustainable practices, at least in the public enterprises under its influence. Analysts can learn to identify, value and endorse companies that derive competitive advantage through sustainable practices. This could then flow through to the private sector as suppliers are brought into the sustainability net cast by publicly listed firms. As we have seen, family owned businesses tend to thrive on Honeybee principles; hence, many would welcome public corporations into the fold of sustainable enterprises. Bringing public companies under Honeybee leadership would ensure that an increasing proportion of the business world operates both profitably *and* sustainably.

The good news is that some financial institutions are becoming increasingly concerned about sustainability. Some leading asset managers will invest their own funds only in sustainable ventures. How sophisticated the criteria are for assessing sustainability is a question for discussion, as is whether the criteria extend beyond being 'green' and 'socially responsible'. However, things may also be changing as far as environmental and social responsibility is concerned. Some research suggests that more financial analysts are indeed shifting their attention away from their less responsible or poorer-quality counterparts to socially responsible, high-quality companies.[50] Perhaps the message is getting through that they are likely to be the better performers.

According to United Nations (UN) research, in 2004 major brokerage houses agreed that environmental, social and corporate governance considerations affect long-term shareholder value. It is noteworthy that no North American brokerage houses agreed to participate in this UN study. However, in 2005 an *Investor Weekly* editorial article reported that three major investment houses predicted that socially responsible investing would soon become mainstream. The editor concluded that globally the trend is for more fund members to head down this path.[51]

Another force for change is the concentration of share ownership in funds with long-term horizons. This is occurring in many countries through pension funds, for example. US and other pension funds have enormous power through the sheer volume of their investments in the capital markets. Pension funds must become concerned with the long-term survival of the businesses they invest in for the funds' own survival.[52] This concentration of power is starting to work against the short-term perspective in an industry that requires long-term assessment of risk. Long-term risk can be missed when short-term financial results drive the agenda. For these reasons, long-term-oriented pension funds hold large parcels of shares across the stock market. Pulling their money out of unsustainable corporations to invest in socially responsible firms could result in a reappraisal of companies' attractiveness as investment vehicles.

Illustrating ethical practices to investing is the Norwegian government 'pension' fund, Norges Bank Investment Management (NBIM).[53] NBIM manages the surplus wealth from Norway's large petroleum income, and has since turned into the government's pension fund. NBIM is the largest European fund, and close to the largest in the world. The fund receives a very high transparency rating of 10, and invests in line with prescribed ethical guidelines. Companies that the fund invests in are closely monitored by an ethics council. NBIM may withdraw its funds from companies operating in conflict with its guidelines. The guidelines cover violation of human rights, corruption, environmental damage, child labour and other ethical considerations. NBIM has withdrawn its investment funds from a wide range of companies in many countries deemed to be violating its ethical code.[54]

> *. . . some financial institutions are becoming*
> *increasingly concerned about sustainability.*

Global financial giant Allianz has adopted a strategy of integrating sustainable concepts and practices into its entire business. This includes insurance underwriting, managing assets and risks and caring for society and the environment. Having sustainability issues integral to the strategy of a leading member of the financial sector has major implications for promoting sustainable organisations among its stakeholders.

Back in 2002 Munich Re, one of the world's largest reinsurers, began investing in shares and corporate bonds that met certain sustainability requirements. Since 2005, this has included government bonds. By 2008, 82 per cent of the company's investments in shares, corporate bonds and government bonds satisfied these sustainability criteria.[55] The criteria are based on those of the Dow Jones Sustainability Index and the sustainability ratings issued by the oekom research agency. Sustainability is also taken into account when Munich Re invests in long-term shareholdings and property.

Clearly, pension funds and other large investment managers already have the power to demand that the corporations in which their funds are invested become more sustainable. Pressure for more sustainable leadership is starting to come from major investors valuing a long-term focus on the environment and society. Eventually it should embrace the remaining 21 Honeybee practices, given that each practice is likely to add value to a business.

One implication of these findings is that analysts will have to adopt a longer time horizon in valuing companies than they have to date. Standard reporting practices will have to be developed to enable appropriate comparisons between companies on multiple criteria. Furthermore, Locust CEOs may have to watch their share prices fall as investors switch to more sustainable stock.

What is business doing?

While financial analysts are slow to incorporate environmental and social criteria into their work, business itself is much more convinced. Together with researchers from the University of Amsterdam, KPMG conducted an international survey of corporate responsibility reporting.[56] The aim was to analyse trends in reporting among the largest companies in the world. Companies included the top 250 firms in the *Forbes* 500 (Global 250) plus the top firms in 16 countries (National 100). Among tshe more than 1600 businesses studied, corporate responsibility reporting had increased to 64 per cent of the Global 250 and to 41 per cent of the National 100 companies by 2005. The researchers concluded, somewhat optimistically, that reporting on environmental, social and economic sustainability measures is now mainstream. Some companies incorporate this information into their annual reports, but about 90 per cent issue separate responsibility reports. In particular, the financial sector stands out with a twofold increase in reporting since 2002.

Why are companies increasingly focusing on non-financial measures? Among KPMG's Global 250 companies, about three-quarters were driven by non-economic considerations.[57] These considerations related to innovation, learning, employee motivation and managing risk. Interestingly, about half of the Global 250 companies reported ethical reasons as the driver of their sustainability initiatives. Certainly sustainability reporting is more widespread in Europe than in the USA. Supporting KPMG's findings is an analysis of non-financial reporting practices among 90 European multinational corporations. Common themes among non-financial practices reported included operational safety in products and working conditions, product quality and innovation, dialogue with communities and stakeholders, protecting the environment, employee skill development and being a responsible citizen.[58]

> *Long-term risk can be missed when short-term financial results drive the agenda.*

Is much of this reporting just a token gesture? Reporting quality varied in the KPMG study, and was regarded as superficial in most cases. Environmental issues were covered in more depth than social and economic criteria, and climate change was mentioned in about 85 per cent of reports. Social topics included labour standards, working conditions, community involvement and philanthropy in about two-thirds of the reports. The researchers suggest that a lack of clear social indicators might be behind the superficial reporting on these criteria. Economic reporting was also regarded as superficial, even though 61 per cent of reports included financial information such as profits and revenues. Only about 25 per cent of the reports discussed the broader economic impact of the business in relation to sustainability. However, increasingly, companies are extending their concept of responsibility to include requirements for suppliers to behave responsibly as well. The concern for a firm's overall ecological footprint is growing.

While it is pleasing to see reporting on social and environmental criteria growing, reporting can also be nothing more than paying lip-service to sustainability. At middle levels of sustainability (see Dunphy's Phase 4 in Chapter 1), sustainability is pursued because it makes economic sense. For companies at Phases 5 and 6 sustainability is core to their strategy not only for financial reasons, but also because it is the right thing to do.

The recent trend to accompany financial reporting with social and environmental responsibility outcomes reflects growing concern for social and environmental issues. Still to come is a similar recognition of the other equally important aspects of sustainable leadership identified in this book.

However, this too should change as it becomes more and more difficult to maintain the myth that the Locust way of doing business produces superior results. Numerous practical examples and a large body of research challenge this belief. Certainly a global acceptance that sustainability is *the* issue of the 21st century will trigger a re-examination of current business models. Prudent and innovative companies will accept this as a strategic opportunity to position themselves at the forefront of change. In Box 5–3, you can read about how Roche has integrated many sustainable leadership practices into its everyday pharmaceutical business to create this future.

Box 5–3: Integrated sustainable leadership practices at Roche

Sustainability is not an option for this global Swiss pharmaceutical company. For Roche, sustainability is not limited to environmental, occupational health or CSR issues. Surprising to many, the finance department fosters a very broad view of sustainability, way beyond mere financial measures. Sustainable leadership is part of doing everyday business for everyone at Roche, which is a leader in the Dow Jones and FTSE4Good sustainability indices.

For many years the company did not let stakeholders know about its success in sustainability. This is now changing as the more than 80,000 employees in about 150 satellite locations participate in the firm's strategy. Once head office is satisfied that the 'satellites' share the strong culture, vision and values and that the management can be trusted, the local offices are granted autonomy to run their business – in a sustainable way. The satellites take ownership and responsibility, and this creates buy-in.

Annual sales revenues at Roche in 2009 were just under CHF50 billion, a 10 per cent increase on 2008. Roche, a world leader in cancer and transplantation diagnostics and drugs, derives its revenues from two divisions: pharmaceuticals and diagnostics. The company regards its strategy of tailoring drugs for individuals, rather than trying broad drugs on every patient, as socially responsible and consistent with its sustainability objectives.

The majority of this publicly listed company's shares are still privately owned. Its strategy requires sustainability to be integrated into its business case. In preparing its strategic plans, sustainability issues relevant to the business throughout the entire value chain are identified. Then key performance indicators are developed to measure progress on sustainability and risk. The company website emphasises its long-term view: [59]

> At Roche we are committed to sustainability and thus to running our business in a way that is ethical, responsible and creates long-term value. And, since it takes up to twelve years to bring a new drug to market, our business model inevitably has a long-term focus. We must be responsive to developments in science and society, generate a level of resources that ensures our independence and be willing to take calculated risks.

Furthermore, trust is an important ingredient in Roche's success. In the company's view:

> The trust of our key stakeholders – shareholders and employees, patients and customers, the medical and scientific community, regulatory and other public authorities and the communities in which our facilities are located – is essential. Our 'license to operate' is based on our ability to generate sustainable value. We do this by focusing on our core purpose and main contribution to society: creating innovative solutions for unmet medical needs. [60]

A shortage of talented employees and the impending retirement of its ageing workforce provide challenges for Roche. Roche has ambitions to grow strongly over the next five years, particularly in Asia. New employees will be sought who fit the social and emotional competencies that this highly successful enterprise needs to remain sustainable.

The future

What might the future look like for sustainable leadership? First, as financial institutions become more aware of the need to manage risk – and consider the better business performance expected under Honeybee leadership – they will exert their power. This process has already started with the UN's Principles for Responsible

Investment (PRI).[61] Developed by an international group of about 70 institutional investors in 2005–06, the principles reflect environmental, social and corporate governance issues relevant to investment practices. Banks and other lenders will increasingly refuse to support Locust businesses because of their increased exposure to liability risks and generally poorer performance over the long term. Or lenders will raise the cost of borrowing capital for Locust firms, thereby increasing their operating costs.

Certainly a global acceptance that sustainability is the issue of the 21st century will trigger a re-examination of current business models.

Second, we expect to see investment managers – starting with pension funds – putting pressure on management to become more sustainable in all senses of the word. Just as private equity locusts force CEOs to resign and break up companies, pension fund managers will insist on long-term sustainable performance. Their money will speak.

Third, all kinds of investors, including 'mums and dads', will punish companies that do not act as good citizens. Investors will shift their money to better corporate citizens that respect customers, the environment and local communities as well as future generations. If the pension funds have not made Locust share prices fall, the rest of the investment community will. CEO compensation will tumble unless organisations deliver sustainable outcomes.

Fourth, organisations not practising sustainable leadership will find it harder to attract talented employees, of which there is a growing shortage worldwide. Workers will abandon non-sustainable employers in favour of companies with a better attitude. This could have catastrophic effects for organisations in countries with an impending shortage of labour or an ageing population. Non-sustainable enterprises will be starved of talent as employees vote with their feet. Human resources directors are already becoming concerned about attracting Generation Y employees because of problems in retaining young workers, particularly in companies lacking in corporate social responsibility.[62] These and other pressures should catapult companies into becoming better citizens.

Fifth, suppliers that suffer under Locust philosophies will also punish these enterprises. Squeezing suppliers' margins until they go out of business will come back to bite a Locust company's balance sheet. The few remaining suppliers will choose whom to deliver their goods and services to and at what price. Many will prioritise the positive and fair long-term relationships they have enjoyed with Honeybee firms. When clients and suppliers grow and learn together, both succeed. What will Locust leadership do in these conditions?

Sixth, customers punish bad firms too. The customer revolt is only just beginning. As banks and other firms reduced their outlets, prices and quality, customers abandoned loyalty for price. Many now buy the cheapest goods wherever they are available. This is a threat to be taken seriously as competition comes from cheap production and service economies – China and India are two current examples. How sustainable is a brand without customer loyalty? Can a firm survive difficult times without the support of its customers? Customer satisfaction, or rather dissatisfaction, is already extending beyond quality, price and service. Customers will also expect firms to be environmentally and socially aware in the future.

In short, many of the once powerless stakeholders are garnering power over firms: power to withdraw their financial and other support and power to withhold their talent and their purchasing power. This will probably not be felt by current Locust CEOs with their 3–4 year tenures. However, within a decade or so companies that fail to plan for the long run and neglect or abuse key stakeholders will find it hard to survive, let alone thrive. Honeybee leadership recognises this fundamental weakness of the Locust approach and has 23 elements in place to deal with it.

As already mentioned, conventional wisdom as promoted by business schools, sections of the media, financial analysts and management consultants is driven and perpetuated to a large extent by dogma and ideology. In other words, mainstream thinking has demonstrated a certain inability, if not unwillingness, to learn from high-performance companies. By failing to take on board the methods and attitudes of successful companies from all over the world, adherents of mainstream thinking are disenfranchising not just those who genuinely care about environmental and social responsibility, but also the constituency they claim to represent above all others – their shareholders.

Leaders therefore need to ask themselves one very simple question. Is their approach delivering the best possible results, and is it sustainable? This requires a cold, hard look at the evidence and a disavowal of ideologically driven (mal)practices. If the honest answer is no, organisations have a legal and an ethical duty to their stakeholders to change, including for their shareholders' benefit.

Changing to Honeybee leadership

How can managers who are committed to maximising shareholder wealth, but feel uncomfortable about bucking mainstream thinking, break out of this ideological cul-de-sac? They could ease themselves and their organisation into the direction of greater sustainability by embracing socially responsible activities as a form of risk management.[63] Once organisational members realise that sustainable practices also enhance bottom lines, additional measures will become easier and easier to sell. Gradually the organisation and its members will move through Dunphy's phases of sustainability, until eventually the vast majority of organisational members cannot conceive that there could be any other way of doing business. After all, surely every organisation wants to pursue best practice, best employer and best shareholder value status?

It is one thing to have a broad vision, but where do you start in order to shift to more sustainable leadership? It is not enough to simply claim that 'all 23 elements are equally important'. Leaders have to start with manageable changes. This is where our pyramid reflecting an integrated 'theory of sustainable leadership' comes in. The theory identifies 23 practices and five performance outcomes driving sustainability, and shows how they work together. In order for Honeybee practices to have the greatest chance of realisation and to be most beneficial, we believe that they need to be implemented in a hierarchical fashion. Foundation practices provide the basis for all higher-level practices and need to be embedded first. They in turn drive the higher-level practices that then influence the key performance drivers.

So, the place to start is by examining the foundation practices in an organisation. Which ones are already in place? Which others can be introduced relatively quickly and painlessly? Changing from Locust leadership to Honeybee practices, like any other form of change management, is challenging. However, it can be done even by publicly listed enterprises, as the example of Westpac in Box 5–4 shows.

Box 5–4: How Westpac moved from Locust to Honeybee practices

In his final CEO report in the 2007 annual report of Westpac, Dr David Morgan described the transformation of one of Australia's four largest banks. Westpac nearly went out of business in the early 1990s following huge financial losses. This near-disaster provided the impetus for changing from an essentially Locust-led business to an essentially Honeybee enterprise. Outgoing CEO Morgan charted the events over nine of those years, from 1999 until 2007, to provide insight into what this employer of about 28,000 people did to become more sustainable. The success shows up in a decade of consistently strong financial performance, becoming an employer of choice and regaining customer trust as well as becoming a global leader in sustainability.

For Morgan, running a large company requires the integration of an economic system with a social system. These two systems have to work together, and success depends on meshing them as seamlessly as possible. An effective strategy is also key. Westpac's strategy was to move away from a shareholder focus to making the needs of employees and customers core.

The strategy focused on three principles. First was establishing long-term relationships with customers across multiple products. Second, getting the right employees (who espoused the right values) in the right places within the company helped meet the objective of superior execution. This involved developing highly committed and skilled staff to drive success. Third, although the business remained focused on its core markets, additional investment occurred in sectors of strong growth where the company had the talent necessary to succeed.

Regaining the trust of customers and local communities was essential. At the time of its losses in the 1990s, the bank ranked close to the bottom on customer satisfaction among banking clients. The community was up in arms about the Locust practices of banks. Workers were laid off, rural branches closed and bank fees were rising to meet short-term financial objectives. This represented a huge problem for a business based on trust. At this time, Morgan realised the importance of meshing the social and economic systems if the bank was to be sustainable. Angry customers, employees and communities do not contribute to a sustainable business. So Westpac's response was to embed responsible business practices in everything it did.

Reshaping the internal culture was also vital. The company had to redefine what it stood for, where it was heading and how to get there. This meant refining the vision and putting strong ethical and customer-oriented values at the heart of the business. Employees were now rewarded on merit for their effort and successes. The employee mix became more diverse by 2007, with women in 42 per cent of management roles compared with only 25 per cent in 1998. The company became more family friendly, particularly in organising workplace childcare and parental leave. Employees were encouraged to speak up without fear of repercussions. David Morgan travelled around the country twice each year to meet the bank's leaders, disseminate the vision and strategy and listen to what they had to say. The new culture was effective in raising employee commitment from 56 per cent to 71 per cent in 2007, placing Westpac at the top of large Australian enterprises. High levels of engagement and commitment were very helpful in making Westpac a preferred employer in a competitive environment for talent.

Did it work? Yes. Between 2002 and 2010, Westpac has been rated at the top of the banking sector globally in the Dow Jones Sustainability Index. Financially, the bank's efforts have paid off handsomely for shareholders. Over Morgan's nine years at the helm the company's shares outperformed the market, with shareholder returns averaging over 18 per cent per annum compound growth.

Interestingly, the outgoing CEO did not mention environmental sustainability in his final report to stakeholders. However, a glance at the company's website shows that the bank also leads in this arena. Westpac was the first Australian bank, and one of ten founding signatories globally, to the Equator Principles. Under the Equator Principles, signatories agree to provide loans only to those projects whose sponsors can demonstrate their ability and willingness to ensure that projects are developed in a socially responsible manner and according to sound environmental-management practices. It also strives to reduce the environmental effects of its own operations.

> The challenge for Westpac is to continue its Honeybee leadership under future CEOs. It is all too easy to destroy a Honeybee culture through short-term thinking and other Locust practices. Will Westpac revert to Locust leadership?

The challenges in changing to Honeybee sustainable leadership practices become readily apparent by reference to the Sustainable Leadership Pyramid. Not only do the changes have to occur in a logical sequence as described above, but they also have to be handled in a Honeybee manner. This means with due consideration for the short-term and long-term effects on all stakeholders, and in a planned, considered way. When the changes are poorly handled, the performance of firms in the midst of a transition to Honeybee practices may actually suffer. This is because overall systems and processes are disrupted, without realising the intended benefits.

That there are degrees of success at different stages of implementing a change to Honeybee leadership could explain why part way through some managers might feel that the firm is not benefiting from the new practices. Or, to put it another way, if managers are unaware that major changes, such as adopting Honeybee principles, will go through stages of relative success, they may interpret levelling-off periods following the initial introduction as indicating failure. This might lead either to stopping the initiative or to proceeding with it in a half-hearted, pessimistic way. Either reaction could put such initiatives in jeopardy.

Any subsequent gains at the level of individual firms will, over the long term, have a multiplier effect across the entire economy. After all, to the extent that Honeybee firms contribute to the economic, environmental and social health of the communities they serve, they are consolidating their own position further. This is because strong communities make better markets for products and services than weak communities. On top of that, Honeybee leadership underpins employers of choice. Honeybee leadership represents a win–win scenario – for a company and all its stakeholders (including employees, customers, suppliers, the local community) and for future generations.

Honeybee leadership is not just for high-margin businesses. According to retailing giant Wal-Mart's former CEO Lee Scott, shifting to Honeybee leadership saves money even within a low-cost strategy, as Box 5–5 shows. Starting in 2005, Wal-Mart changed its business model from a low–cost, transactional approach to a strategy built on embracing longer–term collaborative relationships with various external stakeholders, including suppliers and customers. The core of the strategy remains low cost. However, this huge retailer has shifted towards a sustainable leadership approach encompassing the entire business. According to its 2008 and 2009 annual reports, Wal-Mart was performing well financially compared with its competitors. This is despite the radical changes it was undergoing.

The attempts to reinvent the organisation along more sustainable lines at Wal-Mart and Westpac are heartening. These large, publicly listed corporations are leading the way. Like Wal-Mart and Westpac, we all have a choice between encouraging honeybee behaviours that add value to the world or behaving like locusts that destroy the world!

Box 5–5: Turning over a new leaf at Wal-Mart[64]

Wal-Mart is America's largest discount retailer. Sam Walton built an empire on a low-cost model that many customers loved. In its 2008 fiscal year the company's roughly two million 'associates' increased its 2007 net sales by 8.6 per cent, to US$375 billion. In 2009, net sales increased a further 7 per cent. In both those years most other retailers were experiencing declines in revenue.

Business was not always going smoothly for this company. Around 2005, Wal-Mart was in deep trouble – the subject of hate blogs, claims about poor labour practices and exploiting employees, criticism for placing burdens on the communities in which it operated and on social welfare programs, as well as disrespect for the environment. Customers were deserting Wal-Mart, which had also largely ignored its other stakeholders. Major investors, such as the Norwegian pension fund NBIM, withdrew their investments in Wal-Mart. Investors were questioning the risks of owning a company that reportedly violated human rights in its business operations, employed minors, tolerated dangerous or unhealthy working conditions at many of its suppliers, systematically discriminated against females with regard to pay, and at times even unreasonably punished and locked up some employees.[65] Things were getting serious for this giant retailer.

In a now-famous speech in 2005, the then CEO and president Lee Scott vowed to change the company's ways and turn over a new leaf. By January 2008, this was well underway as Scott reported to Wal-Mart employees. Here is an extract from that speech:

... 27 months ago today, I spoke with you about leadership in the 21st century. I discussed a range of issues where we could lead and set specific goals to guide our progress.

With the environment, we said that our goals are to be supplied 100 per cent by renewable energy, to create zero waste, and to sell products that sustain our resources and our environment. We also pledged to become more engaged with working conditions in factories, to work for more affordable and accessible health care for associates and customers, and to reflect to an even greater extent the diverse needs and nature of the communities we serve.

... The result: Our customers rewarded us with a 2.4 per cent store sales increase in the US as our competitors were having decreases. Internationally, they rewarded us with an 18.2 per cent increase in net sales ... We have helped our customers live better in so many ways. By reducing our prices on hundreds of common prescriptions to $4, we saved our customers in the US, Mexico, Puerto Rico, and Brazil more than $850 million. Here in the US, you sold 145 million compact fluorescent light bulbs. You saved our customers $4 billion over the life of those bulbs. And in the process, you eliminated the need for three coal-fired power plants.

... It is important for all of us to understand that there are a number of issues facing the world that will profoundly affect our lives and our company. I am talking to you about issues like international trade, climate change, water shortages, social and economic inequities, infrastructure and foreign oil.

... In the years ahead, we might not be able do everything that everyone wants us to do. But we will do things that need to be done and that you and your company can do. Wal-Mart can take a leadership role, get out in front of the future, and make a difference that is good for our business and the world.

Lee Scott then boasted that 93 per cent of Wal-Mart associates have health benefits compared with only 82 per cent of US workers generally. Wal-Mart intends to use its know-how to improve the US health care system overall, making it more affordable and accessible to more people. Wal-Mart intends to lead the way in collaborating with other employers and health care providers to reduce the cost of prescriptions using e-prescribing.

The company will also tackle the rising cost of energy, now that US families spend an estimated 17 per cent of their income on energy. Wal-Mart wants to extend its mission of saving shoppers money to saving them energy costs. It will do this by making sure that the products it sells are energy efficient. By partnering with suppliers to reduce prices on energy-efficient appliances, Wal-Mart plans to help customers make better purchasing decisions and so reduce waste. This retailer is even looking at the possibility of getting involved in energy-efficient automobiles and the renewable energy sector. According to CEO Scott, manufacturers could reduce the amount of energy they use by 20 per cent. Certainly, the company is putting its principles into action at an experimental store in McKinney, Texas, that incorporates many energy-saving and environmentally friendly features. The performance of this store is measured against performance in a nearby Wal-Mart super centre.

The supply chain is also a focus, with ethical suppliers being important to the new Wal-Mart. Suppliers who cheat on the environment, regulations and treatment of their people will cheat on the quality of product they supply to Wal-Mart, Lee Scott claimed. Suppliers who are ethical and responsible in how they do business are much more likely to care about quality and, in doing so, care about customers. Customers want products made in a way that is consistent with their own personal values. This retailer supports 'Fair Trade' and 'Rainforest Alliance' and is promoting organic farming techniques.

Starting with its private brands, Wal-Mart will require suppliers to show that their factories meet specific environmental, social and quality standards. Certification and compliance will form part of supplier agreements. If a supplier fails to improve and fix the problem, Wal-Mart will stop working with that supplier.

To the amazement of many stakeholders who knew Wal-Mart well, the then CEO stated:

> Wal-Mart would favour – and in some cases even pay more – for suppliers that meet our standards and share our commitment to quality and sustainability. Paying more in the short term for quality will mean paying less in the long term as a company. Higher-quality products will mean better value, fewer problems, fewer returns, and greater trust with our customers. Saving people money is a commitment to our customers throughout the life of the product.

Finally, CEO Scott made clear that Wal-Mart people are regarded as the heart of the business. They are the ones who will make the changes happen. Again, a major challenge for Wal-Mart is to maintain the new vision and strategy under new leadership.

notes

1   Berry, 2007; Campbell, 2007
2   Van Veldhoven, 2005
3   Schneider *et al.*, 2003
4   Danford *et al.*, 2005
5   Hung, 2006
6   Leslie, Loch and Schaninger, 2006
7   Feuss *et al.*, 2004
8   Kaplan and Norton, 1996
9   Bassi and McMurrer, 2004
10   Pfau and Cohen, 2003
11   Ichniowski and Shaw, 1999
12   Pfeffer, Hatano and Santalainen, 1995
13   For example Lawler, Mohrman and Ledford, 1995
14   Scotti *et al.*, 2003
15   Ichniowski and Shaw, 1999
16   Gould-Williams, 2003
17   Gelade and Ivey, 2003
18   Marchington and Zagelmeyer, 2005
19   Boselie, Dietz and Boon, 2005; Paauwe and Boselie, 2005
20   For example Harley, 2002
21   Miller and Lee, 2001
22   Van Marrewijk, 2004
23   Flamholtz and Kannan-Narasimhan, 2005
24   Gevity Institute, 2006
25   Zatzick and Iverson, 2006
26   Statement at the AGM by Dr Helmut Panke, then chairman of the Board of Management, BMW AG, 16 May 2006, pp. 17-18
27   Gebert, Boerner and Lanwehr, 2003
28   Hee-Jae Cho and Pucik, 2005
29   Grewal and Slotegraaf, 2007, pp. 455 and 478
30   Horgan and Mühlau, 2006
31   Deshpandé, Farley and Webster, 2000
32   For example Ghoshal, 2005
33   Parker, 2007
34   For example Stewart, 2004
35   For example Stiglitz, 2002
36   For example Saving Germany's auto industry, 2004
37   For example Kennedy, 2000
38   For example Drucker, 2003; World Economic Forum, 2004
39   Gumbel, 2005
40   Balzli and Reuter, 2006
41   Kucher and Meitner, 2004
42   World Economic Forum, 2008
43   Gumbel, 2005
44   World Business Council for Sustainable Development and the UN Environment Program Finance Initiative, 2004, p. 4
45   World Economic Forum, 2005
46   Benson, Young and Lawler, 2006
47   World Business Council for Sustainable Development and the UN Environment Program Finance Initiative, 2004
48   Mills *et al.*, 2001
49   For example UN Environment Program Finance Initiative, 2004
50   Hoje, 2003
51   McConnell, 2005
52   Sethi, 2005
53   http://www.norges-bank.no/default_25991.aspx; accessed 9 February 2009

54   View the exclusions at http://www.regjeringen.no/en/dep/fin/Selected-topics/andre/ Ethical-Guidelines-for-the-Government-Pension-Fund_Global-/companies-excluded-from-the-investment-u.html?id=447122; accessed 9 February 2009

55   http://sustainability.munichre.com/en/economy/investor_shares/default.aspx; accessed 9 February 2009

56   KPMG, 2005

57   KPMG, 2005

58   Perrini, 2006

59   http://www.roche.com/home/sustainability.htm; accessed 14 February 2010

60   http://www.roche.com/home/sustainability.htm; accessed 14 February 2010

61   http://www.unpri.org/principles/; accessed 27 January 2008

62   Murray, 2007

63   Godfrey, 2005

64   Based on a speech given by CEO and President Lee Scott at the Wal-Mart US Year Beginning Meeting; January 2008; http://walmartstores.com/FactsNews/NewsRoom/7896.aspx; accessed 12 June 2008

65   See details at http://www.regjeringen.no/en/dep/fin/Selected-topics/andre/Ethical-Guidelines-for-the-Government-Pension-Fund_Global-/Recommendations-and-Letters-from-the-Advisory-Council-on-Ethics/Recommendation-of-15-November-2005.html?id=4 50120&epslanguage=EN-GB; accessed 9 February 2009

Epilogue

After the Global Financial Crisis

You might be wondering what has happened to the organisations mentioned in this book since the global financial crisis (GFC). Although it is too early too tell with any certainty at the time of going to press in early 2010, many Honeybee firms have experienced challenges but appear to be performing better than their competitors. In this brief epilogue, we report on firms mentioned more than once or highlighted in a box in the book where financial information is available.

We begin with the automobile industry, which experienced severe turbulence during 2008 and 2009 when all manufacturers suffered reduced sales. However, the Honeybee-oriented carmakers seem to have suffered less in financial terms than their Locust counterparts. BMW reported only a moderate drop in revenues, posting a small profit at the end of 2009. For Porsche, 2009 was a turbulent time in addition to experiencing a drop in sales. The GFC hit Porsche hard as it tried to refinance a large debt incurred in its earlier attempt to take over VW. Instead, Porsche will become fully integrated into the VW Group in 2010. Nonetheless, the company said that it had employed 3.5 per cent more people at the end of 2009. Toyota posted losses in the third quarter of 2009, but continued to suffer in 2010 because of serious quality problems resulting in major recalls of many of its brands. More recent figures are not available. Honda reported lower net income for 2009, with car sales down 10 per cent and motorcycle sales dropping by 8.5 per cent. However, like Porsche, Honda increased the number of employees during the GFC.

The problems encountered by the Japanese and European car manufacturers are not as great as those experienced by their Locust counterparts GM and Chrysler. Both these firms filed for bankruptcy in 2009 and relied on billions of dollars in government loans to survive into 2010. Ford, which is still associated with the founding family, posted a small profit without relying on any government bailouts.

Moving on to those members of the finance sector that we mention in this book, the banks seem to have posted profits at the end of 2009. Bendigo and Adelaide Bank posted a reduced profit of A$173 million, down 26 per cent on 2009. Munich Reinsurance's 2009 figures show an increased profit of nearly €1 billion over 2008 (€2.56 billion compared with €1.58 billion in 2008). Westpac's net profit decline of 10.7 per cent in 2009 was followed by a substantial profit of about A$1.6 billion reported in its first 2010 quarter. Troubled UBS returned to profitability in the fourth quarter of 2009 following substantial staff and cost cutting, and strengthened governance procedures. In 2009, HSBC and Allianz posted 'solid' results.

Retail performance was mixed. Wal-Mart reported strong performance during the GFC with a 7 per cent increase in net sales, earnings per share up 6 per cent and 33,000 new jobs created in the USA alone. The story was different for the Swiss conglomerate Migros, which experienced a 2.4 per cent drop in its retail sales in 2009 down to CHF21.04 billion. The results for Nordstrom's fiscal year, ending 31 January 2010, show a 10 per cent increase in net earnings over the previous year to US$441 million.

Both the pharmaceutical companies in our sample performed very well in 2009. Novartis posted record results with sales up 7 per cent, enabling it to issue its 13th consecutive dividend increase. Roche reported yet another group sales record and record earnings per share. Clearly, these pharmaceutical giants did not suffer noticeably during the GFC.

During the GFC, the travel business was in trouble as Marriott Hotels and Continental Airlines demonstrate. Marriott's revenues declined from US$12.9 billion in 2008 to US$10.9 billion in 2009. Continental reported a full year loss due to the effects of the GFC of $US295 million.

Companies involved in the construction industry also experienced difficulties in 2009. Global building materials supplier Holcim attributed its loss of revenues in 2009 to the GFC, including the 18 per cent drop in the third quarter. Part of WACKER chemicals is involved in construction with its paints and silicones. Despite lower sales in 2009, WACKER reported stable performance over that fiscal year. Seele, privately held manufacturer of glass and steel façades, roofs and other elements, has not released its 2009 figures.

Manufacturers described in this book who have reported their 2009 results have fared quite well despite the GFC, but most have not issued their results at the time of writing. Aesculap, maker of surgical instruments, reported a 6 per cent increase in sales and a 5 per cent increase in profit in 2009. W.L. Gore & Associates achieved global sales of US$2.5 billion, an increase of about 25 per cent over 2008. Atlas Copco indicated profitability in 2009 and issued dividends. Colgate achieved double-digit earnings growth in 2009. No 2009 financial information has been published for the privately held firms Giesecke & Devrient, Kärcher, Rohde & Schwarz, Sa Paper Preservation House or for the city-owned ZF Friedrichshafen. However, Kärcher had reported its highest ever turnover (€1.4 billion) from record unit sales of 6.38 million in 2008. Finally, ITT Corporation, with approximately 40,000 employees engaged in high-technology engineering and manufacturing, delivered revenues of US$10.9 billion in 2009 after five years of record growth. The company continues to position itself for future growth.

Turning to the information and communications sectors, Huawei reported contract sales of US$30.2 billion in 2009, a 30 per cent increase over 2008. For SAS software the story is also positive. SAS revenues increased in 2008 and grew to US$2.31 billion in 2009 despite the GFC, and the company invested 23 per cent of its revenues in R&D. However, Nokia suffered a serious decline in revenues and profits. Preliminary 2009 figures show net sales are down 19 per cent, with a fall in profits of about 76 per cent.

Three service enterprises remain – Fraunhofer, IBM and UPS. In 2009 IBM achieved record net income of US$13.4 billion, an increase of 9 per cent on 2008. This represented the seventh year of double-digit growth in earnings per share. Reports for the 2009 performance of the remaining two firms are not available. However, commercial research organisation Fraunhofer reported an increase in net profits over 2008 in the third quarter of 2009. Judging by its quarterly reports, UPS's revenues in 2009 are down on 2008.

Honeybee enterprises take a long-term perspective and so should we in evaluating the performance of these enterprises post-GFC. It is too early to assess how they have performed following the GFC.

Appendix A

Sustainable Leadership Questionnaire

We have developed a measuring instrument that assesses the extent to which an organisation complies with the 23 sustainable leadership elements. The outcome indicates whether people surveyed within the organisation perceive each practice as being more Honeybee-oriented or Locust-oriented. The degree of consistency with Honeybee practices as seen by the respondents is indicated graphically in the feedback.

The simple on-line questionnaire can be completed by individuals in different parts of an enterprise (for example sales, service or manufacturing), as well as by people at different levels (for example top team, middle management, frontline staff) and in different locations. If stakeholder surveys are not required, the same instrument can be used as a discussion tool for senior executives to check off how well their firm conforms to individual sustainable leadership practices. Alternatively, both methods can be combined: the perceptions of managers, staff and suppliers from different parts of the business can feed into top-team discussions. These discussions can be facilitated by experts in sustainable leadership, if required.

The Sustainable Leadership Questionnaire can be used to direct and monitor changes to a firm's practices. For example, if some of the foundation elements in the Sustainable Leadership Pyramid are perceived as weak, management can begin to develop and introduce policies and procedures to address the gaps. Similarly, if higher-level practices are of concern, management can check whether all the appropriate foundation elements are in place. The process can also work top down in that, if customer satisfaction or the firm's brand and reputation are slipping, the practices supporting those outcomes can be examined.

For detailed information on the Sustainable Leadership Questionnaire and associated processes, please contact the authors at: slq@the-isl.com.

Appendix B

Approach to Research

Much of the evidence used in *Sustainable Leadership* has come from research into a wide range of organisations on various continents. This consists of both academic research and our own observations derived from face-to-face visits of best-practice organisations, usually to the firm's headquarters. To date we have personally met senior managers in 35 enterprises for between four and 44 hours after analysing information available in the public arena about their business. In many cases we met executives on several occasions, enabling us to track their progress over time.

Some evidence was garnered first-hand by such colleagues as Dr Sooksan Kantabutra from Mahidol University, Thailand, to whom we are very grateful. A few organisations mentioned in this book were researched externally only, using such sources as annual reports, firm websites, media reports and published articles.

As part of the process, we reviewed the published research evidence on the practices we observed then discussed them with the managers, refining the sustainable leadership practices over ten years. Where possible we verified our understandings in discussions with employees, by observing the firm's operations and comparing observations with information contained in extensive written briefing reports that were sent to the firms before the visits.

Enterprises that we visited were selected because they do things differently and were willing to discuss their practices. They represent a wide variety of industries – from construction to applied research, from manufacturers to service providers. The firms differ in terms of such factors as their global presence, longevity, size, type of ownership, (mis)fit with the Honeybee leadership model and performance.

Regarding global presence, a few organisations are primarily national (for example Migros in Switzerland, Bendigo and Adelaide Bank and Westpac in Australia, Sa Paper Preservation House in Thailand, Nordstrom and Wal-Mart in the USA). Most, however, are strong global players (for example BMW, Continental Airlines, Roche, Huawei Technologies, Marriott International Hotels, Munich Reinsurance and SAS).

The firms' ages ranged between approximately 20 to 150 years. Longevity cannot be claimed for the youngest firms, but they were included for other reasons. For example, Seele was chosen because it was profitable and expanding at a time when the rest of the German construction industry was in a decade-long downturn. Novartis, although young itself, was created from the merger of several much older pharmaceutical firms.

The smallest example (Sa Paper Preservation House) employed about 500 people; the largest (IBM) about 330,000. Ownership also varied, ranging from family owned and family run, family owned but run by professional management, publicly listed but still substantially family controlled, publicly listed and not related to the founders, to government-supported and not-for-profit organisations.

As to (mis)fit with the Honeybee leadership model, the majority of organisations could be regarded as Honeybee organisations at the time they were studied. However, we also include some organisations that were Honeybee on some practices and Locust on others, as well as corporations changing to Honeybee practices. However, our examples come mainly from Honeybee organisations in order to show the many different ways in which these practices can be implemented. There is no one-size-fits-all answer on how to achieve sustainability. Within the framework of the Honeybee philosophy, many variations are possible. Family friendly policies in Thailand might take a completely different form from family friendly policies in the USA. The key issue is that they are perceived as family friendly by the relevant stakeholders.

Importantly, the firms we studied included some facing performance issues. As Rosenzweig[1] has pointed out, this is important and addresses a serious deficit he saw in others' work. The problem arises when researchers identify organisations that appear to be best practice at the time, and then examine them for commonalities. The concern is that the commonalities may have been attributed to the organisations precisely because they appeared to be doing well. In other words, it is not certain that these firms ever possessed these characteristics. We included enterprises in various stages of performance at the time.

For *Sustainable Leadership*, we sought as much data independence as possible. For each one of the 23 sustainable leadership elements, we scoured the literature for empirical data on organisational performance based on that factor alone. For example, we examined whether the amount of training that people received affects organisational performance, whether high-trust organisations outperform low-trust organisations and so on. We found notable differences in performance on each of the 23 factors, depending on the nature of a particular practice. For 21 of these practices, the research evidence is strong to very strong and in two cases it is indirect. It seems cogent to argue that organisations that embrace high-performance practices should benefit. Research is still needed into the direct effects of the other two variables on organisational performance, but there is indirect support for their contribution.

We have striven to avoid potential bias, in which errors are distributed in some systematic way.[2] It may be that the research into our 23 factors (all of which involves multiple sources) contains some bias that we were not aware of. It is unlikely, however, that across all 23 elements any such bias would be in the same direction. In other words, while we accept that there may be 'noise' or randomly distributed errors, we strove to prevent systematic bias.

A further challenge has been that the economic high performance of some organisations (for example, those closely held by families) is difficult to verify. It has to be deduced from circumstantial evidence such as growth rates, listings on best-employer rankings, sustainability indices, brand and reputation, longevity (in particular the ability to survive major social or economic upheavals), peer reviews, counter-market performance and other indirect indicators of success. We emphasise that this problem applies to some of the organisations only. While it is entirely possible that we have misattributed high performance to one or other of this group of companies at a particular time, we are confident that most of the ones following Honeybee practices are likely to be high performers over time. If some of them are or become low performers this does not necessarily weaken our argument. As already noted, while companies may have good practices in place, if they make the wrong strategic decisions the best processes will not help them perform well.

Finally, since the observations made about company practices in this book were made, some may have changed some of those practices.

notes

1   Rosenzweig, 2007
2   Rosenzweig, 2007, p. 13

References

Adams, F.A. III, True, S.L. and Winsor, R.D. (2002) Corporate America's search for the 'right' direction: Outlook and opportunities for family firms. *Family Business Review*, 15(4), 269–76.

Addison, J.T. and Belfield, C.R. (2000) The impact of financial participation and employee involvement on financial performance: A re-estimation using the 1998 WERS. *Scottish Journal of Political Economy*, 47(5), 571–84.

—— (2001) Updating the determinants of firm performance: Estimation using the 1998 UK Workplace Employee Relations Survey. *British Journal of Industrial Relations*, 39(3), 341–67.

Aguinis, H. and Kraiger, K. (2009) Benefits of training and development for individuals and teams, organizations, and Society. *Annual Review of Psychology*, 60, 451–74.

Albert, M. (1992) The Rhine model of capitalism: An investigation. *European Business Journal*, 4(3), 8–22.

—— (1993) *Capitalism vs Capitalism: How America's Obsession with Individual Achievement and Short-term Profit has Led it to the Brink of Collapse.* New York: Four Walls Eight Windows.

Alexander, J.A., Weiner, B. and Griffith, J. (2006) Quality improvement and hospital financial performance. *Journal of Organizational Behavior*, 27(7), 1003–29.

Alexiou, C. and Tsaliki, P. (2009) Unemployment revisited: Empirical evidence from 20 OECD countries. *Contributions to Political Economy*, 28(1), 23–34.

Allen, N.J. and Hecht, T.D. (2004) The 'romance of teams': Toward an understanding of its psychological underpinnings and implications. *Journal of Occupational and Organizational Psychology*, 77(4), 439–62.

Allen, N.J. and Meyer, J.P. (1990) The measurement and antecedents of affective, continuance and normative commitment to the organization. *Journal of Occupational Psychology*, 63(1), 1–18.

Amalric, F. and Hauser, J. (2005) Economic drivers of corporate responsibility activities. *Journal of Corporate Citizenship*, 20, 27–38.

Anderson, E.W., Fornell, C. and Lehmann, D.R. (1994) Customer satisfaction, market share and profitability: Findings from Sweden. *Journal of Marketing*, 58, July, 53–66.

Anderson, E.W., Fornell, C. and Mazvancheryl, S.K. (2004) Customer satisfaction and shareholder value. *Journal of Marketing*, 68(4), 172–85.

Anderson, R.C. and Reeb, D.M. (2003) Founding-family ownership and firm performance: Evidence from the S&P 500. *Journal of Finance*, 58(3), 1301–27.

Asch, S.E. (1963) Effects of group pressure on the modification and distortion of judgment. In H. Guetzkow (ed.), *Groups, Leadership and Men*. New York: Russell & Russell.

Atchison, T. (1999) The myths of employee satisfaction. *Healthcare Executive*, March/April, 19–23.

Avery, G.C. (2004) *Understanding Leadership: Paradigms and Cases*. London: Sage.

—— (2005) *Leadership for Sustainable Futures: Achieving Success in a Competitive World*. Cheltenham, UK and Northampton, MA: Edward Elgar.

Babakus, E., Bienstock, C.C. and Van Scotter, J.R. (2004) Linking perceived quality and customer satisfaction to store traffic and revenue. *Decision Sciences*, 35(4), 713–37.

Bakker, A.B., Schaufeli, W.B., Leiter, M.P. and Taris, T.W. (2008) Work engagement: An emerging concept in occupational health psychology. *Work and Stress*, 22(3), 187–200.

Balasubramanian, S.K., Mathur, I. and Thakur, R. (2005) The impact of high-quality firm achievements on shareholder value: Focus on Malcolm Baldrige and J.D. Power and Associates awards. *Journal of the Academy of Marketing Science*, 33(4), 413–22.

Balthazard, P.A., Cooke, R.A. and Potter, R.E. (2006) Dysfunctional culture, dysfunctional organization: Capturing the behavioral norms that form organizational culture and drive performance. *Journal of Managerial Psychology*, 21(8), 709–32.

Balzli, B. and Reuter, W. (2006) Übernahmen: Verraten und verkauft. *Der Spiegel*, 14/2006, p. 84.

Bansal, P. (2002) The corporate challenges of sustainable development. *Academy of Management Executive*, 16(2), 122–31.

Barling, J., Weber, T. and Kelloway, E.K. (1996) Effects of transformational leadership training on attitudinal and financial outcomes: A field experiment. *Journal of Applied Psychology*, 81, 827–32.

Barnett, M.L. and Salomon, R.M. (2006) Beyond dichotomy: The curvilinear relationship between social responsibility and financial performance. *Strategic Management Journal*, 27(11), 1101–22.

Bartel, A., Freeman, R., Ichinowski, C. and Kleiner, M. (2004) Can a work organization have an attitude problem? The impact of workplaces on employee attitude and economic outcomes. Centre for Economic Performance, London School of Economics, CEP Discussion Paper.

Bassi, L. and McMurrer, D. (2004) How's your return on people? *Harvard Business Review*, 82(3), 18.

Batory, S.S., Neese, W. and Heineman, A. (2005) Ethical marketing practices: An investigation of antecedents, innovativeness and business performance. *Journal of American Academy of Business*, 6(2), 135–42.

Batt, R. (1999) Work organization, technology, and performance in customer service and sales. *Industrial and Labor Relations Review*, 52(4), 539–64.

Baum, J.R., Locke, E.A. and Kirkpatrick, S.A. (1998) A longitudinal study of the relation of vision and vision communication to venture growth in entrepreneurial firms. *Journal of Applied Psychology*, 83, 43–54.

Bazerman, M.H. and Gillespie, J.J. (1999) Betting on the future: The virtues of contingent contracts. *Harvard Business Review*, 77(5), 155–60.

Becker, B.E., Huselid, M.A., Pickus, P.S. and Spratt, M.F. (1997) HR as a source of shareholder value: Research and recommendations. *Human Resource Management*, 36(1), 39–47.

Bell, A. (2004) W.L. Gore & Associates, Inc.: Natural leadership. In G.C. Avery (2004), op. cit., pp. 171–87.

Bennis, W. (2003) Flight of the phoenix: Authentic leaders find a way to fly. *Executive Excellence*, Australian edition, 20(5), 2–5.

Benson, G.S., Young, S.M. and Lawler III, E.E. (2006) High-involvement work practices and analysts' forecasts of corporate earnings. *Human Resources Management*, 45(4), 519–37.

Berman, S.L., Wicks, A.C., Kotha, S. and Jones, T.M. (1999) Does stakeholder orientation matter? The relationship between stakeholder management models and firm financial performance. *Academy of Management Journal*, 42, 488–506.

Bernhardt, K.L., Donthu, N. and Kennett, P.A. (2000) A longitudinal analysis of satisfaction and profitability. *Journal of Business Research*, 47(2), 161–71.

Bernthal, P. and Wellins, R. (2006) Trends in leader development and succession. *Human Resource Planning*, 29(2), 31–40.

Berry, L.L. (2007) The best companies are generous companies. *Business Horizons*, 50(4), 263–9.

Bhaskaran, S. (2006) Incremental innovation and business performance: Small and medium-size food enterprises in a concentrated industry environment. *Journal of Small Business Management*, 44(1), 64–80.

Bianco, A., Lavelle, L., Merritt, J. and Barrett, A. (2000) The CEO trap: Looking for superheroes to deliver sky-high growth ensures disappointment. *Business Week*, 11(37), 86–92.

Bird, A. (1995) Performance measurement for the financial services industry, *Community Banker*, 1, 7–10.

Boeker, W. and Goodstein, J. (1993) Performance and successor choice: The moderating effects of governance and ownership, *Academy of Management Journal*, 36(1), 172–86.

Bolton, R.N. and Drew, J.H. (1991) A multistage model of customers' assessments of service quality and value. *Journal of Consumer Research*, 17(4), 375–84.

Boning, B., Ichniowski, C. and Shaw, K. (2001) Opportunity counts: Teams and the effectiveness of production incentives. National Bureau of Economic Research, Inc. NBER Working paper, no. 8306.

Booz Allen Hamilton (2003) Results of global CEO survey. Published in *strategy + business in 2002*.

Boselie, P., Dietz, G. and Boon, C. (2005) Commonalities and contradictions in HRM and performance research. *Human Resource Management Journal*, 15(3), 67–94.

Brammer, S.J. and Pavelin, S. (2006) Corporate reputation and social performance: The importance of fit. *Journal of Management Studies*, 43(3), 435–55.

Bronars, S.G., Deere, D.R. and Tracy, J.S. (1994) The effects of unions on firm behavior: An empirical analysis using firm-level data. *Industrial Relations*, 33(4), 426–52.

Burla, S., Alioth, A., Frei, F. and Müller, W.R. (1994) *Die Erfindung von Führung: Vom Mythos der Machbarkeit in der Führungsausbildung*. Zürich: Verlag der Fachvereine.

Caldwell, C. and Karri, R. (2005) Organizational governance and ethical systems: A covenantal approach to building trust. *Journal of Business Ethics*, 58, 249–59.

Cameron, K. (2006) Good or not bad: Standards and ethics in managing change. *Academy of Management Learning and Education*, 5(3), 317–23.

Cameron, K., Bright, D. and Caza, A. (2004) Exploring the relationships between organizational virtuousness and performance. *American Behavioral Scientist*, 47, 766–90.

Campbell, J.L. (2007) Why would corporations behave in socially responsible ways? An institutional theory of corporate social responsibility. *Academy of Management Review*, 32(3), 946–67.

Carlson, K.A. and Russo, J.E. (2001) Biased interpretation of evidence by mock jurors. *Journal of Experimental Psychology: Applied*, 7(2), 104–11.

Carmeli, A., Gilat, G. and Waldman, D.A. (2007) The role of perceived organizational performance in organizational identification, adjustment and job performance. *Journal of Management Studies*, 44(6), 972–92.

Carmeli, A., Gilat, G. and Weisberg, J. (2006) Perceived external prestige, organizational identification and affective commitment: A stakeholder approach. *Corporate Reputation Review*, 9(2), 92–104.

Carmeli, A., Meitar, R. and Weisberg, J. (2006) Self-leadership skills and innovative behavior at work. *International Journal of Manpower*, 27(1), 75–90.

Carmeli, A. and Tishler, A. (2004a) Resources, capabilities, and the performance of industrial firms: A multivariate analysis. *Managerial and Decision Economics*, 25(6/7), 299–315.

—— (2004b) The relationships between intangible organizational elements and organizational performance. *Strategic Management Journal*, 25(13), 1257–78.

—— (2005) Perceived organizational reputation and organizational performance: An empirical investigation of industrial enterprises. *Corporate Reputation Review*, 8(1), 13–30.

Carpenter, M.A., Geletkanycz, M.A. and Sanders, W.G. (2004) Upper echelons research revisited: Antecedents, elements and consequences of top management team composition. *Journal of Management*, 30(6), 749–78.

Cascio, W. (2002) *Responsible Restructuring: Creative and Profitable Alternatives to Layoffs*. San Francisco, CA: Berrett-Koehler.

Castillo, J. (2003) Challenging the knowledge management mystique: An exploratory study on the performance of knowledge managing companies. *Journal of Management Research*, 3(3), 152–71.

Certo, S.T., Lester, R.H., Dalton, C.M. and Dalton, D.R. (2006) Top management teams. Strategy and financial performance: A meta-analytic examination. *Journal of Management Studies*, 43(4), 813–39.

Champlin, D.P. and Knoedler, J.T. (2003) Corporations, workers, and the public interest. *Journal of Economic Issues*, 37(2), 305ff.

Chan, K.C., Gee, M.V. and Steiner, T.L. (2000) Employee happiness and corporate financial performance. *Financial Practice and Education*, 10(2), 47–52.

Charreaux, G. and Desbrieres, P. (2001) Corporate governance: Stakeholder value versus shareholder value. *Journal of Management and Governance*, 5(2), 107–28.

Chatman, J.A. (1991) Matching people and organizations: Selection and socialization in public accounting firms. *Administrative Science Quarterly*, 36(3), 459–84.

Chen, Z.X. and Aryee, S. (2007) Delegation and employee work outcomes: An examination of the cultural context of mediating processes in China. *Academy of Management Journal*, 50(1), 226–38.

Cheng, Y.C. and Cheung, W.M. (2004) Four types of school environment: Multilevel self-management and educational quality. *Educational Research and Evaluation*, 10(1), 71–100.

Christensen, C.M., Kaufman, S.P. and Shih, W.C. (2008) Innovation killers: How financial tools destroy your capacity to do new things. *Harvard Business Review*, 86(1), 98–105.

Chun, R. (2006) Corporate reputation: Meaning and measurement. *International Journal of Management Reviews*, 7(2), 91–109.

Chun, R. and Davies, G. (2006) The influence of corporate character on customers and employees: Exploring similarities and differences. *Journal of the Academy of Marketing Science*, 34(2), 138–46.

Chung-Leung, L., Yau, O.H.M., Tse, A.C.B., Sin, L.Y.M. and Chow, R.P.M. (2005) Stakeholder orientation and business performance: The case of service companies in China. *Journal of International Marketing*, 13(1), 89–110.

Clutterbuck, D. (1998) Handing over the reins: Should the CEO's successor be an insider or an outsider? *Corporate Governance: An International Review*, 6(2), 78–85.

Collins, J. (2001a) Level 5 leadership: The triumph of humility and fierce resolve. *Harvard Business Review*, 79(1), 67–76.

—— (2001b) *Good to Great: Why Some Companies Make the Leap and Others Don't*. New York: HarperCollins.

Collins, J. and Porras, J. (1994) *Built to Last*. New York: HarperCollins.

Connolly, T., Conlon, E.J. and Deutsch, S.J. (1980) Organizational effectiveness: A multiple-constituency approach. *Academy of Management Review*, 5(2), 211–17.

Cooney, R. (2004) Empowered self-management and the design of work teams. *Personnel Review*, 33(6), 677–92.

Copeland, T. and Dolgoff, A. (2006) Expectations-based management. *Journal of Applied Corporate Finance*, 18(2), 82–97.

Corbett, C.J., Montes-Sancho, M.J. and Kirsch, D.A. (2005) The financial impact of ISO 9000 certification in the United States: An empirical analysis. *Management Science*, 51(7), 1046–59.

Corsten, D. and Felde, J. (2005) Exploring the performance effects of key-supplier collaboration: An empirical investigation into Swiss buyer–supplier relationships. *International Journal of Physical Distribution & Logistics Management*, 35(6), 445–61.

Covey, S. (2003) Seven habits revisited. *Executive Excellence*, Australian edition, 20(5), 7–8.

Cropanzano, R. and Wright, T. A. (2001) When a 'happy' worker is really a 'productive' worker. *Consulting Psychology Journal: Practice and Research*, 53(3), 182–99.

Danford, A., Richardson, M., Stewart, P., Tailby, S. and Upchurch, M. (2005) Workplace partnership and employee voice in the UK: Comparative case studies of union strategy and worker experience. *Economic and Industrial Democracy*, 26(4), 593–620.

Davis, J.H., Schoorman, F.D., Mayer, R.C. and Hwee, H.T. (2000) The trusted general manager and business unit performance: Empirical evidence of a competitive advantage. *Strategic Management Journal*, 21(5), 563–76.

Deepak, S., Singh, J. and Sabol, B. (2002) Consumer trust, value and loyalty in relational exchanges. *Journal of Marketing*, 66(1), 15–37.

De Grauwe, P. and Camerman, F. (2002) How big are the big multinational companies? *Tijdschrift voor Economie en Management*, 47(3), 311–26.

DeGroot, T., Kiker, D.S. and Cross, T. (2000) A meta-analysis to review organizational outcomes under charismatic leadership. *Canadian Journal of Administrative Sciences*, 17(4), 3.

De Leede, J., Nijhof, A.H.J. and Fisscher, O.A.M. (1999) The myth of self-managing teams: A reflection on the allocation of responsibilities. *Journal of Business Ethics*, 21(2/3), 203–15.

Denison, D. (1984) Bringing corporate culture to the bottom line. *Organizational Dynamics*, 13(2), 4–22.

Dennis, B., D'Intino, R.S., Houghton, J.D., Neck, C.P. and Boyles, T. (2008) Corporate social performance: Creating resources to help organizations excel. *Global Business and Organizational Excellence*, 27(2), 26–41.

Deshpandé, R., Farley, J.U. and Webster, F.E. (2000) Triad lessons: Generalizing results on high performance firms in five business-to-business markets. *International Journal of Research in Marketing*, 17, 353–62.

Dess, G.G. and Shaw, J.D. (2001) Voluntary turnover, social capital, and organizational performance. *Academy of Management Review*, 26, 446–56.

DeVaro, J. (2006) Teams, autonomy, and the financial performance of firms. *Industrial Relations*, 45(2), 217–69.

De Vries, R.E., Roe, R.A., Tharsi, C.B. and Taillieu, T.C.B. (1998) Need for supervision: Its impact on leadership effectiveness. *Journal of Applied Behavioral Science*, 34(4), 486–501.

De Wet, J.H.v.H. and du Toit, E. (2007) Return on equity: A popular but flawed measure of corporate financial performance. *South African Journal of Business Management*, 38(1), 59–69.

Djordjević, B. and Djukić, S. (2008) The impact of downsizing on the corporate reputation. *Economics and Organization*, 5(1), 51–62.

Dönch, U. and Frank, S. (2006) Um drei Uhr wecken. *Focus*, 13, 206–9.

Dose, J.J. and Klimoski, R.J. (1995) Doing the right thing in the workplace: Responsibility in the face of accountability. *Employee Responsibilities and Rights Journal*, 8(1), 35–6.

Dröge, C., Claycomb, C. and Germain, R. (2003) Does knowledge mediate the effect of context on performance? Some initial evidence. *Decision Sciences*, 34(3), 541–68.

Drucker, P.F. (2003) Future of management. *Executive Excellence*, Australian edition, 20(5), 3.

—— (2006) They're not employees, they're people. Extract reprinted in *Harvard Business Review*, 84(2), 152.

D'Souza, R.M., Strazdins, L., Clements, M.S., Broom, D.H., Parslow, R. and Rodgers, B. (2005) The health effects of jobs: Status, working conditions, or both? *Australian and New Zealand Journal of Public Health*, 29(3), 222–8.

Dunphy, D. (2003) Corporate sustainability: Challenge to managerial orthodoxies. *Journal of the Australian and New Zealand Academy of Management*, 9(1), 2–11.

Dunphy, D., Griffiths, A. and Benn, S. (2003) *Organizational Change for Corporate Sustainability*. London: Routledge.

Dyer, J.H. and Singh, H. (1998) The relational view: Cooperative strategy and sources of interorganizational competitive advantage. *Academy of Management Review*, 23, 660–97.

Eberl, M. and Schwaiger, M. (2004) Corporate reputation: Disentangling the effects on financial performance. *European Journal of Marketing*, 39(7/8), 838–54.

Edmondson, A.C., Roberto, M.A. and Watkins, M.D. (2003) A dynamic model of top management team effectiveness: Managing unstructured task streams. *Leadership Quarterly*, 14, 297–325.

Elkington, J. (2001) *The Chrysalis Economy: How Citizen CEOs and Corporations can Fuse Values and Value Creation*. Oxford: Capstone Publishing Ltd.

Ettling, J.T. and Jago, A.G. (1988) Participation under conditions of conflict: More on the validity of the Vroom–Yetton model. *Journal of Management Studies*, 25(1), 73–83.

Evans, W.R. and Davis, W.D. (2005) High-performance work systems and organizational performance: The mediating role of internal social structure. *Journal of Management*, 31(5), 758–75.

Ewing, B.T. and Wunnava, P.V. (2004) The trade-off between supervision cost and performance based pay: Does gender matter? *Small Business Economics*, 23, 453–60.

Ferris, G.R., Mitchell, T.R., Canavan, P.J., Frink, D.D. and Hopper, H. (1995) Accountability in human resources systems. In G.R. Ferris, S.D. Rosen and D.T. Basman (eds), *Handbook of Human Resource Management*, pp. 175–96. Oxford: Blackwell Business.

Fessler, D.M.T. (2001) Emotions and cost-benefit assessment. In G. Gigerenzer and R. Selten (eds), *Bounded Rationality: The Adaptive Toolbox*, pp. 191–214. Cambridge, MA: MIT Press.

Feuss, W.J., Harmon, J., Wirtenberg, J. and Wides, J. (2004) Linking employees, customers, and financial performance in organizations. *Journal of Cost Management*, 18(1), 12–22.

Finkelstein, S. and Hambrick, D.C. (1996) *Strategic Leadership: Top Executives and their Effects on Organizations*. Minneapolis: West Publishing Company.

Flamholtz, E. and Kannan-Narasimhan, R. (2005) Differential impact of cultural elements on financial performance. *European Management Journal*, 23(1), 50–64.

Flood, P.C., Hannan, E., Smith, K.G., Turner, T., West, M.A. and Dawson, J. (2000) Chief executive leadership style, consensus decision making, and top management team effectiveness. *European Journal of Work and Organizational Psychology*, 9(3), 401–20.

Florida, R. and Goodnight, J. (2005) Managing for creativity. *Harvard Business Review*, 83(7), 124–31.

Freeman, R.B. and Rogers, J. (1999) *What Workers Want*. Ithaca, NY: Russell Sage Foundation.

Fulmer, I.S., Gerhart, B. and Scott, K.S. (2003) Are the 100 Best better? An empirical investigation of the relationship between being a 'great place to work' and firm performance. *Personnel Psychology*, 56(4), 65–93.

Gallo, M.A. (2004) The family business and its social responsibilities. *Family Business Review*, 17(2), 135–49.

Gandossy, R. and Kao, T. (2004) Talent wars: Out of mind, out of practice. *Human Resource Planning*, 27(4), 15–19.

Gant, J., Ichniowski, C. and Shaw, K. (2002) Social capital and organizational change in high-involvement and traditional work organizations. *Journal of Economics and Management Strategy*, 11(2), 289–328.

Gates, S. (2000) Strategic performance measurement systems: Translating strategy into results. *Bank of America Journal of Applied Corporate Finance*, 13(3), 44–59.

Gebert, D., Boerner, S. and Lanwehr, R. (2003) The risks of autonomy: Empirical evidence for the necessity of a balance management in promoting organizational innovativeness. *Creativity and Innovation Management*, 12(1), 41–9.

Gelade, G.A. and Ivey, M. (2003) The impact of human resource management and work climate on organizational performance. *Personnel Psychology*, 56(2), 383–404.

Gelb, D.S. and Strawer, J.A. (2001) Corporate social responsibility and financial disclosures: An alternative explanation for increased disclosure. *Journal of Business Ethics*, 33(1), 1–13.

Geneen, H. (2000) The essential elements. In P. Krass (ed.) (2000), *The Book of Management Wisdom: Classic Writings by Great Business Leaders*. Indianapolis, IN: John Wiley & Sons.

Gevity Institute (2006) Establishing a link between HR management and firm profitability. Compensation and Benefits for Law Offices, 2–4 January. www.ioma.com; accessed February 2006.

Ghoshal, S. (2005) Bad management theories are destroying good management practices. *Academy of Management Learning & Education*, 4(1), 75–91.

Ghoshal, S. and Bartlett, C.A. (1996) Rebuilding behavioral context: A blueprint for corporate renewal. *Sloan Management Review*, 37(2), 23–36.

Ghoshal, S., Bartlett, C.A. and Moran, P. (1999) A new manifesto for management. *Sloan Management Review*, 40(3), 9–20.

Gittell, J.H., von Nordenflycht, A. and Kochan, T.A. (2004) Mutual gains or zero sum? Labor relations and firm performance in the airline industry. *Industrial and Labor Relations Review*, 57(2), 163–80.

Globescan (2004) Corporate Social Responsibility Monitor: Global public opinion on the changing role of companies. http://www.globescan.com; accessed 19 April 2004.

Godfrey, P.C. (2005) The real relationship between corporate philanthropy and shareholder wealth: A risk management perspective. *Academy of Management Review*, 30(4), 777–98.

Goerke, L. and Pannenberg, M. (2004) Norm-based trade union membership: Evidence for Germany. *German Economic Review*, 5(4), 481–504.

Goh, S.C. and Ryan, P.J. (2008) The organizational performance of learning companies: A longitudinal and competitor analysis using market and accounting financial data. *Learning Organization*, 15(3), 225–39.

Goldenberg, D.I. (2000) Shareholder value debunked. *Strategy and Leadership*, 28(1), 30–6.

González-Benito, J. and González-Benito, Ó. (2005) Environmental proactivity and business performance: An empirical analysis. *Omega*, 33, 1–15.

Gouldner, A.W. (1954) *Patterns of Industrial Bureaucracy*. Glencoe, Il: Free Press.

Gould-Williams, J. (2003) The importance of HR practices and workplace trust in achieving superior performance: A study of public-sector organizations. *International Journal of Human Resource Management*, 14(1), 28–54.

Grewal, R. and Slotegraaf, R.J. (2007) Embeddedness of organizational capabilities. *Decision Sciences*, 38(3), 451–88.

Gudmundson, D., Tower, C.B. and Hartman, E.A. (2003) Innovation in small businesses: Culture and ownership structure do matter. *Journal of Developmental Entrepreneurship*, 8(1), 1–18.

Gumbel, P. (2005) Buyout mania, *Time Europe Magazine*, 29 August. http://www.time.com/time/europe/globalbiz/2005/08/takeover.html; accessed 14 February 2010.

Hambrick, D.C., Finkelstein, S. and Mooney, A.C. (2005) Executive job demands: New insights for explaining strategic decisions and leader behaviors. *Academy of Management Review*, 30(3), 472–91.

Hamel, G. (2003) Radical innovation. *Executive Excellence*, Australian edition, 20(5), 11.

—— (2006) The why, what, and how of management innovation. *Harvard Business Review*, 84(2), 72–84.

Hamel, G. and Prahalad, C.K. (1989) Strategic intent. Reprinted in *Harvard Business Review*, 2005, 83(7), 148–61.

Hamilton, B.H., Nickerson, J.A. and Owan, H. (2003) Team incentives and worker heterogeneity: An empirical analysis of the impact of teams on productivity and participation. *Journal of Political Economics*, 111(3), 465–97.

Handy, C. (2002) What's a business for? *Harvard Business Review*, 80(12), 48–55.

Harley, B. (2002) Employee responses to high performance work system practices: An analysis of the AWIRS95 data. *Journal of Industrial Relations*, 44(3), 418–34.

Harris, J. and Bromiley, P. (2007) Incentives to cheat: The influence of executive compensation and firm performance on financial misrepresentation. *Organization Science*, 18(3), 350–67.

Harrison, J.S., Bosse, D.A. and Phillips, R.A. (2010) Managing for stakeholders, stakeholder utility functions, and competitive advantage. *Strategic Management Journal*, 31(1), 58–74.

Hart, S.L. and Quinn, R.E. (1993) Roles executives play: CEOs, behavioral complexity, and firm performance. *Human Relations*, 46(5), 543–74.

Harter, J.K., Schmidt, F.L. and Hayes, T.L. (2002) Business-unit-level relationship between employee satisfaction, employee engagement, and business outcomes: A meta-analysis. *Journal of Applied Psychology*, 87(2), 268–79.

Hausfeld, J., Gibbons, K., Holtmeier, A., Knight, M., Schulte, C., Stadtmiller, T. and Yeary, K. (1994) Self-staffing: Improving care and staff satisfaction. *Nursing Management*, 25, 74.

Haveman, H.A. (1992) Between a rock and a hard place: Organizational change and performance under conditions of fundamental environmental transformation. *Administrative Science Quarterly*, 37(1), 48–75.

Heath, C. (1999) On the social psychology of agency relationships: Lay theories of motivation overemphasize extrinsic incentives. *Organizational Behavior and Human Decision Processes*, 78(1), 25–62.

Hee-Jae Cho and Pucik, V. (2005) Relationship between innovativeness, quality, growth, profitability, and market value. *Strategic Management Journal*, 26(6), 555–75.

Heffes, E.M. and Sinnett, W.M. (2006) Private companies: In pursuit of sustainable growth. *Financial Executive*, October, 36–42.

Hemp, P. and Stewart, T.A. (2004) Leading change when business is good. *Harvard Business Review* 82(12), 60–70.

Heras, I., Dick, G.P.M. and Casadesús, M. (2002) ISO 9000 registration's impact on sales and profitability: A longitudinal analysis of performance before and after accreditation. *International Journal of Quality and Reliability Management*, 19(6), 774–91.

Heskett, J., Jones, T., Loveman, G., Sasser, W.E. and Schlesinger, L. (1994) Putting the service-profit chain to work. *Harvard Business Review*, March–April, 164–74.

Hewitt and Associates (2001) Survey highlights: Best employers to work for in Australia study 2001, Sydney.

——— (2004) Hewitt study shows companies revamping executive long-term incentive programs. Press release. 8 April.

Hilb, M. (2006) *New Corporate Governance: Successful Board Management Tools*. 2nd edn, Berlin-Heidelberg: Springer.

Hillmer, S., Hillmer, B. and McRoberts, G. (2004) The real costs of turnover: Lessons from a call center. *Human Resource Planning*, 27(3), 34–41.

Hirschhorn, L. (1997) *Reworking Authority: Leading and Following in the Post-Modern Organization*. Massachusetts: MIT Press.

Hitt, M.A., Bierman, L., Shimizu, K. and Kockhar, R. (2001) Direct and moderating effects of human capital on strategy and performance in professional service firms: A resource-based perspective. *Academy of Management Journal*, 44(1), 13–28.

Hodges, M. and Woolcock, S. (1993) Atlantic capitalism versus Rhine capitalism in the European Community. *West European Politics*, 16(3), 329–44.

Hodson, R. (2004) A meta-analysis of workplace ethnographies. *Journal of Contemporary Ethnography*, 33(1), 4–38.

Hoffmann, J. (2004) Co-ordinated Continental European market economies under pressure from globalization: Germany's 'Rhineland' capitalism. *German Law Review*, 8. http://www.germanlawjournal.com/index. php?pageid=11&artID=485; retrieved 2 February 2007.

Hoffmann, K. and Koop, B. (2004) Die 'employee-quality-customer chain'. *Mannheimer Beiträge zur Wirtschafts- und Organisationspsychologie*, 19(1), 3–8.

Hofstede, G. (1993) Cultural constraints in management theories. Reprinted in L.W. Porter, G.A. Bigley and R.M. Steers (eds) 2003, *Motivation and Work Behavior*. New York: McGraw-Hill, pp. 344–57.

Hogan, J. and Mühlau, P. (2003) The adoption of high performance human resource practices in Ireland: An integration of contingency and institutional theory. *Irish Journal of Management*, 24(1), 26–47.

Hogarth, J. (1971) *Sentencing as a Human Process*. Toronto: University of Toronto Press.

Hoje, J. (2003) Financial analysts, firm quality, and social responsibility. *Journal of Behavioral Finance*, 4(3), 172–83.

Holm, S. and Hovland, J. (1999) Waiting for the other shoe to drop: Help for the job-insecure employee. *Journal of Employment Counseling*, 36(4), 156–66.

Horgan, J. and Mühlau, P. (2006) Human resource systems and employee performance in Ireland and the Netherlands: A test of the complementarity hypothesis. *International Journal of Human Resource Management*, 17(3), 414–39.

House, R.J. and Aditya, R.N. (1997) The social scientific study of leadership: Quo vadis? *Journal of Management*, 23(3), 409–73.

House, R.J., Woycke, J. and Fodor, E. (1988) Charismatic and noncharismatic leaders: Differences in behavior and effectiveness. In J.A. Conge and R.N. Kanungo (eds), *Charismatic Leadership: The Elusive Factor in Organizational Effectiveness*. San Francisco: Jossey-Bass.

Howell, J.P., Bowen, D.E., Dorfman, P.W., Kerr, S. and Podsakoff, P.M. (1990) Substitutes for leadership: Effective alternatives to ineffective leadership. *Organizational Dynamics*, Summer, 21–38.

Hubbard, G., Samuel, D., Heap, S. and Cocks, G. (2002) *The First XI: Winning Organisations in Australia*. Brisbane: John Wiley & Sons.

Hubbell, A.P. and Chory-Assad, R.M. (2005) Motivating factors: Perceptions of justice and their relationship with managerial and organizational trust. *Communication Studies*, 56(1), 47–70.

Hult, G.T., Hurley, R.F. and Knight, G.A. (2004) Innovativeness: Its antecedents and impact on business performance. *Industrial Marketing Management*, 33, 429–38.

Hung, R.Y-Y. (2006) Business process management as competitive advantage: A review and empirical study. *Total Quality Management*, 17(1), 21–40.

Hurley, R.F. and Estelami, H. (1998) Alternative indexes for monitoring customer perceptions of service quality: A comparative evaluation in a retail context. *Journal of Academy of Marketing Science*, 26(3), 209–21.

Huselid, M.A. (1995) The impact of human resource management practices on turnover, productivity, and corporate financial performance. *Academy of Management Journal*, 38(3), 635–72.

Huselid, M.A. and Becker, B.E. (2000) Comment on 'Measurement effort in research on human resources and firm performance: How much error is there and how does it influence effect size estimates?' by Gerhart, Wright, McMahan and Snell. *Personnel Psychology*, 53(4), 835–54.

Hutton, W. (2002) *The World We're In*. London: Little, Brown.

Hyundai Motor (2005) A better drive. *The Economist*, 21 May, p. 61.

IBM Global CEO Study (2006) *Expanding the Innovation Horizon*. IBM Global Business Services.

IBM Global Services (2007) *How CIOs can drive growth, business flexibility and innovation in a flex-pon-sive* company*. April. IBM.

Ichniowski, C., Kochan, T.A., Levine, D., Olson, C. and Strauss, G. (1996) What works at work: Overview and assessment. *Industrial Relations*, 35(3), 299–333.

Ichniowski, C. and Shaw, K. (1999) The effects of human resource management systems on economic performance: An international comparison of US and Japanese plants. *Management Science*, 45(5), 704–22.

—— (2003) Beyond incentive pay: Insiders' estimates of the value of complementary human resource management practices. *Journal of Economic Perspectives*, 17(1), 155–80.

Ichniowski, C., Shaw, K. and Prennushi, G. (1997) The effects of human resource management practices on productivity: A study of steel finishing lines. *American Economic Review*, 87(3), 291–313.

Jacobs, R.L. and Washington, C. (2003) Employee development and organizational performance: A review of literature and directions for future research. *Human Resource Development International*, 6(3), 343–54.

Janz, B.D. and Prasarnphanich, P. (2003) Understanding the antecedents of effective knowledge management: The importance of a knowledge-centered culture. *Decision Sciences*, 34(2), 351–84.

Jaruzelski, B., Dehoff, K. and Bordia, R. (2006) Smart spenders: The Global Innovation 1000. Booz Allen Hamilton. http://www.strategy-business.com/media/file/leading_ideas-20080108.pdf; accessed 14 February 2010.

Jenkins, H. and Yakevleva, N. (2006) Corporate social responsibility in the mining industry: Exploring trends in social and environmental disclosure. *Journal of Cleaner Production*, 14, 271–84.

Jing, F. (2009) An investigation of the relationship between leadership paradigms and organisational performance in pharmaceutical sales organisations. Unpublished thesis, Macquarie University, Sydney.

Jones, T.M. (1995) Instrumental stakeholder theory: A synthesis of ethics and economics. *Academy of Management Review*, 20, 404–37.

Jose, A. and Thibodeaux, M.S. (1999) Institutionalization of ethics: The perspective of managers. *Journal of Business Ethics*, 22(1), 133–43.

Kane, R. (1996) *The Significance of Free Will*. New York: Oxford University Press.

Kantabutra, S. (2009) *A Study of the Application of the Sufficiency Economy Philosophy in the Business Sector*. Thailand: Center for the Study of Sufficiency Economy at National Institute of Development Administration.

Kantabutra, S. and Avery, G.C. (2003) Investigating relationships between vision components and hospital ward performance: Proposed model. *International Business and Economics Research Journal*, 2(1), 1–8.

—— (2005) Essence of shared vision: Empirical investigation. *New Zealand Journal of Human Resources Management*, 5. http://www.nzjhrm.org.nz/Site/Articles/2005.aspx; accessed 14 February 2010.

—— (2007) Vision effects in customer and staff satisfaction: An empirical investigation. *Leadership and Organizational Development*, 28(3), 209–29.

Kanter, R.M. (1989) *When Giants Learn to Dance.* New York: Simon & Schuster.

—— (2004) The middle manager as innovator. *Harvard Business Review*, 82(7/8), 150–61.

Kaplan, R.S. and Norton, D.P. (1996) Linking the balanced scorecard to strategy. *California Management Review*, 39(1), 53–79.

Kennedy, A.A. (2000) *The End of Shareholder Value: The Real Effects of the Shareholder Value Phenomenon and the Crisis it is Bringing to Business.* London: Orion Business Books.

Kinnie, N., Hutchinson, S. and Purcell, J. (2000) 'Fun and surveillance': The paradox of high commitment management in call centres. *International Journal of Human Resource Management*, 11(5), 967–85.

Kinnie, N., Hutchinson, S., Purcell, J., Rayton, B. and Swart, J. (2005) Satisfaction with HR practices and commitment to the organisation: Why one size does not fit all. *Human Resource Management Journal*, 15(4), 9–29.

Kirkman, B.L. and Rosen, B. (1999) Beyond self-management: Antecedents and consequences of team empowerment. *Academy of Management Journal*, 42(1), 58–74.

Kleiman, R., Petty, W. and Martin, J. (1995) Family controlled firms: An assessment of performance. *Family Business Annual*, 1, 1–13.

Klein, A. (2004) AAA Overrated. *Sydney Morning Herald*, 27–28 November, pp. 45–8.

Klein, G. (2001) The fiction of optimization. In G. Gigerenzer and R. Selten (eds), *Bounded Rationality: The Adaptive Toolbox*, pp. 103–21. Cambridge, MA: MIT Press.

Kochan, T.A., Gittell, J.H. and Lautsch, B.A. (1995) Total quality management and human resource systems: An international comparison. *International Journal of Human Resource Management*, 6(2), 201–22.

Konar, S. and Cohen, M.A. (2001) Does the market value environmental performance? *Review of Economics and Statistics*, 83(2), 281–9.

Kotter, J.P. and Heskett, J.L. (1992) *Corporate Culture and Performance.* New York: Free Press.

KPMG (2005) *International Survey of Corporate Responsibility Reporting 2005.* Amsterdam: KPMG Global Sustainability Services.

Kristof-Brown, A.L., Zimmerman, R.D. and Johnson, E.C. (2005) Consequences of individuals' fit at work: A meta-analysis of person–job, person–organization, person–group, and person–supervisor fit. *Personnel Psychology*, 58(4), 281–342.

Kucher, A.B. and Meitner, M. (2004) Private equity for distressed companies in Germany. *Journal of Private Equity*, Winter, 55–62.

Kuipers, B.S. and de Witte, M.C. (2005) Teamwork: A case study on development and performance. *International Journal of Human Resource Management*, 16(2), 185–201.

Ladd, J. (1970) Morality and the ideal of rationality in formal organizations. *The Monist*, 54, 488–516.

Lakshman, C. (2006) A theory of leadership for quality: Lessons from TQM for leadership theory. *Total Quality Management*, 17(1), 41–60.

Lämsä, A-M. and Pučėtaite, R. (2006) Development of organizational trust among employees from a contextual perspective. *Business Ethics*, 15(2), 130–41.

Lane, C. (2000) Globalization and the German model of capitalism – erosion or survival? *British Journal of Sociology*, 51(2), 207–34.

Lapidus, R.S., Roberts, J.A. and Chonko, L.B. (1997) Stressors, leadership substitutes, and relations with supervision among industrial salespeople. *Industrial Marketing Management*, 26, 255–69.

Lardner, J. (2002) In praise of the anonymous CEO. *Business 2.0*, 3(9).

Laroche, P. (2004) Presence syndicale et performance financiere des entreprises: Une analyse statistique sur le cas Français. (With English summary.) *Revue Finance Controle Strategie*, 7(3), 117–45.

Larsson, R., Brousseau, K.R., Kling, K. and Sweet, P.L. (2007) Building motivational capital through career concept and culture fit: The strategic value of developing motivation and retention. *Career Development International*, 12(4), 361–81.

Latting, J.K., Beck, M.H., Slack, K.J., Tetrick, L.E., Jones, A.P., Etchegaray, J.M. and da Silva, N. (2004) Promoting service quality and client adherence to the service plan: The role of top management's support for innovation and learning. *Administration in Social Work*, 28(2), 29–48.

Lau, R.S.M. and May, B.E. (1998) A win-win paradigm for quality of work life and business performance. *Human Resource Development Quarterly*, 9(3), 211–26.

Lawler, E.E. III, Mohrman, S.A. and Ledford, G.E. Jr (1995) *Creating High Performance Organizations: Practices and Results of Employee Involvement and Total Quality Management in Fortune 1000 Companies.* San Francisco, CA: Jossey-Bass.

Lawson, B. and Samson, D. (2001) Developing innovation capability in organizations: A dynamic capabilities approach. *International Journal of Innovation Management*, 5(3), 377–400.

Leana, C.R. and Rousseau, D.M. (2000) (eds) *Relational Wealth*. Oxford: Oxford University Press.

Lee, J. (2004) The effects of family ownership and management on firm performance. *SAM Advanced Management Journal*, 69(4), 46–53.

Lerner, J.S. and Tetlock P.E. (1999) Accounting for the effects of accountability. *Psychological Bulletin*, 125(2), 255–75.

Leslie, K., Loch, M.A. and Schaninger, W. (2006) Managing your organization by the evidence. *McKinsey Quarterly*, 3, 64–75.

Levering, R. (2000) *A great place to work: What makes some employers so good – and most so bad?* San Francisco: Great Place to Work Institute.

Levitan, S.A. and Werneke, D. (1984) Worker participation and productivity change. *Monthly Labor Review*, 107(9), 28–33.

Lewis, B. (1999) The best managers offer responsibility rather than blame to their employees. *Infoworld*, 21(40), 104.

Li, J. (2006) The interactions between person-organization fit and leadership styles in Asian firms, an empirical testing. *International Journal of Human Resource Management*, 17(10), 1689–706.

Liker, J.K. and Choi, T.Y. (2004) Building deep supplier relationships. *Harvard Business Review*, 82(12), 104–13.

Ling, Y-H. and Jaw, B-S. (2006) The influence of international human capital on global initiatives and financial performance. *International Journal of Human Resource Management*, 17(3), 379–98.

Liu, W., Lepak, D.P., Takeuchi, R. and Sims, H.P. (2003) Matching leadership styles with employment modes: Strategic human resource management perspective. *Human Resource Management Review*, 13, 127–52.

Longenecker, C.O., Neubert, M.J. and Fink, L.S. (2007) Causes and consequences of managerial failure in rapidly changing organizations. *Business Horizons*, 50(2), 145–55.

Lopez, S.P., Peon, J.M.M. and Ordas, C.J.V. (2005) Human resource practices, organizational learning and business performance. *Human Resource Development International*, 8(2), 147–64.

Lord, R.G. and Maher, K.J. (1991) Leadership and information processing: Linking perceptions and performance. *People and Organizations*, Vol. 1, Boston, MA: Unwin & Hyman.

Love, E.G. and Kraatz, M. (2005) How do firms' actions influence corporate reputation? The case of downsizing at large U.S. firms. Academy of Management Conference, Honolulu, 5–10 August.

Loveman, G.W. (1998) Employee satisfaction, customer loyalty, and financial performance: An empirical examination of the service profit chain in retail banking. *Journal of Service Research*, 1(1), 18–31.

Lowe, K.B. and Galen Kroeck, K. (1996) Effectiveness correlates of transformational and transactional leadership: A meta-analytic review of the MLQ literature. *Leadership Quarterly*, 7(3), 385–426.

Lucier, C., Spiegel, E. and Schuyt, R. (2002) *Why CEOs fall: The Causes and Consequences of Turnover at the Top*. Sydney: Booz Allen Hamilton.

McCauley, D.P. and Kuhnert, K.W. (1992) A theoretical review and empirical investigation of employee trust in management. *Public Administration Quarterly*, 16(2), 265–85.

McColl-Kennedy, J.R. and Anderson, R.D. (2002) Impact of leadership style and emotions on subordinate performance. *Leadership Quarterly*, 13, 545–59.

McConaughy, D.L., Matthews, C.H. and Fialko, A.S. (2001) Founding family controlled firms: Performance, risk, and value. *Journal of Small Business Management*, 39(1), 31–49.

McConnell, B. (2005) Arising to mainstream. *Investor Weekly*, 509 (15–21 September), 2.

MacIntosh, E. and Doherty, A. (2007) Extending the scope of organisational culture: The external perception of an internal phenomenon. *Sport Management Review*, 10, 45–64.

McKinsey (2006) The McKinsey global survey of business executives: Confidence index, January 2006. *McKinsey Quarterly*, web exclusive, January 2006. http://www.mckinseyquarterly.com; accessed 14 February 2010.

McLain, D.L. and Hackman, K. (1999) Trust, risk and decision making in organizational change. *Public Administration Quarterly*, 23(2), 152–76.

McNabb, R. and Whitfield, K. (1997) Unions, flexibility, team working and financial performance. *Organization Studies*, 18(5), 821–39.

Malik, F. (2002) Perpetuierung falscher Corporate Governance. *Manager Magazin*. http://www.manager-magazin.de/koepfe/mzsg/0,2828,217433,00.html; accessed 27 November 2002.

Management Services (2002) Ethical issues score badly in poll of small businesses. 46(5), 7.

Manz, C.C. (1986) Self-leadership: Toward an expanded theory of self-influence in organizations. *Academy of Management Review*, 11(3), 585–600.

—— (1990) Beyond self-managing work teams: Toward self-leading teams in the workplace. In R. Woodman and W. Pasmore (eds), *Research in Organizational Change and Development*, Vol. 4, pp. 273–99. Greenwich, CT: JAI Press.

—— (1996) Self-leading work teams: Moving beyond self-management myths. In R.M. Steers, L.W. Porter and G.A. Bigley (1996), *Motivation and Leadership at Work*, 6th edn, pp. 581–99, New York: McGraw-Hill.

Manz, C.C., Mossholder, K. and Luthans, F. (1987) An integrated perspective of self-control in organizations. *Administration and Society*, 19, 3–24.

Manz, C.C. and Sims, H.P. (1986) Leading self-managed groups: A conceptual analysis of a paradox. *Economic and Industrial Democracy*, 7, 141–65.

Marchington, M. and Zagelmeyer, S. (2005) Foreword: Linking HRM and performance – a never-ending search? *Human Resource Management Journal*, 15(4), 3–8.

Marcoulides, G.A. and Heck, R.H. (1993) Organizational culture and performance: Proposing and testing a model. *Organization Science*, 4(2), 209–25.

Marriott, J.W. Jr and Brown, K.A. (1997) *The Spirit to Serve: Marriott's Way*. New York: Harper.

Martignon, L. (2001) Comparing fast and frugal heuristics and optimal models. In G. Gigerenzer and R. Selten (eds), *Bounded Rationality: The Adaptive Toolbox*, pp. 148–71. Cambridge, MA: MIT Press.

Martinez, R.J. and Norman, P.M. (2004) Whither reputation? The effects of different stakeholders. *Business Horizons*, 47(5), 25–32.

Martz, B., Neil, T.C. and Biscaccianti, A. (2003) TradeSmith: An exercise to demonstrate the illusion of control in decision making. *Decision Sciences Journal of Innovative Education*, 1(2), 273–87.

Matzler, K., Hinterhuber, H.H., Daxer, C. and Huber, M. (2005) The relationship between customer satisfaction and shareholder value. *Total Quality Management and Business Excellence*, 16(5), 1–10.

Mayer, R.C. and Davis, J.H. (1999) The effect of the performance appraisal system on trust for management: A field quasi-experiment. *Journal of Applied Psychology*, 84(1), 123–36.

Medley, F. and Larochelle, D. (1995) Transformational leadership and job satisfaction. *Nursing Management*, 26(9), 64JJ–64NN.

Meindl, J.R. (1998) Invited reaction: Enabling visionary leadership. *Human Resource Development Quarterly*, 9(1), 21–4.

Meyer, C.B. and Stensacker, I.G. (2006) Developing capacity for change. *Journal of Change Management*, 6(2), 217–31.

Meyer, M.W. (2005) Can performance studies create actionable knowledge if we can't measure the performance of the firm? *Journal of Management Inquiry*, 14(3), 287–91.

Michie, J. and Sheehan-Quinn, M. (2001) Labour market flexibility, human resource management and corporate performance. *British Journal of Management*, 12(4), 287–307.

Miller, D. and Le Breton-Miller, I. (2003) Challenge versus advantage in family business. *Strategic Organization*, 1(1), 127–34.

Miller, D. and Lee, J. (2001) The people make the process: Commitment to employees, decision making, and performance. *Journal of Management*, 27, 163–89.

Miller, K.I. and Monge, P.R. (1988) Participation, satisfaction, and productivity: A meta-analytic review. *Academy of Management Journal*, 29, 727–53.

Mills, J., Cocklin, C., Fayers, C. and Holmes, D. (2001) Sustainability, socially responsible investment and the outlook of investment professionals in Australia. *Greener Management International*, 33, 31–45.

Mintzberg, H. (2004) *Managers not MBAs: A Hard Look at the Soft Practice of Managing and Management Development.* UK: FT Prentice-Hall, Pearson.

Mintzberg, H., Simons, R. and Basu, K. (2002) Beyond selfishness. *MIT Sloan Management Review*, Fall, 67–74.

Mitchell, L.E. (2001) *Corporate Irresponsibility: America's Newest Export.* New Haven: Yale University Press.

Mitra, D. and Golder, P.N. (2006) How does objective quality affect perceived quality? Short-term effects, long-term effects, and asymmetries. *Marketing Science*, 25(3), 230–47.

Mokhtar, M.Z., Karbhari, Y. and Naser, K. (2005) Company financial performance and ISO9000 registration: Evidence from Malaysia. *Asia Pacific Business Review*, 11(3), 349–67.

Montgomery, D.B. and Ramus, C.A. (2007) Including corporate social responsibility, environmental sustainability, and ethics in calibrating MBA job preferences. Research Paper #1981, Research Paper Series. CA: Stanford Graduate School of Business.

Morishima, M. (1991) Information sharing and firm performance in Japan. *Industrial Relations*, 30(1), 37–62.

Muller, P. and Pénin, J. (2006) Why do firms disclose knowledge and how does it matter? *Journal of Evolutionary Economics*, 16(1), 85–108.

Müller, W.R. and Hurter, M. (1999) Führung als Schlüssel zur organisationalen Lernfähigkeit. In G. Schreyögg and J. Sydow, *Managementforschung 9: Führung – neu gesehen.* Berlin: De Gruyter.

Mumford, M.D., Scott, G.M., Gaddis, B. and Strange, J.M. (2002) Leading creative people: Orchestrating expertise and relationships. *Leadership Quarterly*, 13, 705–50.

Murray, B. (2007) Engaging Generation X and Y. *Strategic Communication Management*, 11(5), 2.

Nadler, D. and Tushman, M. (1990) Beyond the charismatic leader: Leadership and organizational change. *California Management Review*, 32, 77–97.

Naor, M., Goldstein, S.M., Linderman, K.W. and Schroeder, R.G. (2008) The role of culture as driver of quality management and performance: Infrastructure versus core quality practices. *Decision Sciences*, 39(4), 671–702.

Nasrallah, W., Levitt, R. and Glynn, P. (2003) Interaction value analysis: When structured communication benefits organizations. *Organization Science*, 14(5), 541–57.

Naveh, E. and Marcus, A. (2005) Achieving competitive advantage through implementing a replicable management standard: Installing and using ISO 9000. *Journal of Operations Management*, 24(1), 1–26.

Neck, C.P. and Houghton, J.D. (2006) Two decades of self-leadership theory and research: Past developments, present trends, and future possibilities. *Journal of Managerial Psychology*, 21(4), 270–95.

Nelson, J. (2005) Clayton Christensen. *New Zealand Management*, 52(4), 41–3.

Neves, P. and Caetano, A. (2006) Social exchange processes in organizational change: The roles of trust and control. *Journal of Change Management*, 6(4), 351–64.

Nicholls, J. (2005) Corporate social responsibility and small and medium-sized enterprises. In C.S. Brown (ed.) (2005), *The Sustainable Enterprise: Profiting from Best Practice*. London: Kogan Page.

Odo Securities (2008) *Innovation: ESG, no oil but lots of ideas!* Paris: Odo Securities.

OECD (2001) Annual projections for OECD countries. *Economic Outlook* No. 40, December.

—— (2004) *Investment in human capital through post-compulsory education and training*, http://www.oecd.org/document/9/0,3343,en_2649_34573_2082818_1_1_1_1,00.html; accessed 14 February 2010.

oekom research and Morgan Stanley Private Wealth Management (2004) Sustainability as a style of investment offering double dividends. http://www.oekom-research.com/ag/Performance_Study.pdf; accessed 27 December 2006.

Ogbonna, E. and Harris, L.C. (2000) Leadership style, organizational culture and performance. *International Journal of Human Resource Management*, 11(4), 766–88.

Ogden, S. and Watson, R. (1999) Corporate performance and stakeholder management: Balancing shareholder and customer interests in the UK privatized water industry. *Academy of Management Journal*, 42, 526–38.

O'Regan, N. and Ghobadian, A. (2005) Strategic planning: A comparison of high and low technology manufacturing small firms. *Technovation*, 25, 1107–17.

Orlitzky, M. (2005) Payoffs to social and environmental performance. *Journal of Investing*, Fall, 48–51.

Orlitzky, M., Schmidt, F.L. and Rynes, S.L. (2003) Corporate social and financial performance: A meta-analysis. *Organization Studies*, 24(3), 403–41.

O'Sullivan, M. (2003) The political economy of comparative corporate governance. *Review of International Political Economy*, 10(1), 23–72.

Oswald, S., Stanwick, P. and LaTour, M. (1997) The effect of vision, strategic planning, and cultural relationships on organizational performance: A structural approach. *International Journal of Management*, 14, 521–9.

Paauwe, J. and Boselie, P. (2005) HRM and performance: What next? *Human Resource Management Journal*, 15(4), 68–83.

Parker, L.D. (2007) Financial and external reporting research: The broadening corporate governance challenge. *Accounting and Business Research*, 37(1), 39–54.

Pascale, R.T. and Athos, A.G. (1981) *The Art of Japanese Management*. New York: Warner Books.

Perel, M. (2005) You can innovate in hard times. *Research Technology Management*, 48(4), 14–23.

Perrini, F. (2006) The practitioner's perspective in nonfinancial reporting. *California Management Review*, 48(2), 73–103.

Perry, J. (2005) Excellence through quality. *CMA Management*, 78(8), 26–9.

Peters, T. (2003) Brand inside: Meter your energy, spirit, and spunk. *Executive Excellence*, Australian edition, 20(5), 16.

Pettigrew, A.M. and Whipp, R. (1991) *Managing Change for Competitive Success*. Oxford: Blackwell.

Pettigrew, A.M., Woodman, R.W. and Cameron, K.S. (2001) Studying organizational change and development. *Academy of Management Journal*, 44(4), 697–713.

Pfau, B.N. and Cohen, S.A. (2003) Aligning human capital practices and employee behavior with shareholder value. *Consulting Psychology Journal*, 55(3), 169–78.

Pfeffer, J., Hatano, T. and Santalainen, T. (1995) Producing sustainable competitive advantage through the effective management of people. *Academy of Management Executive*, 9(1), 55–72.

Pfeffer, J. and Sutton, R.I. (2006) Evidence-based management. *Harvard Business Review*, 84(1), 62–74.

Pfeifer, P.E. (2005) The optimal ratio of acquisition and retention costs. *Journal of Targeting, Measurement and Analysis for Marketing*, 13(2), 179–88.

Pitelis, C.N. (2004) (Corporate) governance, (shareholder) value and (sustainable) economic performance. *Corporate Governance: An International Review*, 12(2), 210–23.

Politis, J.D. (2006) Self-leadership behavioural-focused strategies and team performance: The mediating influence of job satisfaction. *Leadership and Organization Development Journal*, 27(3), 203–16.

Porter, M.E. and Kramer, M.R. (2006) Strategy and society: The link between competitive advantage and corporate social responsibility. *Harvard Business Review*, 84(12), 78–92.

Poutziouris, P. (2001) The views of family companies on venture capital: Empirical evidence from the UK small to medium-size enterprising economy. *Family Business Review*, 14(3), 277–91.

Power, J. and Waddell, D. (2004) The link between self-managed work teams and learning organizations using performance indicators. *Learning Organization*, 11(3), 244–59.

Poza, E.J., Alfred, T. and Maheshwari, A. (1997) Stakeholder perceptions of culture and management practices in family and family firms: A preliminary report. *Family Business Review*, 10(2), 135ff.

Preston, L.E. and Donaldson, T. (1999) Stakeholder management and organizational wealth. *Academy of Management Review*, 24(4), 619–20.

Prieto, I.M. and Revilla, E. (2006) Assessing the impact of learning capability on business performance: Empirical evidence from Spain. *Management Learning*, 37(4), 499–522.

Purcell, J., Kinnie, N., Hutchinson, S., Rayton, B. and Swart, J. (2003) *Understanding the People and Performance Link: Unlocking the Black Box.* Report of the Chartered Institute of Personnel and Development, London.

Quinn, R.E. and Spreitzer, G.M. (1997) The road to empowerment: Seven questions every leader should consider. *Organizational Dynamics*, 26(2), 37–49.

Rafferty, A.E. and Griffin, M.G. (2004) Dimensions of transformational leadership: Conceptual and empirical extensions. *Leadership Quarterly*, 15, 329–54.

Ramsay-Smith, G. (2004) Employee turnover: The real cost. *Strategic HR Review*, 3(4), 7.

Rappaport, A. (2006) 10 ways to create shareholder value. *Harvard Business Review*, September, 66–77.

Rauch, A., Frese, M. and Utsch, A. (2005) Effects of human capital and long-term human resources development and utilization on employment growth of small-scale business: A causal analysis. *Entrepreneurship*, 29(6), 681–98.

Recardo, R.J. (2000) Best practices in organizations experiencing extensive and rapid change. *National Productivity Review*, Summer, 79–85.

Reichheld, F.F. and Sasser, W.E. (1990) Zero defections: Quality comes to services. *Harvard Business Review*, 68(5), 105–11.

Reisel, W.D., Chia, S-L. and Maloles III, C.M. (2005) Job insecurity spillover to key account management: Negative effects on performance, effectiveness, adaptiveness, and esprit de corps. *Journal of Business and Psychology*, 19(4), 483–503.

Rey, M. and Nguyen, T. (2005) *Financial Payback from Environmental and Social Factors*. Report by AMP Capital Investors, Sydney, 7 April.

Roberts, P.W. and Dowling, C.R. (2002) Corporate reputation and sustained superior financial performance. *Strategic Management Journal*, 23, 1077–93.

Robinson, H.S., Carrillo, P.M., Anumba, C.J. and Al-Ghassani, A.M. (2004) Developing a business case for knowledge management: The IMPaKT [*sic*] approach. *Construction Management and Economics*, 22, 733–43.

Romero, E.J. and McFarlin, D. (2004) Are the great places to work also great performers? *Academy of Management Executive*, 18(2), 150–2.

Rosenzweig, P. (2007) Misunderstanding the nature of company performance: The halo effect and other business delusions. *California Management Review*, 49(4), 6–20.

Rousseau, D.M. (2006) Is there such a thing as 'evidence-based management'? *Academy of Management Review*, 31(2), 256–69.

Rousseau, D.M. and Batt, R. (2007) Global competition's perfect storm: Why business and labor cannot solve their problems alone. *Academy of Management Perspectives*, 21(2), 16–23.

Ruf, B.M., Muralidhar, K., Brown, R.M., Janney, J.J. and Paul, K. (2001) An empirical investigation of the relationship between change in corporate social performance and financial performance: A stakeholder theory perspective. *Journal of Business Ethics*, 32(2), 143–56.

Rust, R.T. and Zahorik, A.J. (1993) Customer satisfaction, customer retention and market share. *Journal of Retailing*, 69(2), 193–215.

Safford, G.S. III (1988) Culture traits, strength, and organizational performance: Moving beyond 'strong' culture. *Academy of Management Review*, 13(4), 546–58.

Sako, M. (1992) *Prices, Quality and Trust: Inter-firm Relations in Britain and Japan*. Cambridge: Cambridge University Press.

Saruta, M. (2006) Toyota production systems: The 'Toyota Way' and labour-management relations. *Asian Business & Management*, 5, 487–506.

Saving Germany's auto industry (2004) *Business Week*, 1 November, p. 72.

Scarnati, J.T. (1998) Beyond technical competence: Fear – banish the beast. *Leadership and Organization Development Journal*, 19(7), 362–5.

Schlenker, B.R. (1997) Personal responsibility: Applications of the Triangle Model. *Research in Organizational Behavior*, 19, 241–301.

Schneider, B., Hanges, P.J., Smith, D.B. and Salvaggio, A.N. (2003) Which comes first: Employee attitudes or organizational financial and market performance? *Journal of Applied Psychology*, 88(5), 836–51.

Schnietz, K.E. and Epstein, M.J. (2005) Exploring the financial value of a reputation for corporate social responsibility during a crisis. *Corporate Reputation Review*, 7(4), 327–45.

Scotti, J., Behson, S., Farias, G., Petzel, R., Neumam, J.H., Keashly, L. and Harmon, J. (2003) Effects of high-involvement work systems on employee satisfaction and service costs in veterans' healthcare. *Journal of Healthcare Management*, 48(6), 393–406.

Scotti, J., Harmon, J. and Behson, S. (2007) Links among high-performance work environment, service quality, and customer satisfaction: An extension to the healthcare sector. *Journal of Healthcare Management*, 52(2), 109–23.

Seibert, S.E., Silver, S.R. and Randolph, W.A. (2004) Taking empowerment to the next level: A multi-level model of empowerment, performance, and satisfaction. *Academy of Management Journal*, 47(3), 332–49.

Sethi, S.P. (2002) Corporate codes of conduct and the success of globalization. *Ethics and International Affairs*, 16(1), 89–106.

—— (2005) Investing in socially responsible companies is a must for public pension funds – because there is no better alternative. *Journal of Business Ethics*, 56(2), 99–129.

Sheridan, J. (1992) Organizational culture and employee retention. *Academy of Management Journal*, 35(5), 1036–56.

Shuttleworth, C.D., Aynsley, A.M.R. and Avery, G.C. (2008) The role of reflection in leading sustainable organizations: A preliminary study. *International Journal of Interdisciplinary Social Sciences*, 3(7), 187–94.

Simonson, I. (1989) Choice based on reasons: The case of the attraction and compromise effects. *Journal of Consumer Research*, 16, 158–74.

Sitzia, J. and Wood, N. (1997) Customer satisfaction: A review of issues and concepts. *Social Science Medical*, 45, 1829–43.

Sood, A. and Tellis, G.J. (2008) Do innovations really pay off? Total stock market returns to innovation. http://papers.ssrn.com/sol3/papers.cfm?abstract_id=1121005; accessed 19 February 2010.

Sorensen, S. (2002) The strength of corporate culture and the reliability of firm performance. *Administrative Science Quarterly*, 47(1), 70–91.

Sosik, J.J. (2005) The role of personal values in the charismatic leadership of corporate managers: A model and preliminary field study. *Leadership Quarterly*, 16, 221–44.

Spector, P.E. (1986) Perceived control by employees: A meta-analysis of studies concerning autonomy and participation at work. *Human Relations*, 39(11), 1005–16.

Srivastava, A., Bartol, K.M. and Locke, E.A. (2006) Empowering leadership in management teams: Effects on knowledge sharing, efficacy, and performance. *Academy of Management Journal*, 49(6), 1239–51.

Stadler, C., Matzler, K., Hinterhuber, H. and Renzl, B. (2006) The CEO's attitude towards the shareholder value and the stakeholder model: A comparison between the Continental European and the Anglo-Saxon perspectives. *Problems and Perspectives in Management*, 4(3), 41–8.

Stalk, G. Jr and Lachenauer, R. (2004) Hardball: Five killer strategies for trouncing the competition. *Harvard Business Review*, 82(4), 62–71.

Stavrou, E., Kassinis, G. and Filotheou, A. (2007) Downsizing and stakeholder orientation among the Fortune 500: Does family ownership matter? *Journal of Business Ethics*, 72(2), 149–62.

Stern, N. (2007) *The Economics of Climate Change: The Stern Review.* Cambridge: Cambridge University Press.

Stewart, T.A. (2004) Winning attitudes. *Harvard Business Review*, 82(4), 10.

Stiglitz, J. (2002) *Globalization and Its Discontents.* London: Penguin.

Sveiby, K-E. (2007) KM in a Norwegian hospital. http://www.sveiby.com/articles/index.html; accessed 21 February 2010.

Tanriverdi, H. (2005) Information technology relatedness, knowledge management capability, and performance of multibusiness firms. *MIS Quarterly*, 29(2), 311–34.

Tarí, J.J. and Sabater, V. (2006) Human aspects in a quality management context and their effects on performance. *International Journal of Human Resource Management*, 17(3), 484–503.

Tetlock, P.E. (1985) Accountability: The neglected social context of judgment and choice. *Research in Organizational Behavior*, 7, 297–332.

Thomas, D.E. (2007) How do reputation and legitimacy affect organizational performance? *International Journal of Management*, 24(1), 108–16.

Thoms, P., Dose, J.J. and Scott, K.S. (2002) Relationships between accountability, job satisfaction, and trust. *Human Resource Development Quarterly*, 13(3), 307–23.

Todd, P.M. (2001) Fast and frugal heuristics for environmentally bounded minds. In G. Gigerenzer and R. Selten (eds), *Bounded Rationality: The Adaptive Toolbox*, pp. 51–70. Cambridge, MA: MIT Press.

Tontini, G. (2007) Integrating the Kano model and QFD for designing new products. *Total Quality Management*, 18(6), 599–612.

Trevino, L.K., Weaver, G.R., Gibson, D.G. and Toffler, B.L. (1999) Managing ethics and legal compliance: What works and what hurts. *California Management Review*, 41(2), 131–51.

Tzafrir, S.S. (2005) The relationship between trust, HRM practices and firm performance. *International Journal of Human Resource Management*, 16(9), 1600–22.

UBS (c. 2004) *The Making of UBS*. Zurich: UBS AG.

Ulrich, D., Allen, J., Brockbank, W., Younger, J. and Nyman, M. (2009) *HR Transformation: Building Human Resources from the Outside in*. New York: McGraw Hill.

UN Environment Program Finance Initiative (2004) *The Materiality of Social, Environmental and Corporate Governance Issues to Equity Pricing*. http://www.unepfi.org/fileadmin/publications/amwg/amwg_materiality_equity_pricing_report_2004.pdf; accessed 1 February 2010.

Van Aken, J.E. (2007) Design science and organization development interventions: Aligning business and humanistic values. *Journal of Applied Behavioral Science*, 43(1), 67–88.

Van Herpen, M., Van Praag, M. and Cools, K. (2005) The effects of performance measurement and compensation on motivation: An empirical study. *De Economist*, 153(3), 303–29.

Van Kemenade, E., Pupius, M. and Hardjono, T.W. (2008) More value to defining quality. *Quality in Higher Education*, 14(2), 175–85.

Van Marrewijk, M. (2004) The social dimension of organizations: Recent experiences with Great Place to Work® assessment practices. *Journal of Business Ethics*, 55, 135–46.

Van Veldhoven, M. (2005) Financial performance and the long-term link with HR practices, work climate and stress. *Human Resource Management Journal*, 15(4), 30–53.

Venohr, B. and Meyer, K.E. (2007) The German miracle keeps running: How Germany's Hidden Champions stay ahead of the global economy. Working paper, Academy of International Business, Indianapolis. http://papers.ssrn.com/sol3/papers.cfm?abstract_id=991964; accessed 14 February 2010.

Vermeier, W., van de Velde, E. and Corten, F. (2005) Sustainable and responsible performance. *Journal of Investing*, 14(3), 94–101.

Verschoor, C.C. (2004) Does superior governance still lead to better financial performance? *Strategic Finance*, October, 13–14.

Vogus, T.J. and Welbourne, T.M. (2003) Structuring for high reliability: HR practices and mindful processes in reliability-seeking organizations. *Journal of Organizational Behavior*, 24(7), 877–903.

Von Paumgarten, P. (2003) The business case for high-performance green buildings: Sustainability and its financial impact. *Journal of Facilities Management*, 2(1), 26–34.

Vora, M.K. (2004) Creating employee value in a global economy through participation, motivation and development. *Total Quality Management and Business Excellence*, 15(5/6), 793–806.

Waldman, D.A., Javidan, M. and Varella, P. (2004) Charismatic leadership at the strategic level: A new application of upper echelons theory. *Leadership Quarterly*, 15, 355–80.

Wall, T.D. and Wood, S.J. (2005) The romance of human resource management and business performance, and the case for big science. *Human Relations*, 58(4), 429–62.

Wang, E., Chou, H-W. and Jiang, J. (2005) The impacts of charismatic leadership style on team cohesiveness and overall performance during ERP implementation. *Project Management*, 23, 173–80.

Weihrich, H. (1999) Analyzing the competitive advantages and disadvantages of Germany with the TOWS matrix: An alternative to Porter's model. *European Business Review*, 99(1), 9–22.

Westhead, P., Cowling, M. and Howorth, C. (2001) The development of companies: Management and ownership imperatives. *Family Business Review*, 14(4), 39–85.

Wezel, F.C. and Saka-Helmhout, A. (2006) Antecedents and consequences of organizational change: 'Institutionalizing' the behavioral theory of the firm. *Organizational Studies*, 27(2), 265–86.

Wheatley, M.J. (2003) Prepare for the future: Engage people in meaningful work. *Executive Excellence*, Australian edition, 20(5), 10–11.

Wilhelm, K., Kovess, V., Rios-Seidel, C. and Finch, A. (2004) Work and mental health. *Social Psychiatry and Psychiatric Epidemiology*, 39(11), 866–73.

Wittmeyer, C. (2003) The practice of management: Timeless views and principles. *Academy of Management Executive*, 17(3), 13–14.

Wood, S. (1996) High commitment management and payment systems. *Journal of Management Studies*, 33(1), 53–77.

World Business Council for Sustainable Development and the UN Environment Program Finance Initiative (2004) *Generation Lost: Young Financial Analysts and Environmental, Social and Governance Issues.* Young Managers Team. http://www.wbcsd.org; accessed 14 February 2010.

World Commission on Environment and Development [Bruntland Report] (1987) *Our Common Future*. Oxford: Oxford University Press.

World Economic Forum (2004) Voice of the leaders survey. http://www.weforum.org./security/survey; accessed 14 February 2010.

—— (2005) Mainstreaming responsible investment. http://www.weforum.org./pdf/mri.pdf; accessed 14 February 2010.

—— (2008) The global impact of private equity. http://www.weforum.org/pdf/cgi/pe/Full_Report.pdf; accessed 14 February 2010.

Yang, J., Rui, M. and Wang, J. (2006) Enhancing the firm's innovation capability through knowledge management: A study of high technology firms in China. *International Journal of Technology Management*, 36(4), 305–17.

Yaniv, E. and Farkas, F. (2005) The impact of person–organization fit on the corporate brand perception of employees and of customers. *Journal of Change Management*, 5(4), 447–61.

Yu, G-C. and Park, J-S. (2006) The effect of downsizing on the financial performance and employee productivity of Korean firms. *International Journal of Manpower*, 27(3), 230–50.

Zatzick, C.D. and Iverson, R.D. (2006) High-involvement management and workforce reduction: Competitive advantage or disadvantage? *Academy of Management Journal*, 49(5), 999–1015.

Index

Made in the USA
Lexington, KY
19 May 2019